AMERICAN ABUNDANCE

THE NEW ECONOMIC AND MORAL PROSPERITY

LAWRENCE KUDLOW

60 FIFTH AVENUE, NEW YORK, NEW YORK 10011

CIP Data is available.

Printed in the United States of America

10 9 8 7 6 5 4 3 2

ISBN 0–8281–1117–0

For my beloved Judy,

*who pulled me back from the edge, whose inner strength
and faith in God are shining lights, and who is the
center of my very being.*

TABLE OF CONTENTS

ACKNOWLEDGMENTS

When Wade Dokken, the CEO of American Skandia Marketing, suggested last summer that I put a book together that would include my previously published newspaper and magazine articles, as well as other writings, and new materials, my instinctive first reaction was that old bugaboo fear. It would be too much work, and too much stress, with far little time, especially for someone still in the early stages of sobriety, two years and four months abstinent as of this writing. Yet I have learned to cope, manage and push the fears back, in large measure by taking suggestions from people I respect and trust. Wade is one such person. He is a brilliant marketing man, the best I've ever seen, who from scratch has built a fast-growing insurance based variable annuity and mutual fund business located in Shelton, Connecticut. For me personally, his caring compassion, and his encouragement and support for all aspects of my new life, including the welcoming support from his wife Susan, must be acknowledged with all the heartfelt gratitude and humility I can muster. It is part of the miracle.

Also part of the miracle, I wish to express my gratitude and thankfulness to Arthur B. Laffer, who brought me in to his prosperous economic consulting firm in San Diego after I completed a five-month stay at Hazelden. At that point in late November, 1995, I had no prospects, no confidence, no ambition and no sense that I could do the job. But Art and his wife Tracy brought Judy and me out West, made us welcome guests in their home, and afforded us a heaven sent opportunity to re-start our life. For their friendship, support, and mentoring, I shall always be grateful. Sometimes stern, sometimes playful, with plenty of tough love and a heart of gold, Art always made me toe the line in the office and in recovery. It was exactly what I needed. He is an extraordinary human being.

Let me also express thanks to Robert Caldwell, the editor of the San Diego *Union-Tribune*'s Sunday Insight section. In early 1996, Bob reopened the door to journalism by publishing my articles in his paper, the only conservative daily in California. He is a hard working, straight-up gentleman of the old school, who believes in free markets and free people, and I am grateful for his support.

Also, I wish to thank my old friend Victor Canto and his wife Anna, who were so helpful in getting Judy and me settled into the pleasant life of Rancho Santa Fe, where we lived during our California year. Victor and I both have new jobs now, but we continue to talk by phone on a regular basis. Also part of the extended Laffer family, Charlie Parker and Bill Shiebler have supported me through the good times and the rough times. Thank you.

In late January 1996, when I still had no idea which end was up, barely two months out of Hazelden, I took a call from Mary Lou Forbes, the editor of the *Washington Times* Commentary section. She welcomed me back, expressed support for my journey, and asked if she could publish part of the first essay I wrote for Laffer, Canto and Associates. I cried then just as I am now as I write this. Of course I agreed and expressed my gratefulness. Mary Lou is low profile, but she is a remarkable woman. With the single exception of the powerful *Wall Street Journal*, Mary Lou runs the most important op-ed pages in America. I am proud and honored to be part of her stable of contributors. Every one of my articles that she has published over the past two years is included in this volume. And let me also say thanks to her deputy, Frank Perley, who is tough about meeting deadlines, as he must be. And Donald Lambro, who may just be the best political economic reporter in Washington today, and who has been a great friend.

In the spring of '96 David Asman of the *Wall Street Journal* called to assign me a piece for his op-ed page and again I was overcome with emotion. The *Journal* is the most important newspaper in the country. The conservative, free-market, supply-side views of its editor, Robert Bartley, have transformed government policy over the past three decades. For any serious policy-oriented economist, the *Journal*'s op-ed page is the number one platform. David Asman, who I first met in Buenos Aires, Argentina during the early Cavallo days in 1991, has been a great friend, supporter and editor. His insights have always made the pieces more lucid and hard-hitting. Recently departed for Fox television, he was a great op-ed page editor. So was Amity Schlaes, who published me during the early 1990s, and became a good friend. And to Bob Bartley, who will undoubtedly go down as the most influential newspaper editor of the second half of the twentieth century, I also wish to express my sincere thanks and gratitude.

A good chunk of my heart and soul will always remain with William F. Buckley's *National Review*, where I worked as economics editor in 1994 and the first half of 1995. I will always be grateful for that experience, where I learned to write and think more clearly under the tutelage of editor John O'Sullivan. The *NR* group is a wonderful collection of bright, warm-hearted and dedicated people. The magazines niche in history will always be secure. So much has been written about the brilliance of Bill Buckley, the guiding spirit of modern conservatism, but my link to him is as much emotional as it is intellectual. Sitting with Bill at the editorial dinners in his Manhattan home is a wonderful and fascinating experience. But there's another side to Bill's persona, a very caring and fatherly and compassionate side, which prompted him to call and write me at Hazelden to see if I would be okay. I will never forget that. Nor will I ever forget the motherly care of Pat Buckley. To both of them, my sincere gratitude and thanks for their help and their affection.

Recently I have been re-invited to the *NR* editorial board meetings, and I am thankful for the opportunity to contribute. Nevertheless, my feelings of shame for having badly let the magazine down during my crash and burn period in the spring of '95 still weigh heavily on me. I take this opportunity to again make amends, not only to Bill and John, but to Dusty, Ed, Dorothy, Linda, Kate, Rich, Ramesh, Drew, Matt, David, Karina, Jeffrey and Rick. For some reason you have remained my friends, supporting me in my recovery journey. I cannot thank you enough. Also in the *NR* circle, many thanks for the friendship of Van Galbraith, and Neal Freeman. Neal's Washington, DC TV show *Money Politics*, which was a victim of the 1990 credit crunch, was a wonderful experience. He has invited me from time to time this year to appear on Technopolitics, and I am grateful. Neal has been a friend and a mentor; he and Jayne have been wonderful.

Many of my best writing ideas have come during the CNBC weekend talk show "Strictly Business," which I helped to start in 1991, and which is still going strong today, the longest running show on that network. For all those years Bill Griffeth has been the moderator, a calm, steady, and knowledgeable veteran TV journalist and author. Bill has been a great friend, and it was he who shepherded me back into regular participation last April. For this I wish to express deep gratitude. I love that show, and we cover a lot of ground; its a battleground of ideas among Jimmy Rodgers, Bill Wolman, Bill Griffeth and me. Indeed, I owe special thanks to the entire CNBC network for supporting me and re-opening the door. To Jack Reilly, and Peter Sturtevant, and Larry Moscow, and Peggy Giordano, and Ron Insana, and Mark Haines, and Sue Herrera, and Ted David, and Kathleen Hays, people Ive worked with for years, and more recent colleagues Joe Kernan and David Faber on "Squawk Box" and Terry Keenan on "Market Wrap," and Maria Bartiromo and Tyler Mathisen on "Business Center." And, of course, Kerima Green, who now produces "Strictly Business," and Marge Martin in makeup, whose transforming skills are legendary. To all of them, many, many thanks.

I would also like to thank Brian Lamb of C-Span for bringing me back on his network and his early morning talk show "Washington Journal." C-Span has become a central part of the public policy discussion, and for someone like myself the reopening of that door has been a blessing. Also, Brian's "Booknotes" program on Sunday evenings, and its accompanying book of the same name, moved me to actually believe I could put this book together. Thank you.

So much of my blood, sweat and tears remain in the hallways and corridors of Bear Stearns, where I spend eight years as their chief economic scribbler. Alan Greenberg treated me with respect and support, and he was particularly kind to Judy during the worst period. For all that I express appreciation and thanks. And to the whole supply-side economics gang, who down through the years provided the tough thinking, the fact checking and the analytical support. They have all remained good friends: John Ryding, Melanie Hardy, Lincoln Anderson, Michelle Colley, David Malpass, David Goldman, Tim Kearney, Kim Griffin and Liz Passanante. In particular, as I restarted my professional life, John Ryding has been a loyal and supportive colleague, going beyond the normal boundary of friendship to keep me up to speed. I refer to him as the "British genius," and he has made a tremendous name for himself in the economics field. Many, many thanks.

And I must also express deep appreciation and thanks to the big-time institutional money managers, most of whom I met during the Bear Stearns days, who placed their confidence and trust in me over the past two years by signing me on as an economic consultant. Few people outside the professional investment management business understand the extraordinary high quality of those who are on the investment hot seat and manage our nation's pension and retirement accounts. I am honored to remain in their circle. This is not the place to list the names of all my clients, but I do want to mention a few who have been virtually family members and gave me constant support and encouragement: Patricia and John Chadwick, Tim Dalton, Mark Kurland, Harlan Cadinha, George Yeager, David Marks, Dick Weisman, Nick Forstmann, Charlie Mires, Bill Stephens, Pat Small, Keith Anderson and Rob Kapito, Scott Grannis, Mark Bavoso, Frank Husic, and Catherine Wood. To these close friends, many thanks. And to my dear friend, John Sites, who is always checking up on me, whether in Hazelden or Shelton, thank you for your friendship and support.

I am also deeply grateful to Ed Crane and Steve Moore at the Cato Institute, and Jim Miller and Liz Tobias at Citizens for a Sound Economy, and David Gerson and Jim Glassman of the American Enterprise Institute. They all helped bring me back into the public policy field in Washington, an area of work that I love. Steve Moore has been a deal friend. Ger and I go all the way back to the early OMB days in late 1980. Jim Glassman and I have many shared experiences. I also wish to thank Wayne Angell for his spiritual thoughts and his personal friendship. And also John McLaughlin, who provided many opportunities on his television shows and who keeps track of me with support and friendship.

Jack and Joanne Kemp have been great friends to Judy and me down through the years, and we are deeply grateful for that. It was Jack who provided my entrée to the Reagan Administration, and I have been honored to be part of his circle for nearly twenty years. He called me during the first week in Art Laffer's shop, to say hello and welcome me back. When I saw him at the Republican Convention in August '96 in San Diego, after he was nominated Vice President, he gave me a big hug in full public view. This is a measure of the one of the truly great men in American public life.

Steve and Sabina Forbes have also been great friends, providing warmth and support. Steve and I went through the crucible of the Whitman campaign in '93, and we proved the point that tax-cutting growth politics still work. Now he is out and about on the national trail, but he still checks in periodically to see how I'm doing. Thank you.

Back in early 1993, my long-time friend and mentor Jeffrey Bell brought Father C. John McCloskey into my life. Since then Fr. John has been with me, body and soul and mind, without interruption, no matter what happened or where I was. He taught me that Jesus went through his passion, and his redemption, for the benefit of all mankind, including me. I have come to believe this with all my heart and soul, and it sustains me on a daily basis. For this, and the journey into the Catholic church, I am grateful. It too is part of the miracle.

Finally, to Russell Forrest of Center City, Minnesota, who taught me to accept powerlessness, ask for help, and follow directions, and to understand that illness, not badness, brought me to Hazelden. I am eternally grateful.

Many thanks to my editor, Ron Balmer, of Forbes/American Heritage Custom Publishing division. Ron's strong belief in free-market economics has made us soulmates. We did a lot of work in a short period of time, but somehow with his help it all got done. Also thanks to Chris Cimino at Forbes/American Heritage Custom Publishing division, for keeping the project on schedule.

Also many thanks to John Walker, one of the best financial relations people in the business. I have known John for many years, and his advice and guidance has always been on the mark. This book could never have been done without him.

In the office at American Skandia, Jeremy Hildreth, an émigré from the University of Pennsylvania and the Cato Institute in Washington, DC, has been enormously helpful as my economic assistant and software data maven. For his tender young years, he is far too knowledgeable and bright, but that is why he is an invaluable resource. Many thanks.

And to Susan Varga, an incredibly cheerful, kind, productive and efficient personal assistant and business manager, many, many thanks. She came on board last spring, and my myriad of professional operations have never been run more smoothly. None of this would be possible without her help and guidance. I am grateful.

I apologize to readers who have plowed through all these gratitudes and thank yous. But you see, living at Hazelden all those months, after crashing and burning from alcohol and cocaine addiction, I feared that my life and career were over. I was utterly defeated by the disease of addiction. I lost my Wall Street position, my magazine editorship, my television shows, was humiliated in the press, and very nearly lost my wife. It is my sincere hope that fellow-suffering alcoholics and chemical dependants will learn to trust God, as I have, so they may avoid the kind of bottom that I experienced. Today, nearly two and half years later, I have learned just how good and gracious and affectionate and caring people can be, so I have come to cherish my friendships, taking no one and nothing for granted. And that is one of the reasons for this book and my new life: I am trying to give some of it back. With God's grace, this too will be part of the miracle.

—*Lawrence Kudlow*
Redding, Connecticut
October 31, 1997

THE LONG WAVE OF PROSPERITY: OVERTURNING THE OLD KEYNESIAN ORDER

On the eve of the 21st century the United States finds itself in a long wave of prosperity that began fifteen years ago and could conceivably continue without serious interruption until 2020 or 2030. Stock prices are higher, economic growth is faster, both inflation and unemployment are lower, technological change is more pervasive, the dollar is stronger, social conditions are more hopeful, the public spirit is more confident and the nation's future is brighter than anyone thought possible fifteen or twenty years ago when pessimism and anxiety were the dominant strains in American life.

As a young economist working first at the New York Federal Reserve Bank in the early 1970s, and later that decade on Wall Street, I enhanced my reputation and my visibility as a card-carrying pessimist, especially during the Carter years. But pessimism has never truly sat well with me; as though bound by a shirt collar that was too heavily starched, it made me feel uneasy and irascible. This was, after all, my country and my future. Wasn't there a way out that could set things right?

Then came Reagan, and it was he who restored the country to greatness. Today I am just as honored and grateful that I went to work for him as I was seventeen years ago. It was Reagan who turned pessimism into optimism through a set of economic policies that brought back the classical free-market model of sound money to eliminate inflation and tax cuts to unleash the entrepreneurial forces of growth. It was Reagan who changed our foreign policy from "passive balance of power" defeatism to a forceful articulation of America's democratic values, and the build-up of military hardware to back up those values, thereby ending the Cold War and the imperialism of Soviet Communism. It was Reagan who restored the U.S. role in the world to that of the only true global economic and military super-power. It was Reagan who revitalized the basic U.S. traditions of free markets and free elections, that is to say, of political, economic and religious *freedom*, and turned them into a broad beacon of light—a spirit, really, that with the marvels of advanced high-speed communication technologies was broadcast throughout the world and proceeded to transform the institutions and behavior of people in every nation and geographical region on the planet.

It was Reagan, and his Great Britain colleague Margaret Thatcher, who turned back the tide of Keynesian governmental fine-tuning and central planning, confronting the constant chorus of pessimistic criticism from distinguished Ivy establishmentarians such as Samuelson, Modigliani, Solow, Tobin, Thoreau, Galbraith, Kennedy and others who had wrapped themselves in the comfortable and smug self-knowledge that economics could only be managed by distinguished university dons; free-markets and the unfettered actions of ordinary people in commerce, trade and finance was a dangerous thing, something that must be tightly controlled, lest it lead to unmanageable chaos.

Pessimistic liberals loudly proclaimed that tax cuts would create excess demand and drive up inflation, but they did not. Instead, the investment side of the economy came alive, making goods and services more available, and inflation quickly declined. Big government elites said the deregulation of energy prices would lead to oil costs rising to $100 per barrel, but oil prices fell to $12 instead. Union liberals screamed that the PATCO strike would wreck airline safety, but instead the skies remained safe while the militant Big Labor tide was reversed. Carter alumni argued that the strong dollar would stop our exports and hollow out our industries, but exports soared, high technology transformed the entire economy into the strongest in the world, and the strong dollar vanquished inflation. Numerous Wall Streeters insisted that trade deficits and budget deficits would bankrupt the nation, but massive foreign investment inflows poured into our economy to capture high capital returns and rebuild our industries, while the budget deficits were put to productive use by funding the rapid inflation decline which deflated budget revenues, the military build-up to end the Cold War, and the tax cuts to re-start the engines of growth. Liberal professors preached the triumph of top-heavy state-directed capitalism in Japan and social market capitalism in Germany, but American growth and wealth-creation has far outstripped those two stagnant economies.

Pessimists jumped for joy at the market crash in October, 1987 (as they did in October 1997), only to be chagrined when the market and the economy soared to new high levels during the 1990s. Liberal Democrats were briefly enthralled when President Clinton raised taxes and attempted to nationalize health care in 1993–94, but were horrified when a free market Republican brigade took over Congress in 1994, pledging to reduce taxes and spending, and roll back the welfare state planning and control system that decimated the American social and moral order over the past thirty years.

Then the hard core Democratic left walked away from Clinton as he sounded more and more Republican in the '96 campaign, and of course he won without them. Indeed, Clinton actually deserves a bit more credit than even conservatives are willing to give him, for despite his tax hike and nationalized health care proposal in '93, Clinton and Treasury Secretary Robert Rubin cooperated with Greenspan to appreciate the dollar and reduce the inflation rate to essentially zero by '97. Declining inflation has had a pervasive tax cut effect throughout the economy, boosting real incomes, real wages, real profits and real stock market returns, perhaps neutralizing the prior income tax hike. Pessimists then warned that lower inflation would raise unemployment and deflate the economy; even some conservatives are adopting a similar mantra. But real economic growth has flourished during the last downturn of inflation in 1997, while unemployment has fallen, once again disproving the Phillips curve theory that inflation and unemployment must always trade off inversely in a heads-I-win-tails-you-lose zero-sum game.

(It is worth noting, however, that a year after Clinton's '93 tax hike long term Treasury rates moved up from 5.75% to 8.25%, while the producer price index accelerated from minus 4.7% to plus 4.2%. The stock market advance stagnated in '94, with the nervous Dow bouncing around 3600 while 70% of the listed New York Stock Exchange company shares declined. The trend of real economic growth slowed from 3.3% to 1.7%. Clinton's tax-rate hike was clearly detrimental to the economy until the next wave of disinflation offset it in '96 and '97.)

But Clinton did get rid of the partisan Japanese-bashing Mickey Cantor and brought in Charlene Barshefsky to be the top trade negotiator, who promptly negotiated an information-tech free-trade deal in Singapore and a communications-tech deal in Geneva, correctly labeling them "global tax cuts." Now she is working to get fast-track trade negotiating authority approved by Congress. This will allow Clinton to bring Chile into the NAFTA free-trade zone, and from Chile he can link to the Mercosur countries of Brazil, Paraguay, Argentina and Uruguay. So Reagan's vision of hemispheric free trade, supported by a common currency area based on the dollar, could come to fruition under Clinton. On trade and inflation Clinton sounds like Reagan. He even signed a tax cut bill this year that, warts and all, reduced the tax-rate on capital gains, lowered inheritance penalties and expanded IRA savings plans, all things the Gipper would have supported.

It is a tribute to Reagan's political and economic longevity that Clinton has tried to adopt the Californian's sunny demeanor and at least some of his policy approaches. Without question Reagan created the economic high ground on which Clinton's favorable polls now rest. But more importantly, the success of the Reagan-inspired economic cycle proves that establishment "experts," especially the professoriat of the elite Eastern universities, with their Keynesian economic models and their liberal political leanings, were proven wrong again and again and again. Their pessimism was not rooted in objective forecasting or historical study, but instead it was a desperate attempt to rationalize and protect their own high standing in the ivied economic and intellectual sanctuaries of privilege and comfort to which they have become so accustomed. "What?" they seemed to be saying. "Is it possible that these roust-about radical upstarts who are attempting to revive classical free-market thought actually believe they will overturn the established Keynesian order, in which we have labored so long and so successfully? Just who do these upstarts think they are?"

Well, we *are* trying to overthrow the Keynesian political economic order. Tax-cut politics removes both the resources and the raison d'être of government spending, fine-tuning, targeting, engineering, and controlling, all the policy levers of modern Keynesian government management. By cutting taxes and shifting resources to the private sector citizenry, classical economics undercut the power and the purpose of Big Government. People who are permitted to keep more of what they earn, so they will have more money to spend and invest more wisely than government will, with a greater sense of the virtue of personal responsibility and accountability to their families, businesses, and communities, and a stronger sense of the virtue of self-government, will supply the essential growth dynamic of entrepreneurial capitalism *on their own*. They will have no need for the Daddy state or the entitlement state or the targeted subsidy state or the education state or the multicultural state or any of the corruption-laden functions that the Big Bureaucracy and its Keynesian think tank and university allies have cooked up over the past thirty some years.

This is why the high dons of Keynesianism, after 50 years of using budget deficits to finance additional government spending, suddenly turned face and became "deficit hawks," the protectors of fiscal solvency. Really, however, they wanted desperately to stop tax cuts. So, they pretended to be aghast at Reagan's "financial profligacy," and they fought all tax cuts, past, present, and future, in the name of "fiscal balance." Of course, these bright men of the establishment knew exactly what they were doing. It hadn't a thing to do with deficits, which were never of any real financial or economic consequence according to Robert Eisner, economics professor at Northwestern

University, a past president of the American Economics Association, and one of the leading lights of the liberal economic establishment. In Congressional testimony, on the op-ed pages of the *New York Times* and the *Wall Street Journal*, on "Crossfire" and other public policy television shows, Eisner derided government accounting procedures and deflated the deficit and debt issue through ridicule as much as analysis. The real political battle was over tax cuts, not deficits.

I can remember testifying at a Senate Budget Committee hearing one morning during the Bush recession of 1990. The Democrats then held both houses of Congress and this particular hearing was chaired by Jim Sasser of Tennessee (now ambassador to China), ably assisted by Paul Sarbanes of Maryland. More to the point, my fellow panelists were economic professors Paul Samuelson of MIT and James Tobin of Yale, both Nobel Prize winners and both charter members of the Keynesian high table. It was a long morning and I was completely outranked and out-credentialed by these two famous experts. The subject was what to do about the economic slump. My answer was to repeal the Bush tax increase passed that summer, including the income tax hike, the luxury sales tax increase (boats, furs, jewelry, big cars, which reduced demand and threw thousands of blue collar workers out of their jobs), the punitive deepening of the alternative minimum tax and, especially, roll back the capital gains tax hike of 1986, and index it to inflation, in order to spur the lagging animal spirits of entrepreneurship.

Messrs. Samuelson and Tobin made it plain that they have never met an across-the-board tax cut they liked. They pounced on me, Reagan, supply-side, entrepreneurs, incentives and the 1980s. It was all a sham, a disaster, a financial catastrophe that destroyed the nation and its economy. Never mind that Professor Tobin was a member of the Council of Economic Advisors under President Kennedy, when JFK cut the top marginal income tax rate from 90% to 70%, using rhetoric crafted by Jim Tobin and Walter Heller in 1962 that sounded nearly identical to the economic rationale we supplied Reagan in the early '80s. Professor Samuelson was at least willing to consider a temporary investment tax credit, but not permanent tax-rate cuts on capital or income. However, the two distinguished Nobelists were in complete agreement on the need for a government stimulus package, only a modest one of $50 billion or $60 billion in view of the deficit problem, but a spending program that would revive aggregate demand and consumption. And if that didn't work, more government spending would be necessary, along with rapid money supply growth from the Fed, in order to foreclose the possible depression that might come from Reagan's policies.

Actually, just as a minor factoid, though Bush economics were pure root canal austerity, a complete departure from Reagan, the recession, nonetheless was mild and shallow, lasting only nine months, and it did not interrupt the long wave of prosperity. More important, in my brief brush with the great and the near great of the economics establishment, it was very clear to me that nothing in the 1980s, or the '70s for that matter, had even remotely encouraged them to revisit their government-sponsored demand-side approach to the economy. It was as though neither the failure of the stagflationary 1970s, nor the recovery boom of the 1980s, ever existed. But I also learned from this episode that this and many other scrapes with the Keynesian old-guard was not really about numbers, or facts or history. It was about theological doctrine: populist tax cuts versus government management. Most of all, it was about power and influence. Distinguished men such as Samuelson and Tobin, men who have taught students and published serious works for decades, were not about to admit they might have even occasionally been wrong, and they were not about to give up their *position*. Certainly not to some free-market, tax-cutting upstart. Or anyone else who departs from the orthodoxy.

Turning back to the *economics* of taxation, reduced tax-rates and higher after-tax returns are absolutely crucial to successful entrepreneurial activity. As Arthur Laffer has put it many times over the years, "When you tax something, you get less of it. When you tax something less, you get more of it." Tax-rate cuts promote growth *and* reduce inflation. Tax-rate reduction unlocks existing capital and creates new capital. Tax cuts provide the necessary after-tax returns to attract capital and commercialize new ideas. Tax cuts also make labor more productive.

Changes in tax-rates cause shifts in economic behavior. Ordinary people know, even if mainstream economists do not, that it must pay to work, produce and invest. If it does pay, in after-tax returns, then people *will* take risks, be more creative, inventive and innovative. On the margin, they will choose work over leisure, production over consumption, investment over hoarding, risk-taking over the safety of Treasury bills. In 1981, the top income tax-rate was 70%, leaving the salaried worker only 30 cents on the extra dollar earned. By 1987, with the top rate dropping to 28%, the extra dollar earned was worth 72 cents, a whopping 140% incentive to increase risk-taking and production. It was this incentive effect that rescued the economy from deep recession, and drove the stock market from 750 in mid-1982 to 2700 at the peak in 1987, a remarkable 260% rise which symbolized the surge of U.S. wealth creation.

Tax cuts will, over time, pay for themselves. The Laffer Curve, originated by Arthur B. Laffer in the mid-1970s, shows that when tax rates fall from the punitive zone, then expanded incentives to work, produce and invest will generate more economic activity and higher tax revenues. Tax rates and tax revenues have an inverse relationship: lower tax-rates produce higher tax receipts. It's nothing more than classical price theory. In business, if you raise prices too high, then sales revenue falls. If product prices are lowered, however, then product marketing will penetrate a wider base, thereby increasing sales volume and sales revenues. Over the course of Reagan's tax reforms in the 1980s, inflation-adjusted real tax revenues increased by 31% between 1982 and 1989. Reagan left the budget deficit at 2.9% of GDP in fiscal year 1989, almost exactly where he inherited it at 2.7% in 1981. In between, however, he sharply cut tax rates to promote growth and spent heavily on defense to defeat the Soviet Union. In fact, on a national income account's basis, the combined Federal, state and local budget deficit in 1989 was only $118 billion.

What's more, tax reduction is consistent with, even a necessary condition for, budget restraint. Just as in business, nothing reduces expenses and overhead faster than declining revenues and profits, so it is when the initial impact of tax reduction temporarily lowers revenues in government. Show me a committed tax-cutter and I'll show you a shrinking government, at least as a share of GDP. Actually, Reagan was much more successful in holding down budget growth than even many conservatives, including my former OMB boss David Stockman, believe. In fact, a recent study by the centrist Urban Institute, no friend of supply-side economics, ranked Reagan second only to FDR (believe it or not), and tougher than Calvin Coolidge (who tied for seventh), in reducing the domestic budget share of GDP during the 20th century.

Reagan himself understood all this. In his autobiography, *An American Life*, the former President put it very well: "The twenty-five percent tax cut, followed by the Tax Reform Act of 1986, touched off a *surge of growth in America that brought down inflation* (italics mine), brought down interest rates, brought down unemployment, and created a cascade of additional tax revenue for government. Realizing they could keep more of what they earned, people went out and made more money."

In other words, cut taxes, maintain sound money (preferably by linking the dollar to a gold price rule, as has been the case since 1981, under both Paul Volcker and Alan Greenspan at the Fed), and good things will happen. Indeed they did. According to the business cycle gurus of the National Bureau of Economic Research in Cambridge,

Massachusetts, the recovery cycle of the past fifteen years (1982–97) is the longest period of prosperity in the 20th century. Real economic growth has averaged 3% per year for fifteen years, while 34 million new jobs have been created, bringing unemployment below 5%. The inflation rate has descended from 15% in 1980 to about 1½% today (producer prices are actually deflating by 1½% over the past nine months, providing a tax cut effect that is boosting real income, real wages, real profits and real investment returns), while interest rates have dropped from 15% to 20% all the way down to about 6%. King Dollar has once again taken its place as the world's reserve currency, really the only adult currency in global financial markets.

Meanwhile, 700,000 new business start-ups per year, with each small firm creating an average of three to four new jobs, have become the backbone of the new economy. Spurred by stable interest rates, zero inflation and high capital returns, consumers on the margin would rather invest for the long-term than spend now. So production (about 5%) exceeds consumption (3½%), putting a lie to the constant whine that America consumes too much. Business profits have risen from less than 5% of GDP to over 9%, something that is only possible through increased productivity, which in the real high-tech business world is probably increasing at a 2% to 3% rate, rather than the government's estimate of only 1%. Using S&P 500 companies, the trend rate of return on capital assets has grown from 12% to nearly 17%, with recent quarterly results coming in close to 20%. Undoubtedly another recession will occur in my lifetime, but at present there's still no downturn in sight.

As mentioned earlier, the stock market during the first wave of Reagan's supply-side policies increased by an astonishing 260%. After the Republicans took Congress in 1994, thereby ending the threat of future tax increases, and opening the way for flat tax reduction and simplification, what I will call the second wave of free-market policies, a new stock market boom took the Dow from 3700 to 8000 at the peak in 1997, a gain of nearly 120%. All told, the 15-year bull market has increased the Dow by six-fold, a 500% gain in real (inflation-adjusted) terms, creating a staggering $12 trillion in new household net worth (a figure not even included as savings in our goofy GDP accounting system). As a proxy for our nation's wealth and well-being, the stock market charts the recovery of American optimism, American values and America's place in the world.

According to recent surveys over 40% of the U.S. population, roughly 125 million people, nearly equal to the entire workforce, own stock market shares through brokerage accounts, bank deposit plans,

IRAs, mutual funds, Keoghs, 401K plans, variable annuities or other retirement plans. This number has doubled in the past seven years, with the largest percentage of new owners coming from women (49%) and nonprofessional salaried workers (38%), both groups earning $75,000 or less in yearly income. This is the most successful experiment of democratic capitalism in economic history. And with so many Americans owning a piece of the rock, it is not likely that they'll let their elected leaders stray far from the free-market policy model that has generated so many new jobs and produced so much new wealth. If stock owners/voters keep Washington on a short free-market leash, then the long bull market wave of prosperity will continue for some time to come. How deliciously ironic. Karl Marx is both dead and wrong. By the end of the 20th century *workers* came to be the owners of the means of production. So capitalism became stronger and more democratic. It was Marxism that withered away.

A key part of the Reagan-launched long wave of prosperity is the absolutely crucial role played by information age technological innovation and investment, which has completely transformed every nook and cranny of the economy through a multitude of spillover effects, new applications, adaptations and refinements of existing technologies. University of California-Berkeley economist Paul Romer calls this the law of *increasing* returns, which he believes replaces the rather dismal economic law of diminishing returns. In short, Romer argues that the spillover effects of technological application are virtually limitless. There are no one-time effects of technological advance, but rather a nuclear combustible throw-weight chain of events throughout the economy that was initially prompted by the commercial use of an invention or an innovation.

This high-tech influence on the economy is not new in economic history. The United States experienced a similar burst of high-tech innovation during the 19th century, where the post Civil War economy was propelled forward for nearly sixty years (ending in the 1930s depression) by railroadization, steam and steel, automobiles, electricity, chemistry and then the telegraph and the telephone. Today's technological wave is based on knowledge and information, with micro-chips, micro-processors, cell phones, personal computers, fiber optics, high-definition televisions, the Internet, DNA analysis, biotechnology, molecular engineering and on and on.

Today's burst of technological advance is in many important ways even greater than that of the 19th century. Then, the new products were more physical, finite, and heavy industry-directed. Now, the new breakthroughs are more located in cyberspace and the microcosm, completely downsized, operating in the limitless sphere of knowledge, information and communication. Hence the spillover effect is probably greater now, and thus the economic effects are more far-reaching and long-lived. At this point in our economy, even with numerous measurement inadequacies, government figures show that high-tech production and investment contribute roughly one-third of the nation's economic growth. Not even scored in the national income accounts, the U.S. software business is thought by many private analysts to be the nation's third largest industry.

Joseph A. Schumpeter, who in my view is the most important economist of the 20th century, and certainly my favorite dead economist, called this economic transformation "Gales of Creative Destruction," where the new is constantly replacing the old: new ideas, new inventions, new innovations, new people, new firms, new business practices, new profits, and new capital. Innovation plays the central role in Schumpeter's theory, and the entrepreneur and the risk-taker are the key players. Schumpeter put human creativity at the center of the economy, thereby improving the dismal science of economics by giving it a human face. Schumpeter also believed it must pay to be a risk-taker, and so he emphasized the role of "entrepreneurial profits," which today would largely encompass what we call capital gains.

Essentially, Schumpeter believed that an increase in knowledge, plus the profit motive, will induce an entrepreneur to undertake something new and unfamiliar, usually borrowing money to build his innovative product. When the products of entrepreneurs are commercialized and sold to the marketplace, the total output and wealth of the economy are increased by far more than the old products or capital that were replaced or destroyed. What's more, Schumpeter not only believed that bursts of technological innovation are the single most important forces that create and drive a dynamic growth economy, he also asserted that technological innovation leads to *more output, with better quality, at lower prices.* According to the U.S. Labor Department, personal computer prices have fallen nearly 100% since the early 1980s. High-tech capital equipment prices are dropping about 30% per year. The first cellular telephone I bought in 1986 cost nearly $3,000. But the model I purchased last winter cost about $200, with more battery time and superior memory capabilities.

This thought, that technological breakthroughs lead to stronger growth with lower prices, is essential to understanding what many today call the "new paradigm," where rapid economic growth can coexist with declining inflation, thereby repealing old-think Keynesian economic models that argue for a Phillips curve trade-off between unemployment and inflation, or the non-accelerating inflation rate of unemployment (NAIRU), or output gaps, or a growth speed limit or other demand-side austerity nostrums of an allegedly static economic structure. Really, the so-called new paradigm is a new spin on an old principle. The classical description of inflation is a decline in the monetary standard leading to too much money chasing too few goods. In today's environment, with the golden yardstick of monetary value hovering at a low $320 per ounce, indicating a strong dollar, we are presently experiencing *hard money chasing more technologically-driven goods and services*. This, of course, has led to zero inflation and price stability, a point missed by demand-side monetarists and Keynesians who still worry about capacity utilization, despite the fact that high-tech innovation has substantially increased the economy's investment-side potential to grow.

Actually, Schumpeter was the original free-market supply-sider. He believed that taxes " . . . interfere with the results of business processes . . . when the highly progressive income tax exceeds 25%, (it) may enforce dissaving and disinvestment . . . will block progress and indus-trial efficiency . . . and must blunt the profit margins by taxing away gains necessary to call forth the efforts of the individual recipients." Schumpeter also believed that government policies must take care to nurture the entrepreneur, and the profit returns due the entrepreneur, not only by holding down taxes, but also by keeping money value stable through the gold standard, by eliminating barriers to domestic and foreign trade, and by abolishing governmental controls and regulations.

For me, the key Schumpeter book is *Business Cycles*, an abridgement approved by the Schumpeter Committee of Harvard University and published by Porcupine Press in Philadelphia, Pennsylvania. Schum-peter was an Austrian trained economist who attended the University of Vienna, at age 30 taught at Columbia University in New York, briefly served as Austrian finance minister, then taught at the University of Berlin, and finished his life as a Harvard economics professor from the early 1930s until his death in 1950. His other books include *The Theory of Economic Development* (1926), *Capitalism, Socialism and Democracy* (1942), and *History of Economic Analysis*, edited from a manuscript by Elizabeth Boody Schumpeter in 1954, after her husband's death. The original two-volume edition of *Business Cycles* was originally published in 1939, and it is there that he charts the long-wave cycles of creative destruction, technological innovation and entrepreneurial risk-taking. (I am indebted to Dallas Fed economist Michael Cox for renewing my interest in Schumpeter and for directing me to *Business Cycles*. I am also deeply indebted to New York economist David Goldman, an old friend and colleague, for helping me work through the key themes and applications of Schumpeter's theories and other academic works.)

Actually, as an avid reader of political and economic history, I cannot resist the temptation to go beyond Schumpeter and rank those economists who I believe to be the most important of the 20th century. This, of course, is a purely personal view, and I define "most important" to mean those economists who charted, analyzed, evaluated, and promoted the free-market supply-side ideas that I believe are essential to the growth dynamic of economic health and prosperity, and to social progress. In other words, the classical free-market upstarts.

20TH CENTURY ECONOMIC GREATS

1. Joseph Schumpeter

2. Robert A. Mundell
   Arthur B. Laffer

3. Milton Friedman
   Friedrich Hayek
   Ludwig von Mises

After Schumpeter, my two most important 20th century (living) economic greats are Bob Mundell and Art Laffer, two "roust-about radical upstart" friends of mine, who were first joined at the hip about twenty years ago by economic journalist Jude Wanniski (who also made an important contribution in his book, *The Way The World Works*, published in 1978, where he blamed the highly protectionist Smoot-Hawley tariff increase as one of the major causes of the 1930s depression). Meanwhile, it was the Laffer-Mundell model of tax-rate reduction and a sound dollar re-linked to gold that formed the basic economic policy vision of Ronald Reagan, and which forms the basic intellectual thrust of my own thinking, and this book. Of the two, Mundell is more the academic, and his most important book, at least to me, is *Monetary Theory: Inflation, Interest, and Growth in the World Economy*, written in 1971 when he was an economics professor at the University of Chicago. Today he teaches at Columbia University, and he quite generously participates in various monetary conferences, including a regular monthly dinner he co-hosts with *Wall Street Journal* editor Robert Bartley, sponsored by the free-market Manhattan Institute.

Mundell has always been a hard money advocate, a student of the classical gold standard and the post World War II Bretton Woods dollar-gold fixed exchange rate system. He strongly believes that today's world of currency chaos and floating exchange rates is badly in need of currency reform and cooperation, especially in the aftermath of the recent Southeast Asia crisis. He favors the common currency experiment in Europe, and believes that Germany will be the monetary strongman, linking the new Euro to gold and closely coordinating it with the U.S. dollar. He also likes the growing dollarization of the U.S. and the Western Hemisphere, and hopes that The People's Republic of China and Hong Kong, nations both linked to the dollar, will serve as an example for all the Asian Tigers.

Years ago Mundell wrote extensively on the world's balance of payments system, and through this vehicle he strongly criticized Keynes' notion that over-saving led to the Depression, and always remains a recessionary threat. Instead, Mundell argued that paltry investment returns at home will lead people to make use of efficient international financial markets by investing abroad; there is no such thing as over-saving. However, low taxes, diminished regulations, and price stability at home will lead to more efficient markets and high returns, thereby repatriating international flight capital.

Most important, Mundell has always stressed that paper money must be anchored by a clear standard of value, and that yardstick of value should be gold. This "domestic price rule" approach requires central banks to maintain a steady exchange rate between their currency and the price of gold. In this way the supply of new money creation will be in balance with the economy's demand for money, and the absence of excess liquidity will lead to a stable price level and a zero inflation rate. Essentially, Mundell turned the Keynesian demand model on its head. Instead of the Keynesian nostrum that taxes should be raised to curb "excess demand" (or "overheating"), Mundell argues that inflation is a monetary problem that can only be cured by an increase in dollar value. Instead of the Keynesian view that easy money will stimulate growth and employment, Mundell believes that only tax-rate reductions (including lower tariffs) restore incentives to enhance the supply of new jobs, investment, and output. In other words, Mundell's great contribution is his redefinition of the optimal mix of policy instruments: *taxes* must be applied to the economy, *money* impacts inflation. Judging by the long wave of prosperity, which was based on Mundell's policy mix of tax-rate reduction and a strong dollar, the Keynesian model has been put to rout. Recall that in the 1970s, easy money drove up inflation and rising taxes put a brake on growth.

Art Laffer's views on money are similar (though not identical) to Mundell's, but Laffer made his mark in tax policy. In simple and direct terms, he established the relationship between taxes and growth. Known as the "tax wedge" model, Laffer established that high marginal tax-rates create a barrier, or a wedge, between work effort (or investment risk) and reward. The larger the wedge (such as the 90% income tax-rate in the 1950s, or the nearly 80% tax rate in the 1930s, raised by Hoover from 25%), the lower the supply of work effort or investment capital. Laffer formalized this theory into a parabolic curve called the Laffer curve, which showed that punitively high tax-rates, or excessively low tax-rates, will yield diminished tax revenues. But a proper tax-rate (I believe Art would place the theoretically optimal rate no higher than 25% and no lower than 10%) will maximize the flow of tax revenues as it spurs economic growth.

In the late 1970s Art Laffer explained his curve to Ronald Reagan, arguing that a reduction of the top income tax-rate from 70% to 50%, or even less, would rejuvenate the economy by restoring economic incentives and, over time, would be self-financing. Reagan bought into the analysis and, at Laffer's suggestion, endorsed the Kemp-Roth across-the-board income tax-cut plan, which became the centerpiece of his successful 1980 Presidential campaign. Later on, Laffer served on Reagan's Presidential Economic Advisory Board, and remained a close Reagan advisor. Years before, Laffer taught at the University of Chicago, and then the University of Southern California. For over two decades he has run a successful economic research and consulting firm in southern California (I spent 1996 as a full-time staffer), turning out hundreds of papers on virtually every aspect of domestic and international economics.

My third tier of 20th century economic greats includes two Nobel Prize winners, Milton Friedman and Friedrich Hayek, as well as Hayek's fellow Austrian economist Ludwig von Mises. While I do not subscribe to Friedman's quantity theory of money (monetarism only works when tied to gold), I salute Milton for his staunch free-market credo. In 1980 he starred in the remarkable PBS television series, "Free to Choose," which was taken from the book of the same name, co-authored by Milton and his wife Rose. This book, and the television series, had a significant impact on the public, as Milton described free-markets and their application to economic problems in a clear and calm manner. Its impact was revolutionary, and undoubtedly helped Reagan to get elected. The Nobel Prize was awarded to Friedman, now professor emeritus at the University of Chicago, for his permanent income hypothesis, which essentially argued against Keynesian demand management, government stimulus, and the illusory effects of cheap money. Friedman's *Monetary History of the United States*, co-authored with Anna Schwartz, is also a classic.

While Hayek and von Mises have written extensively on economics, I include them on my list of economic greats principally because of their devotion to the philosophy of free markets, free people, and economic liberty. In *The Constitution of Liberty*, Hayek outlines the virtues of the "spontaneous order" of the market economy, arguing that markets are a discovery process and no one has sufficient knowledge to control prices, manage central planning or even develop useful or accurate econometric models. Von Mises, in his opus *Human Action*, places individual behavior and choice squarely at the center of the economy; he denigrates all government efforts to control or dominate economic forces. Both Hayek and von Mises were bitter foes of John Maynard Keynes. They also staunchly opposed all forms of socialism, and wrote extensively in economic, philosophical and historical terms about the evils of statism and socialist central planning. The list of their publications is virtually endless, but reading the work of these two great thinkers is well worth the while.

Can my 20th century economic greats overturn the Keynesian order? Well, they've made significant progress, and more is to come. And they are getting a lot of help from free-market economists such as Jack Kemp, Dick Armey, Steve Forbes, Phil Gramm, Robert Bartley, James Buchanan, Martin Feldstein, Robert Barro, Gary Becker, Robert Lucas, Jerry Jordan, Michael Cox, Bob McTeer, Martin Anderson, Jim Miller, Ed Crane, Steve Moore, Charles Murray, Jim Glassman, Chris DeMuth, Dan Mitchell, Paul Craig Roberts, Alan Reynolds, Larry Hunter, Richard Rahn, Steve Entin, Steve Hanke, John Ryding, Larry Mone, Victor Canto, Tom Sowell, Walter Williams, Walt Wriston, and many, many others who carry the fight on a daily basis. It's an impressive platoon. In the spirit of Schumpeter's gales of creative destruction, slowly but surely the new thinkers are replacing the old, transforming the economics profession as well as the economy.

What I do know, however, is that ordinary men and women who are not trained economists can use the free market supply-side ideas of the new economic thinkers by creating their own economic forecasts and their own investment strategy. Call it a stock market investing tool kit, for this is, after all, a book about the stock market and what makes it tick.

Let's start with the basic model. First, free markets work best when money is sound, tied to the golden standard of value, producing stable monetary purchasing power, price level stability, and zero inflation. Interest rates, especially long-term rates, are closely tied to inflation risk expectations formed in the financial markets. Hard money tied to gold generates stable and low interest rates and zero inflation. Second, entrepreneurs, risk-takers, investors, producers and workers provide maximum effort when tax-rates are low and after-tax returns are high. With the right incentive structure, economies will grow and flourish, throwing off rising profits and substantial capital returns. All of which are then capitalized into rising stock market price valuations.

Third, economic and market efficiency is greatly enhanced by minimal government interference and regulation, including government budget spending, which is best measured as a share of the economy (GDP). Fourth, international transactions (exports and imports, including capital flows) flow freely when tariffs (taxes) are lowest. And fifth, new technological innovations, which develop best in an efficient free-market setting, will power a free economy to new heights.

The best advice I can give to Main Street investors, as discussed in the articles published in this book, is to keep track of real world economic developments and government policy announcements to see whether events are moving toward the free market model (bullish) or away from the model (bearish). In the 1970s, for example, taxes, inflation, interest rates and regulations were all rising, and this stagflationary period produced the worst stock market since the 1930s. From 1966 through 1981, real (inflation-adjusted) stock prices declined 0.35% per year. Although numerous high-tech innovations were patented and developed in the 1970s, dismal after-tax economic returns and sky-high interest rates prevented these high-tech breakthroughs from being funded and commercialized.

During the 1980s, however, taxes, inflation, interest rates and tariffs all declined substantially and this triggered the first wave of bull market prosperity. From 750 in 1982 to the 2700 Dow peak in 1987, real stock market gains averaged 38% per year. Information Age high-tech took off and wealth creation soared.

During the late '80s, one of the key variables of the free-market model, inflation and the dollar, went in the wrong direction. As Treasury Secretary James Baker devalued the dollar, gold prices shifted back up to $500, and inflation and interest rates soon followed. Long-term bond yields are the key discounting factor in the net present value of future earnings (and stock market prices). So when Treasury rates moved from 7% to 10%, the expected future earnings decline prompted the October '87 market crash and led directly to the '87–'90 bear market (which, fortunately, did not break the long-term uptrend).

Also, a key variable in stock market investing is *the effective tax-rate on real capital gains.* Capgains is essentially a tax on risk-taking and wealth creation, and is therefore very closely linked to the stock market, which is a barometer of future wealth and economic growth. Remember, the capital gains tax has never been indexed to offset the effects of inflation. So, a simple approach to calculating the real capgains tax burden on the market (and the economy) is to take the inflation rate, plus a 3% historic real rate of return, times the Federal capital gains tax-rate, all divided by the 3% real rate of return. (I am indebted to my dear friend John Ryding for this formulation, and for his many other analytical contributions.)

Down through the years, actually going back to 1947, changes in the real capgains tax-rate have always anticipated stock market trends. During the hard money 1950s and early 1960s, an effective capgains tax rate of less than 40% was a huge factor in the postwar bull market (1949–68). However, during the inflationary 1970s, the effective capgains tax-rate averaged over 100%, at times reaching 200%, thus leading to the long bear market.

Since 1978, the Federal capital gains tax-rate has averaged about 28% (though it's had its ups and downs). As inflation receded from 15% to an average 3½% in the '80s, the effective burden on real gains fell below 60%, a huge improvement from its 100% to 200% rate in the '70s. Hence the bull market. The tax burden rose during the late '80s inflation-ridden market slump, but in recent years inflation has dropped below 2%, with gold around $320, and this year the Federal capgains tax was cut to 20%, so the effective tax-rate on real capital gains has fallen to an historically low 22.5%. Looking ahead, this is very, very bullish. Probably 10,000 to 15,000 bullish on the Dow over the next five to ten years, provided that the dollar remains stable and tax-rates are not raised (both reasonably good bets).

Really, the most important moving part in the free-market model and the stock market investing tool kit is the inflation rate. Tax, tariff and regulatory policies emanate from Washington, and while the direction of policy does shift periodically, changes tend not to be frequent. The inflation path, however, requires constant monitoring, for it can change quickly if excess money creation from the Fed causes the gold price to rise and the dollar to fall. So the key trick in the tool kit is inflation forecasting, especially the threat of *rising* inflation risk, for that will drive up bond rates and reduce the discounted net present value of future earnings. Put simply, expected inflation, expected bond yields, and expected corporate earnings are where the rubber meets the road for stock market prices. They are all of a piece.

Down through the years I have come to believe that gold is the single best leading indicator of inflation—the mother of all inflation barometers. Just as the Laffer-Mundel model predicted twenty years ago, movements in the gold price inform us about the Fed's supply of money, and the market's demand for money, and whether the two are in balance. A rising gold price (inflation) tells us that money supply is excessive (and needs to be withdrawn by the Fed) A falling gold price (deflation) tells us that money is too scarce (and needs to be expanded by the Fed). Tax cuts, by the way, will increase money demand (arguing for more money from the Fed), while tax hikes will lower money demand (arguing for less money from the Fed).

Rising gold suggests an increase in the inflation rate, a rise in the real capgains tax, an upturn of bond yields, a decline of future corporate earnings and therefore a stock market drop. From the same reasoning, declining gold prices (up to a point) are bullish for stocks. Best of all would be a *stable* gold price, probably in a range of $300 to $350. No one knows for sure what the "exact" right gold price should be. My advice is to simply track the trend. Upward is almost always bad for stocks, downward almost always good.

However, for those investors who prefer to cross-check gold with other leading indicators of inflation, I suggest a related but slightly expanded approach: the theorem of four dead bodies. Once again, look to free markets. In this case, financial and commodity markets. Inflation-sensitive market prices, including broad commodity indexes, the dollar exchange rate, and the Treasury yield curve spread, along with gold, will tell the inflation risk story.

Suppose you are walking in the city one day and you see a dead body in an alley. It could be a murder, but it might also be a death from natural causes. If you found two dead bodies, your suspicions would be raised, but you still cannot be absolutely sure if a murder has been committed. However, if you find *four* dead bodies lying side-by-side in the alley, there can be no mistake; there's been major foul play. So you take action, presumably placing an immediate call to the police.

So it is with inflation-sensitive market price indicators. If gold and commodity price indicators are rising, and the dollar exchange rate is falling, and the spread between 10-year Treasury rates and the Federal funds rate is widening, so the four indicators are moving together, then you would suspect that future inflation will be higher than current inflation, and the stock market is about to be murdered. But if only one, or perhaps two of the price indicators are signaling danger, it may be fine to worry, but the evidence is not yet conclusive. These forward-looking indicators are part of what supply-side economists call a "market price rule." Free-market prices capture all available information, as well as the forecast bets of millions of profit-seeking investors around the world. All this data is reflected in the *price* of inflation-sensitive market indicators. (I am indebted to Manuel H. Johnson, former vice-chair of the Fed, and Robert E. Keleher, now senior economist at the Joint Economic Committee of the U.S. Congress, for their 1996 book, *Monetary Policy, a Market Price Approach*, and for their friendship and guidance on this and many other subjects down through the years.)

MARKET PRICE INDICATORS
TO FORECAST INFLATION AND THE STOCK MARKET
(Four Dead Bodies)

1. Gold
2. Commodity Indexes
    Commodity Research Bureau (CRB)
    Goldman Sachs
    Journal of Commerce
3. U.S. Dollar Index (FINEX)
4. Treasury Yield Spread
    10-year rate minus Fed funds rate

Of course, there's never been a perfect mousetrap, and neither the market price rule approach nor the overall free market model is going to capture every twist and turn of the stock market. Nevertheless, the investment policy tool kit will serve as a useful guide for picking up trends, and that I believe is what good investing is all about. The key point is that Main Street investors can profitably use the very same free-market policy agenda that Reagan successfully implemented, and the very same classical free-market ideas put forth by my 20th century economic greats. What worked for national policy worked to improve the economy, and economic improvement is what's been driving the stock market. Importantly, low taxes, sound money, free trade and regulatory restraint are the key building blocks. This is the model.

Actually, long-term stock market trends suggest that the bull market prosperity of the past fifteen years is closer to the norm for the United States; the dreary bear market from the mid-'60s to the early '80s was really more of an exception. Market surveys by Chicago-based Roger Ibbotson, and Jeremy Siegel of the University of Pennsylvania, show that over the long run U.S. stocks appreciate by about 7% per year in real, inflation-adjusted, terms.

From Ibbotson's work, the stock market has increased at a real yearly rate of 7% since 1926, so that $1,000 invested back then in large company stocks would be worth $1,371,000 today. Had the same $1,000 been invested over the 70 year period in small company stocks it would be worth nearly $5 million today. A recent study by a mutual fund trade group shows that since 1970, a period encompassing twelve bad years and fifteen good ones, a $5,000 yearly investment in an average performing mutual fund would have grown to $840,000 today, for an 11.7% average annual return, a pretty comfortable retirement nest egg. Jeremy Siegel goes all the way back to 1802, and from that point until now the average annual return for all stocks has been 6.99%, adjusted for inflation. That's 195 years.

So John Maynard Keynes was dead wrong again. In the long run we are personally responsible and accountable for our own well-being and for the well-being of our spouses and families. And the best way for ordinary people to plan for retirement, and create wealth along the way, is through the magic of the stock market. War time inflation such as occurred in the World War II 1940s and the Vietnam '60s and '70s are always bad periods for the market. But we are not at war now, nor are we likely to enter a global conflagration any time in the foreseeable future. What's more, we have learned about the perils of protectionism and global trade wars from the dreadful 1930s experience, and today the emphasis is on expanding world free trade, not curtailing it. The ravages of inflation two decades ago have completely changed the tune of world central bankers and finance ministers, who are now ever vigilant over price increases and, at least arguably, have recommitted world money to a price rule approach linked to gold.

Here at home the combination of economic prosperity and budget restraint is bringing on a new era of surplus politics. My estimate of the budget suggests that over the next ten years we can expect surpluses as far as the eye can see, rising to as much as $200 billion to $300 billion per year. This will open the door and provide the resources for a thorough revamping of our indecipherable tax system and the inefficient Social Security system, which has not been materially changed since its inception over sixty years ago.

I believe that gales of creative destruction will sweep through the Federal system of taxes and retirement, and when the change is completed we will have a flat and simple income tax system with a top rate of no higher than 25%, along with a privatized retirement system that enables the workforce to invest its own payroll tax contributions in the stock market. Over the next years stock market ownership will rise to 150 million people or more, and they will be sure to protect their retirement nest egg by keeping government on a short free-market wealth-creating leash. Mr. Ibbotson's work suggests that historical stock market returns will bring the Dow Jones index to 53,000 by the year 2020. Unbelievable? Maybe so. But no one in their right mind on Wall Street in the 1970s would have ever predicted an 8000 Dow. And we did that last summer.

So I remain steadfastly optimistic; my uneasy and irascible pessimism is a thing of the distant past. President Reagan's vision tapped into a rich vein of optimism that lies deep within all of us. And optimism is the essence of leadership. The free market movement began by Reagan, a vineyard I have labored in virtually all my professional life, is slowly but surely overturning the old Keynesian order of government planning and elitist rule. In its place is the emergence of a long wave of prosperity based on Information Age high-tech innovation and a populist democratic capitalism that has created more abundance than anyone dreamed possible. That's the word, abundance. American abundance: the new economic and moral prosperity. Keep the faith. Faith is the spirit.

PART ONE

KUDLOW ON
POLICY AND POLITICS

1.1 REAGANOMICS: WHAT WORKED? WHAT DIDN'T?

A KEYNOTE ADDRESS FOR
THE CENTER OF THE AMERICAN EXPERIMENT

July 15, 1997

In defending President Reagan and the economic policies he started 15 years ago, I knew I was on to something last autumn during the presidential campaign of '96. Many feel that it was a fairly lackluster campaign. From the Republican perspective it clearly was. Probably the most interesting aspect of it, however, was that candidate Clinton essentially ran on a platform that emphasized smaller government, lower taxes, and traditional family values. And just like the politician who made these three issues winning issues, Ronald Reagan, Clinton won easily.

A lot of conservatives in Washington and other places are resentful and angry and even pessimistic over the current state of affairs. I am not, and I am glad that Mr. Clinton continues to run and govern on what are essentially Reagan principles. Admittedly they are Clinton's own interpretation of those principles, but imitation is the sincerest form of flattery. It shows the power and force of Reagan's ideas and vision.

In fact, that power may be spawning new Clintons. There's one in Great Britain today, Mr. Tony Blair, Prime Minister, who sounds more like Margaret Thatcher than John Major did. One could even argue that Clinton sounds more like Reagan than George Bush did. Regrettable, but true. A week or two after Blair was elected, he gave a speech to a socialist enclave in Northern Europe. At the conclusion of the speech he was roundly booed, which should be regarded as tremendous progress. If someone like me gave a speech before a bunch of socialists and was booed, it would be one thing, but for that to happen to Tony Blair, Labor Party PM, is quite a different matter. In that respect, we have come a long way, and it makes it all the easier to defend Reagan's legacy because it is a living legacy. Its spirit, principles and ideas are very much alive today and are the dominant influence on both political parties.

We've come a long way in economic terms from the period of the late 70s and early 80s. When I went to work on the Reagan OMB treasury transition in November 1980, I was a young man in my early 30s. The economy and the world situation then were a lot different than they are today. It is almost hard to imagine what it was like. The

3

United States had lost its place in the world. The Soviet Union was gaining not only in the territorial battleground, but also in the logical battleground and certainly in the media battleground. We were in a very precarious international place. In economic terms, we had just weathered our second oil shock and our inflation was running upwards of 12–15%. Distinguished Wall Street economists like Henry Kaufman were talking about the end of our financial markets as we knew them, with long term federal bonds at double digit yield levels. The economy basically stopped growing in 1978 and didn't begin to grow again until 1983. It was one of the longest business downturns in history.

Today it is a different ball game. The Cold War is over, the United States is supreme. American ideas, values, and economics dominate the world scene. I believe firmly, with respect to the great success President Clinton has had in this economy, that it was President Reagan that gave him the ground he is standing on.

I credit Reagan's policies to vanquish inflation which is the most pervasive influence, good or bad, on any economy. Reagan appointed Volker. Reagan appointed Greenspan. Reagan gave both of them the authority to do what it took and, of course, aided them with his own efforts to de-regulate the economy. We forget that it was Reagan who turned around the labor situation by standing up to the air traffic controllers in the PATCO dispute, settling it firmly in the favor of the American people and against a sort of materialistic union movement which, to the detriment of the economy, had gotten far too big for its britches.

It was Reagan who gave the primary thrust to de-regulating energy. He argued with Department of Energy economists in 1981 that the price of oil would not go to $80 or $100 a barrel, and that if our policies of disinflation and currency stability, along with the tax and de-regulatory efforts, were successful, oil would go to $20 or $25 a barrel.

The President was instrumental in de-regulating the transportation industry, and the banking and financial services industry. He was instrumental in setting the forces that led to the de-regulation of telecommunications and, more recently, utilities. All of these policies are still playing out, even through one or two generations of policy people in the federal departments and agencies.

It was Reagan who was four-square behind the notion of free trade. We had a hell of a time getting Canadian free trade, but we did. Reagan really did that with the force of his personality. That was expanded later to Mexican free trade and what we now call NAFTA. It was Reagan who floated the notion of hemispheric free trade, the notion that at some point in the future Canada, the United States, Mexico, and all of Latin America would be linked into a free trading zone.

Of course, in an area which goes beyond my expertise, it was Reagan who stood up to the Soviet Union time and time again. But it wasn't possible to just stand up to them. We had to have behind our moral force and our military and diplomatic initiatives an economy that would show the Soviet Union we meant business when we said we would out-spend and out-arm them if we had to.

This is where the controversial supply-side tax cuts came into place, along with the other economic innovations to which I haved referred. Income tax rates were up 70%. They had been raised by Republicans and Democrats from the late 60s through the late 70s, and the combination of double digit inflation and un-indexed, highly progressive marginal income tax rates created what we used to call tax bracket creep. That is to say, as you earned more you were pushed into the higher tax brackets, and inflation pushed you into still higher tax brackets. Families earning real incomes of $30–$35,000 a year were paying at the top end of the tax rate system and it was one of the reasons the economy had stagnated. We had the worst of all worlds. We had high inflation and high unemployment at the same time.

So a band of supply-siders, of which I was a part, helped President Reagan enact the Kemp-Roth tax cut bill in 1981, which later evolved into the flat tax reform of 1986. The top rate was reduced, in steps, from 70% to 28%, which spurred economic growth. There was a lot of doom and gloom in the 80s while economic growth was recovering. People focused on budget deficits and trade deficits and the early stages of transforming our industrial economy into an information age economy. They said the dollar was too high, or the dollar was too low. Hardly anybody in those days would focus on the main chance—that the economy was recovering and jobs were growing. The expansion of the 1980s lasted over seven years and created roughly 20 million new jobs. The economy grew at a 4% annual rate and the inflation rate was just over 3%. The unemployment rate was taken down from a peak of 11% to about 5½ or 5¼% at its lowest point. It was the longest peacetime expansion in history. My friend, *Wall Street Journal* editor Robert Bartley, referred to it in his book *The Seven Fat Years*—a biblical reference, and a very appropriate one.

People will continue to criticize President Reagan and the rest of us for the deficit problem, so I want to comment on it briefly before moving on to other more interesting topics. Deficits, in my view, are a fiscal policy tool. By themselves, they have no moral content. Nations that run recurring deficits over decades and decades are probably nations that are going to have trouble. But as historian John Steele Gordon has written in his recent book *Hamilton's Blessing*, there are times throughout American history when deficit finance and the accumulation of debt has served very important national purposes. Certainly Hamilton's consolidation and selling of debt was one of the cornerstones to setting our fragile new Republic on solid ground in the 1790s and led to 40 years of prosperity. Certainly debt was floated in the Civil War and in World War I and World War II. Indeed, the highest debt to GDP ratio occurred during and after World War II, when it ran upwards of 115 or 120% of our gross domestic product. We needed that to win the war and maintain our freedom. Likewise, I believe we needed to employ deficit financing in the 80s to win the Cold War and bolster our *economic* freedom.

Moreover, I believe the single largest cause of the deficit was the sharp reduction of inflation, from a zone of 12–15% in 1980 and 1981, to a zone of 2–3% in 1986. The government had been living on inflated revenues and inflated personal income revenues for over a decade, from LBJ through Nixon and Ford, to Jimmy Carter. The government's appetite for inflated revenues was virtually insatiable, and it supported, nourished, and ultimately overfed the rise of the entitlement state. Reagan inherited that.

Rising inflation was a huge effective tax increase on the economy, on top of the already high actual tax rates. So, getting inflation down was a huge tax cut, though it probably resulted in a loss of nominal GDP income of close to a trillion dollars from what might have been the case if the inflation had continued at a 10–12% annual rate. If the choice is to finance a deficit in order to lower inflation and improve the economy, or to oppose a deficit and maintain the inflation that was destroying our economy, I would take the former any time. Reagan made a brilliant economic and political decision to give Volker the green light to do what he had to do.

The supply-side tax cuts are usually blamed for the deficit, but the facts are really not supportive of that position. That's the interesting part. We've learned now that even in the first couple of years of the tax rate cuts, we only lost about $30 or $40 billion in personal income flows from what might have been the case. A lot of studies have been done on this, and over the course of the expansion from 1982 to 1989, it turns out that revenues nearly doubled in nominal terms, and in real terms went up by 35%! If it were true that tax cuts caused lost revenues and deficits, then why did the level of revenues go up so much during that period?

6

My answer is that the Laffer curve worked. Arthur Laffer, a dear friend with whom I worked in California, argued that reducing tax rates from a punitively high range will not only encourage more entrepreneurship, more work effort, more risk taking, and more capital formation, but will also pay off in a relatively short period of time with better economic growth and a higher revenue volume. That is exactly what happened in the 1980s, so I really don't accept the criticism that the tax cuts caused the deficit expansion (although I recognize that mine is a controversial view). I believe it was the sharp inflation drop that was truly responsible. However, both were necessary for our economic security, and the re-invigoration of our economic security was a crucial tactic in the effort to reclaim our national and international physical security. When President Reagan went to Reykjavik in 1986, he was able to stand tall with an economy that was in its third solid year of growth at a time when the rest of Europe, for example, was still in a recession. Gorbachev knew, in that negotiation and subsequent ones, that Reagan had his economy behind him. It was clear we could afford to do, and spend, whatever it took if that's the game the Sovs wanted to play. They folded their hand, and part of the reason for that was the recovery of our domestic economy.

The last issue on the deficit, of course, is the build up of military spending. The Weinberger Defense Department spent about 1.6 trillion real dollars. This was part of the game plan actually begun under President Carter, who in the last year of his administration finally understood that the Soviets were not our friends. But it was left to Reagan to really boost defense spending, and that boost was not only a crucial factor in the end of the Cold War, but the fundamental reason why we never had a hot war. Instead, we got just a glimpse, a snapshot, of the awesome military power that we created in the 80s when we triumphed so quickly and decisively in the Persian Gulf War in early 1991.

People say this is the legacy we're handing to our children and our grandchildren—this debt which is really about 50% of gross domestic product, very much at the low end of the historical range. I say that what we are really leaving to the next generation is a strong economy with maximum opportunity—the leader in the information age and high technology transformation which will be the 21st century's economic story. *That* is what we have bequeathed to future generations—a world that is not only prosperous, but peaceful. And I wouldn't underestimate the peaceful part as something which will have a flow-back effect to the prosperous part of that legacy.

These are Reagan's legacies.

We will pay the debt down in the next 20 or 30 years. Slowly but surely, any clever treasury secretary with some good debt management policy advisors can begin to redeem the debt by slowing down its issuance, as current Treasury Secretary Robert Rubin has been doing. He's paid down about $65 billion worth of debt so far in FY 1997 by simply not re-opening a number of Treasury note and bond issues. This is the right way to do it. There is no obsession here. It doesn't interfere with any market forces. It's just done as a matter of course.

More interesting is that except for about eight months (late 1990 and early 1991) during a Bush administration that neglected Reagan's economic principles, the U.S. economy has been in continuous growth and prosperity for nearly 15 years. That is an awesome achievement. We have created more than 36 million new jobs, 20 million of which came in the 1980s alone. We are experiencing the greatest bull market in stocks in our nation's history. It shows no signs of fatigue or end and it has, so far, according to Federal Reserve statistics, created $17 trillion in new household worth. $17 trillion is about two and a half times the entire European GDP, and we did that in just the last 15 years. According to the published data, real GDP since 1982 has grown 3% at an annual rate and the inflation rate has been slightly above 3% at an annual rate. I believe both of these measures will be re-calculated to better reflect the high technology investment, production, services and spillovers of the information age.

Some economists like Leonard Nakamura, of the Philadelphia Federal Reserve, and Michael Cox, of the Dallas Federal Reserve, argue that over this period we have underestimated productivity by at least 1% and maybe 2%. Therefore, we have underestimated real GDP by at least one percentage point, maybe two, and we have overestimated the inflation rate by at least one percentage point and maybe two. When some historian, let's say in the year 2050, looks back on this period using a refined measurement process which captures all the contributions to the economy of high technology advances, it may turn out that the 80s and 90s were a period when the American economy grew at close to 5% a year with about 1% inflation and 3% productivity growth. For years I resisted this, but I have now come to believe that Jack Kemp was right. We *can* grow at 5% per year and it is just a matter of time before some national politician runs for high office on that very plank.

Along the way, we have so democratized and de-regulated financial markets, as well as other sectors, that today, according to surveys, there are roughly 125 million people invested in the stock market. That number is almost identical to the entire work force of this country. So, virtually all working Americans and, by implication, their children, are invested in the stock market. They've got a piece of the rock. This is the greatest advance of democratic capitalism in world history. This is not a market of rich people. This is not a market of elites. This is a market of ordinary people saving through stockbrokers and mutual funds and IRAs and 401(k)s and you name it. That $17 trillion increase in net worth, a function of the stock market's wealth creating process, is real money.

This is one reason why Americans are at their highest level of confidence in years. Roughly speaking, we are as confident today as we were about ten years ago at the height of the Reagan boom, and as we were in the early and mid 60s at the height of the Kennedy/Johnson era.

Let me make a couple of forecasts. By the end of President Clinton's term of office (which I think will occur on the regularly scheduled date of January 2001), I believe we will have had three more years of uninterrupted economic growth. There will have been no recession. This will have given us roughly 18 years of prosperity. I believe at the end of his term we will have a zero inflation rate. I believe at the end of his term we will have a 4% unemployment rate, and if I am wrong it will be because it's lower than that. I believe at the end of his term we will have a 5% Treasury bond rate, a 4% mortgage rate, and a Dow Jones average somewhere near 12,000. That will merely be a step on the way to the 40,000 Dow I think likely by the year 2020.

What's more, in furtherance of Reagan's spirit and legacy, I believe we will be running budget surpluses of $100 to $150 billion a year, the first of which will appear in FY 1998 (which starts at the end of this calendar year). We have solved the problem. Supply-siders argued that by some manner of flexibly freezing federal spending and by maintaining incentives to grow the economy, we would solve the problem. We are solving the problem. We have the lowest deficit in the industrial world. In fact, only the United States meets the G7 Eurodollar deficit requirements.

There is a fad in Washington right now that if there are surpluses we must spend them immediately. Others think we should use the surpluses to retire the debt. Well, I don't agree with either position. I think we should turn the money back to the taxpayers.

I am reminded of two of my favorite heads of State who inherited large deficits and debt and were able to retire them through supply-side means. One was the famous Victorian British Prime Minister William Ewart Gladstone. Gladstone was the Chancellor of the Exchecquer when Peel repealed the Corn Laws. Those were steep tariffs, as were the tax rates of the day. Gladstone also eliminated most taxes throughout the U.K. when he was Prime Minister and in so doing grew the British economy to a point that virtually all of England's Napo-leonic War-related debt could be retired. In this country in the 1920s, Calvin Coolidge, who followed Harding, lowered the Coolidge-Mellon income tax rates and, at the same time, extinguished post-WWI debt and put the budget in a surplus. *First* he cut taxes, *then* he waited for economic growth, *then* he retired the debt. *First* Gladstone cut tariffs, *then* he waited for economic growth, *then* he paid down the debt.

I emphasize this because the Reagan agenda has a number of unfin-ished elements. I regard myself as a conservative, free-market reformer and I think there is no better time to reform than during periods of prosperity. It is very difficult to make large scale reforms when econ-omies are turning down and people are unhappy and social conditions are contentious. But when the people have more confidence, when the jobs are plentiful, when prosperity exists, it's a great time to make the reforms that need to be made.

A list of such reforms, which I believe follows directly from Reagan's agenda (and which, incidentally, Clinton may have some sympathy with), includes, first and foremost, tax streamlining. The Reagan 1986 Tax Reform Bill was a great step in this direction. A lot of loopholes were closed. A multitude of tax brackets were collapsed into two—the good old 28 and 15% brackets—and the spirit of tax reform was sufficiently and surprisingly bipartisan. I don't remember the final votes on the bill, but people like Senator Bradley and Congressman Gephardt were tax reform Democrats in those days, and it isn't at all clear to me that President Clinton couldn't become one now. You know, Jack Kemp has actually met with Clinton to discuss tax reform. That is an interesting odd couple and some good might come out of it. The biggest impediment to an administration plan to streamline the tax code and lower tax rates is Clinton's own Treasury Department. It is an odd story. As much as I admire Robert Rubin, who I think has done a wonderful job working with Clinton and with FED Chairman Alan Greenspan to keep the inflation rate down, as much as I admire Mr. Rubin and Mr. Clinton for their spectacular free trade policies—they have done a terrific job following in Reagan's footsteps—Rubin is a class warrior and a revenue redistributor when it comes to tax policy. He is not a capital formation, pro-growth reformer.

I think we should create a tax system—and I believe Reagan strongly advocated this—where entrepreneurs and ordinary men and women will be permitted to spend their own money. They will spend it more wisely than government will. The root of this is not only an economic vision of incentives, but also a vision of personal responsibility and accountability—a spiritual vision in addition to an economic incentive vision.

What is more, I heard President Reagan say repeatedly that the ideal tax code is one in which all income is taxed once, and only once. Such a system would stop taxing saving and investment three and four times as wages, as salaries, as dividends, as interest, as capital gains, as inheritance taxes. These are reforms that are currently out there, and all fall very much under the Reagan rubric.

On the other hand, I believe the biggest mistake President Reagan made was signing the 1983 Social Security Reform Bill, because it triggered a series of payroll tax increases, thereby burdening even more the already burdened middle class. Moreover, it offset and diluted his own income tax reform plan. And finally, it didn't take any small steps in the direction of a privatized social security system which would link our contributions to the investment markets. The rate of return offered by these markets, of course, is superior to that of the Treasury bill market (which has itself diminished). One of the great tragedies, I think, of the last 15 years is that all of us sitting in this room have been denied by the federal Social Security system the opportunity to invest our Social Security contributions in this phenomenal bull market. States and localities have for years invested retirement money in the stock market and have seen terrific performance as a result. It is a pity that the general citizenry is not allowed to do the same. I wish Reagan had moved toward privatization. I and others recommended it at the time, but it, along with tax streamlining, remains an unfinished agenda item.

Additionally, I think we can still make quite a few reductions in the level of federal spending. A lot of unnecessary departments and agencies could be cut out entirely. Reagan would have preferred a significantly smaller government, meaning not only fewer dollars spent every year, but also fewer federal departments and agencies. Unfortunately, there were only two terms, and only so much time in the day, within which to achieve these goals.

Finally, I think an unintended result of Reagan's policies was the extraordinary explosion of this high technology information age which has become the backbone of the economy in the 1990s. It started really in the mid to late 70s, but so much of the new computing devices, both hardware and software, that were developed in the 70s were not sufficiently commercialized, brought to market, and distributed until the 80s. I have to believe it was no coincidence that lower inflation, lower taxation, less onerous interest rates, and so forth, combined to bring these things to commercial success. It's as if Joseph Schumpeter became an advisor to Reagan, though he never had a formal place at the table.

Schumpeter, of course, is my favorite dead economist. He was the foremost proponent of the entrepreneurial theory of growth and, particularly, of the technological innovation theory of growth which plays such a huge role in our present economy. At hand is the greatest burst of high tech innovation and risk taking and commercialization in our nation's history, or at least in the last 100 years. A lot of experts who know more about this than I do have argued that information age technological innovations are more powerful than the steam engines, railroads, automobiles, and other industrial breakthroughs of the 19th century because the information age breakthroughs have more spill-overs and more applications for more people and more businesses. I think that's true. We know they have raised productivity and our economy's potential to grow.

Schumpeter must have had lunch with Alan Greenspan, too, which is a very important point. We are headed towards literally zero inflation. Price indexes are now registering zero inflation. The producer price index has not grown in twelve months. That is a phenomenal achievement. Schumpeter always believed that an entrepreneurial economy would create innovations. Those innovations, when put into business, would do two things: they would raise output and lower prices. So another spillover from the Reagan revolution may be the end of the Phillips curve. Unlike many Wall Street bond traders and many economists at the Federal Reserve, Reagan believed you could have good economic growth, low unemployment, and price stability all at the same time. He believed that, and he encouraged Volker and Greenspan to keep their eye on gold as a reference point for the value of money. We are as close to a Bretton Woods gold system as we've ever been, and it has helped entrepreneurs. Schumpeter, in at least some imaginary sense, is telling Greenspan, "Don't worry about economic growth. It is all coming from the investment side, from the techno-logical side, from the innovation side. It won't *cause* inflation, it'll actually lower it." Last week Compaq announced strong earnings, a tougher marketing process, and lower prices. It is just what Intel said two or three months ago. That is Schumpeter's influence. And with Greenspan having gone back to the hard money philosophy of Reagan, I think short-term interest rates will likely go down, not up. Another spillover from the Reagan years.

Finally, we have the notion that prosperity and price stability improves the national soul—one of my favorite topics. The data actually show that malignant social trends have reversed of late, at least a bit.

Crime rates are down. Property crime rates are way down, but violent crime rates are down as well. Teenage pregnancy is starting to turn down. Family break-up is starting to turn down, as is divorce. Much drug use is also waning.

I am indebted on this point to historian David Hackett Fischer. Fischer has written a great new book called *The Great Wave* in which he talks a lot about how rising inflation causes social deterioration and how falling inflation or stable inflation (what he calls price equilibrium) causes an improvement in the moral fiber and the moral character of nations. In particular, Fischer discusses the Victorian Age. For 76 years, from 1820 to 1896, prices were stable and inflation was non-existent. I mentioned Mr. Gladstone, my favorite Prime Minister from that period, who contributed to that situation in England. In the United States, except during the Civil War, the case was the same. Our inflation rate was zero during that period. Fischer points out that during the Victorian equilibrium we saw a decline of crime, a decline of murders, a decline of alcohol consumption, a decline of illegitimacy. We also, during that period, had an increase in real wages. We also had a decline of income inequality, and Fischer concludes—and I wish to agree strongly—that we had a decline of social despair and a rise of moral value during the Victorian equilibrium.

I believe, along with Nobel Prize-winning historian Robert Fogel, that we are in the midst of another such great awakening, a great spiritual awakening, in this country. Much of this has nothing to do with economics, but much of it does, because it sure is easier to attend to our spiritual flaws and defects if we have a job and a more secure financial future and some money in the bank and some retirement investments that are rising in a bull market.

We are in a period of great change and transformation. Our evaporating inflation rate and our rising economic growth rate are mirrored in the phenomenal increase in the stock market which is a metaphor for our times. We can look forward to improving social, family, and spiritual conditions. We have a marvelous confluence of events: stable prices and free trade, information age entrepreneurship, the promise of new tax reform and social security privatization, and the end of the false paradigm of the trade-off between growth and inflation. We now know we can have low unemployment and zero inflation at the same time. An era of renewed moral and spiritual values, an era of global peace and prosperity, is upon us. I think we are about a third of the way into this long cycle, and I believe strongly that it was Mr. Reagan who began it.

We are changing. We are reforming. We are transforming. It is all of a piece. This is a story about the economy, but it is a story that is much bigger than the economy. This is a story, really, about our unlimited potential to use our God given talent and creativity. I can't predict how long this will go on. There is no end in sight in terms of the stock market and the economy. But I will argue that with the help of millions of people around this country and billions of people around the world, it was Ronald Reagan who led this revolution, who established this new higher ground, who provided us with the spirit, the vision, and the road map which is today still being followed by the most successful politicians on the world scene. So let me say personally, keep the faith. And in the words of my favorite president from California, the best is yet to come.

EXCERPTS FROM A FOLLOW-UP QUESTION & ANSWER SESSION

MITCH PEARLSTEIN: I want you to know that was absolutely compelling. It was wonderful. We have a question in the back.

DAN: Dan from Cargill. That was a very bullish and very positive forecast to the year 2000. What do you think are the biggest threats to that forecast coming true?

LAWRENCE KUDLOW: The biggest single threat I can think of just off the top of my head is the physical condition of Alan Greenspan. He is a very healthy 71 year old, recently re-married, God bless him, and he is active on that tennis court on the roof of the Federal Reserve Board in Washington. He is, in my opinion, the best Fed chairman of my professional lifetime, and probably in the whole history of the institution. We want to keep him healthy. Clinton just indicated in a *Business Week* article that he would re-appoint Greenspan in June of 2000 and that is very reassuring. And, you know, I often wonder. We always look at various indicators of the economy's health and the money supply and gold and commodities, but somewhat glibly, yet somewhat seriously, I would suggest watching Alan Greenspan's EKG. It's a very important factor in the outlook.

CLARKSON: Mr. Kudlow, you threw out a lot of statistics but the one that I was just stunned by and wondered why lightening didn't come down and strike was your assertion that Secretary Rubin has paid off $65 billion of debt this year. Why wasn't there one of these ceremonies with Clinton walking across the White House lawn in front of the troops, or a mortgage burning ceremony on the steps of the White House? It seems like the Congress and the President are slavering and lathering over the fact that the deficit is disappearing.

LAWRENCE KUDLOW: I appreciate the sentiment, but I think the reason Clinton didn't slaver and lather over it is that he is a very successful politician. It is not that big a deal and I think the President knows full well that his political bread is buttered by prosperity. I think Clinton, more than most *Republican* politicians, understands the force of Reagan's growth message and his politics of optimism. I suppose I neglected to focus on that; I had a lot of ground to cover in this speech. It was Reagan who taught us about the politics of optimism, as well as the politics of growth. Regrettably, neither George Bush nor Robert Dole was able to digest the politics of optimism. Mr. Clinton was. Regrettably, many of my conservative intellectual friends today have themselves forgotten. Fortunately, there are still a few of us left to spread that word.

MITCH PEARLSTEIN: Mr. Kudlow, we have about two minutes. Why don't I ask you if you want to make any final comment, perhaps on that last point about the politics of optimism.

LAWRENCE KUDLOW: I wrote a couple of long editorial columns on it this year, and I'll probably revisit it again. I believe that in free democracies, optimists win and pessimists lose. I learned that from Reagan, but I have seen enough of it in my own political meanderings to be convinced. Democracies are about optimism and progress. Second, I believe that optimists are profoundly small-D democratic, profoundly populist. They believe in ordinary people. Pessimists are people who believe in elites and governments. They believe that famous Ivy League college professors are smarter than ordinary men and women. A pessimist believes the government has to tell you how much money you get and where to spend it. An optimist believes that you should keep more of what you earn and that it is totally up to you how you use it. To understand the deep-rooted optimism of Ronald Reagan is to understand that he really was the first populist Republican politician of stature in this century, or at least since Coolidge. Populists who believe in people are optimists, and I think American politics during this long wave of prosperity (to which I find no end in sight) will revolve around those leaders who take an optimistic view and who are, therefore, populist believers in markets and ordinary people, and those who take a rather pessimistic or cynical view, who are more elitist, and who believe that experts and governments must make decisions for us. What is interesting to me about this debate between optimism and pessimism and populism and elitism is that it's difficult to tell which politicians in which parties are going to buy into which view. In that important sense, I believe Reagan was a true bi-partisan president and the older I get, it seems, the more I tend to look at these issues in a bi-partisan, almost non-political sense. I think this era of prosperity and optimism opens up tremendous opportunities for either political party or, for that matter, new political parties. It was Reagan who taught me about optimism and populism and freedom and I think that is a lesson successful politicians must learn.

1.2 Bush Would Continue the Nation's Growth; Dukakis Would Stifle It

November 3, 1988

George Bush is going to win this election by a popular and electoral landslide. With the nation in prosperity, and with an opportunity to build and enlarge on the successes of the 1980s, to reach our fullest potential in the 1990s and beyond, there is simply no reason to change horses in midstream.

Throughout his campaign, Vice President Bush has emphasized private enterprise, wealth creation and individual initiative as the key to economic growth.

Consistent with this view, Bush has pledged to maintain the current low tax rates which have completely reenergized the economy, created new rewards and incentives for work effort and investment, and generated the longest peacetime expansion ever.

The new dynamic has created 17½ million new jobs, reduced the unemployment rate to 5½ percent and slashed female, black and Hispanic unemployment by half.

Inflation has declined from 14 percent to 4 percent and interest rates have eased by half.

Living standards have increased substantially, as real after-tax income has increased by 28 percent since 1980, 15 percent on a per capita basis.

What's more, the reinvigorated economy has generated a surge on investment, where total business spending has risen to 12.3 percent of gross national product, a postwar high, and business equipment spending has jumped to 9.2 percent of GNP, also a postwar high.

Bush will also maintain low inflation, teaming with Federal Reserve Board chairman Alan Greenspan, moving toward a commodity price guideline to regulate money supply to keep the dollar sound and continue international policy coordination with the Group of 7.

These market-oriented policies, and the robust economic performance which has plainly resulted from them, are now being replicated around the globe.

Regrettably, to his political misfortune, Gov. Dukakis has an entirely different and mistaken point of view.

In his dreary and austere vision, a group of Harvard dons stand on one side, ready with their industrial-policy central-planning proposals to control domestic business and create barriers to foreign trade and investment, and a group of IRS tax enforcers stand on the other ready to disrupt families and businesses in pursuit of a few more nickels of revenue.

All this will stifle jobs, not expand them.

Dukakis' is a vision of wealth and income redistribution of increased government spending and taxing and controls. This comes through clearly in his opposition to the Bush proposal for capital gains tax reduction, where Dukakis uses the tired old rhetoric of "tax breaks for the rich."

He would have the federal government mandate a flood of new costs for businesses in health care, higher minimum wage, expensive retraining and reregulation. Moreover, Dukakis had repeatedly emphasized in this convention speeches and the debates, a laundry list of big-ticket budget proposals.

Priced out by Congressional budget experts for the 1980–1993 budget cycle, Dukakis' new spending plans would add at least $200 billion, including $13 billion for child care; $9 billion in food assistance, $10 billion in homeless housing, $75 billion in middle-income housing assistance, $34 billion in education spending, $31 billion for Head Start, $27 billion in long-term health care and $11 billion in clean-coal technology.

This $200 billion of budget busters will play to the worst instincts of the Democratic-controlled Congress, and would of course completely violate the Gramm-Rudman deficit-reduction target now in place in Congress. Which is why Dukakis—unlike Bush—has never endorsed Gramm-Rudman or the targets, much less a balanced budget amendment or a line-item veto.

Though Dukakis has tip-toed around the cost of these proposals—he is indeed the stealth candidate—they are very much a part of his campaign litany. Just as it was his policy in Massachusetts, where from 1982 to 1988 spending rose by 62 percent versus 43 percent at the federal level.

Dukakis has no serious deficit-reduction plan—except of course to raise taxes, which is the hidden agenda. Though he repeatedly denies it, that is the heart of the Dukakis deficit plan. His senior economic advisers, Messrs. Reich, Bluestone, Thurow and Summers, all favor tax increases.

In particular, a tax surcharge on the highest incomes to penalize the rich, which would then kill the geese that lay the golden eggs and end the long economic expansion by removing the low-tax incentives and rewards that stimulate economic vitality.

Also, Dukakis' advisers favor a stock transfer tax and a tax on interest payments to foreigners.

On trade, Dukakis has taken a protection against foreign investment and ownership.

Underscoring this mistake, in the most recent issue of *Institutional Investor* magazine, Dukakis tells us that to revitalize industries and give them time to modernize, he proposes temporary tariff protection.

But temporary tariffs, which are bad enough, will turn into permanent tariffs. This would head us down precisely the wrong road.

On the right side of the issue, George Bush supports free trade and opening markets, such as provided by the Canada-U.S. agreement.

On the budget deficit, Bush's flexible freeze will adhere to the Gramm-Rudman deficit-reduction targets by holding overall government spending growth to about 4 percent.

Tough budget limits, alongside normal economic growth, will permit revenues to expand at a faster rate than budget outlays, without new legislated tax increases.

In sum, George Bush's economic policies will continue the cycle of enterprise and wealth creation, the backbone of employment, sustained economic growth and prosperity. Thus far, we have revived the economy; now we must build on these successes to reach our fullest potential.

This is George Bush's optimism for the future. We are on the right path. There is no reason to change direction.

1.3 THE DARMAN-BRADY RECORD OF FAILURE

September 6, 1992

During his term in office, President Bush has been preoccupied with international affairs—and with good reason. But with all of the changes occurring in the world, Mr. Bush essentially turned the economy over to Treasury Secretary Nicholas F. Brady and Richard G. Darman, the budget director. Their record is littered with failure, virtually destroying Mr. Bush's domestic Presidency.

If Mr. Bush is to succeed in restoring trust and credibility around the growth package he announced in Houston, then the most constructive course of action for Mr. Darman and Mr. Brady would be to immediately resign their positions and let James A. Baker 3d, the White House chief of staff, take over with a new team.

Over the three and a half years that Mr. Brady and Mr. Darman have been in charge, the economy registered a paltry 0.7 percent annual rate of real economic growth, with only a 0.5 percent rate of job creation. Unemployment rose two and a half percentage points and living standards, as measured by real after-tax income per capita, failed to rise at all. These economic losses had a bone-crushing effect on the budget, including $260 billion in foregone revenues, $60 billion in higher outlays and a $320 billion rise in the budget deficit.

By consistently failing to match the economy's post-World War II 3 percent potential for growth, Americans have lost $980 billion in goods and services and have forfeited roughly eight million jobs since Mr. Bush took office.

Equally poor is the Brady-Darman record on budget matters. During the 1991–96 period, Federal spending is projected to run $178 billion—and the deficit $809 billion—above the levels contained in the original November 1990 budget agreement.

By rolling back key tax incentives and creating a fiscal environment completely hostile to risk-taking, entrepreneurship and growth, Mr. Brady and Mr. Darman have actually raised the budget deficit to breathtaking levels, moving it to an estimated 5.7 percent of the economy in 1992, from 3 percent of G.D.P. in 1988. By placing deficit reduction ahead of economic growth, in the end Mr. Brady and Mr. Darman got neither.

If Mr. Bush had a completely new economic team, headed by Mr. Baker, he could restart economic policy and show the American people a clear agenda of growth, job opportunity and capital formation. Unless the voters see a new group of senior people in charge of economic policy, Mr. Bush will find it virtually impossible to gain credibility for his growth package on the campaign stump and in the all-important debates.

What's more, Mr. Bush must flesh out his new plan with far more specifics. He should draw from a detailed proposal submitted recently by Housing Secretary Jack F. Kemp and others from the growth wing of the Republican Party.

Their plan combines permanent across-the-board tax cuts for family income, capital investment and business with a government spending freeze, health care cost control, privatization and asset sales, along with enterprise zones and welfare reform. I estimate that with these incentives and a restructured government, the economy over five years could generate roughly 4 percent annual growth and the budget deficit could be virtually eliminated.

With a new economic staff and a new growth agenda, Mr. Bush can credibly respond to the voter revolt against high taxes and overly expensive government. By replacing Mr. Darman and Mr. Brady, he will break the stranglehold on change and new ideas. Most of all, Mr. Bush will show the American people a clear set of reasons to elect him to a second term.

1.4 IT'S CAPITAL FORMATION, STUPID

December 12, 1992

True enough, serious tax and regulatory mistakes in recent years, committed by a Republican president and a Democratic Congress, ended the Seven Fat Years of the longest peacetime expansion in history. But let's not forget that the volume of wealth creation, business creation and job creation during the 1983–89 period was a great achievement. What's more, free-market principles of limited government, lower tax rates, deregulation, disinflation and falling interest rates provided a global standard of economic success that has been copied in virtually all corners of the world, including Latin America, Western and Eastern Europe, the former Soviet Union, parts of Africa, and most of Asia.

Let's also not forget that American workers are the most productive in the world. According to a recent study by the McKinsey Global Institute, assisted by Little Rock's leading pessimist, Nobelist Robert Solow, a full-time American worker produced $49,600 of goods and services in 1990. In dollars of equivalent purchasing power, a German worker produced $44,200, a Japanese worker $38,200 and a British worker only $37,100. The study also found that German and Japanese factory workers produced just 80% as much, on average, as American workers on an hourly basis. This is why U.S. real exports have doubled in just the past six years.

What's more, except for Japan's lead in machinery, electrical engineering and transport equipment, the U.S. boasts superior productivity over Japan and Germany in every category, including: basic materials, metal products, chemicals, petroleum, rubber, plastic products, wood, paper products, textiles, apparel, leather, food products, beverages, tobacco and total manufacturing.

And, according to a recent New York Times story, the McKinsey study corroborates earlier research by economists William Baumol and Edward Wolff at New York University, Dale Jorgenson at Harvard, Robert Summers and Alan Heston at Penn, as well as Michael Porter of the Harvard Business School. Moreover, the reasons for American productivity superiority include Washington's relatively hands-off attitude compared with Tokyo or Bonn, which allows American companies much greater freedom to change prices, lay off workers, or

22

enter or exit lines of business. Furthermore, America's competitors are much more likely to prop up older industries, sacrificing higher living standards for all to preserve jobs for some.

Monday's lead story on The Wall Street Journal's front page reported that American high-tech companies have regained the lead in semiconductors, and are poised to surpass the Japanese in high-definition TV, electronic books and wireless phones. The U.S. now runs a healthy surplus in advanced technology, moving from a low of $15.6 billion in 1986 to $36 billion in 1991. And this year, U.S. chip makers will reclaim the global lead from Japan.

Turning back to the domestic scene, one notes that the Little Rock pessimists ignored the following socioeconomic facts:

- During the Seven Fat Years of the 1980s, real after-tax income rose 16% for all Americans, including a 12½% gain for the median of all Americans.

- According to studies by the Treasury Department and the Urban Institute, America during the 1980s experienced remarkable upward mobility, as 86% of the lowest quintile moved up, 60% moved out of the second lowest quintile, and 47% moved above the middle quintile. The top 1% actually did the worst.

- The largest relative income gains were generated by women, with an 11% gain in median women's income as a percentage of male income.

- The income tax share paid by the upper 1% of income earners increased 54%, moving from 18.2% in 1981 to 28% in 1988.

- Meanwhile, real gross business fixed investment as a share of gross domestic product was 11½% from 1981 to 1989, compared with 10½% between 1971 and 1979 and 10¼% between 1965 and 1969.

Moreover, as virtually every statistic released in recent months shows clearly, the U.S. economy is getting better, not worse.

Real GDP so far this year has risen at a 2.8% pace (3.6% excluding net exports), and other hard economic data measured against year-earlier levels show across-the-board gains: economic profits, adjusted for hurricanes Andrew and Iniki (up $74 billion); hurricane-adjusted cash flows (up $76 billion); nonfinancial productivity (up 3.5%); retail sales (up 8%); apparel store sales (up 11%); automobile sales (up 13%); income (up 4.9%); nondefense capital goods orders (up 8%); business startups (up 13%); construction (up 6%); housing starts (up 13%); semiconductor book-to-bill ratio (up 12%).

23

Initial unemployment claims are down 150,000. Producer price inflation is only 1.3%; consumer price inflation, 3%; and business output inflation, 1.5%. Interest rates are low—3¼% Treasury bills, 6¾% 10-year Treasury notes, and mortgage rates of around 8%. Even the banking system is recovering from three years of overregulation; bank profits in the third quarter reached a record $8.5 billion (nearly twice that of a year ago), and equity capital as a share of total bank assets has reached 7.39%, the highest level since 1966.

Next year will be the best year for business since 1987–88, with GDP growth of perhaps 3½% or better, largely because this year Washington failed to legislate any new punitive tax and regulatory costs, and thus the private business sector has finally adjusted to the policy shocks and damage inflicted on business over the five prior years. In other words, it is late 1992, not 1932.

Finally, the constantly heard mantra of "worker as victim who needs to be retrained in order to create jobs" is sheer economic nonsense. Workers do not create jobs; businesses create jobs. Former presidential candidate Paul Tsongas put it best last winter when he said that the trouble with Democrats is that they like employment, they just don't like employers.

The great economic issue facing the U.S. in the last decade of the 20th century is not infrastructure or job training—it is the need for capital supplies and capital formation. Workers need capital for new business formation, capital for new technology, capital for job training and retraining, capital for education, capital to convert the defense industry, capital for expanded health care, capital for the inner cities, capital to compete with Europe, Asia and Latin America, and, most of all, for job creation and wealth creation and income creation for all Americans.

Right now this nation has an abundance of capital. More than 100 million Americans, either through direct ownership of stocks and bonds (or mutual funds), or indirect ownership through pension funds and retirement plans, have roughly $1.25 trillion of unrealized capital gains. But this is dead money, locked up by punitive tax rates on investment and the threat of still higher future rates.

If, however, the tax rate on capital were lowered by 50% or more for all assets—both old and new, broadly defined—then the unlocking, realizing and reinvesting of $1.25 trillion would unleash such a flood of business and job creation that the economy would be propelled ahead by at least 4% a year, while the budget deficit would drop by roughly $200 billion through 1996, with plenty of secondary and tertiary resource multipliers to provide the wherewithal to begin solving any number of social problems along the way.

Furthermore, lowering the cost of capital by allowing for inflation-adjusted economic depreciation of capital equipment would reduce the cost of capital and stimulate investment far more effectively than a temporary marginal investment tax credit.

With the correct diagnosis, and the right incentives, any problem can be solved by creative men and women. America today has a shortage of capital, not a shortage of taxes or regulations or government direction. By solving the capital shortage through human action and free-market resource utilization, the Little Rock pessimists would soon discover the benefits of optimism and growth, the twin political pillars of the last successful decade.

1.5 WILL THE 104TH CONGRESS PRODUCE A BULL MARKET?

February 6, 1995

Given all the talk about the need for real political change, it's remarkable how few people recognize it when it finally occurs. Wall Street, taking its cue from the Federal Reserve, continues to fret that moderate economic growth will reignite inflation, missing the bigger Washington picture. Most business and financial journalists, usually more insightful than the general news reporters, believe that despite November 8, it will remain business as usual in Washington.

The evening-news anchors have adopted the Democratic mantra crafted by White House Chief of Staff Leon Panetta and House Minority Leader Richard Gephardt: The Contract with America is a repeat of Reaganomics (as if the longest peacetime expansion in history were a bad thing), with tax cuts for the rich, more defense spending, and big deficits.

Yet significant social and economic policy change is occurring not only in Washington but across the country. Capital punishment and the death penalty have re-emerged as crimefighters. Vouchers and school choice have moved to the head of the class for education reform. Workfare and eligibility limits to ameliorate welfare dependency are cropping up everywhere. Affirmative-action quotas are under assault in the workplace. Victimization pleas are increasingly unfashionable.

Spiritually based self-help books stand atop the best-seller list, including the extraordinary treatise written by the Pope. Religious worship is increasingly popular, and small reading groups are popping up everywhere to study C. S. Lewis, G. K. Chesterton, Malcolm Muggeridge, and the Old and New Testaments.

What does all this have to do with the stock market? Plenty. As the right kind of change percolates upward from the grass roots, carrying with it the message that middle-class families and their small businesses are the backbone of America, that spiritual faith is the glue that holds both together, and that people will spend their own money more wisely than government does, policies in Washington are about to undergo the most significant change since the 1930s.

Government bureaucracy is out; the private marketplace is in. Keynesian fiscal fine-tuning is out; Schumpeter's entrepreneurship, innovation, and risk taking are in. Federal mandates are out; states' rights are in. This movement began in the Reagan Eighties but was interrupted during the dreary Bush-Clinton period. Now it is re-energized and re-staffed and ready to roll into the twenty-first century.

The 104th Congress has already begun to implement the new agenda. It is an agenda based on traditional Western values. It is a growth and opportunity agenda. It is a free-market agenda. It is a bullish agenda.

On the first night of the new Congress, the House ruled out tax increases, created honest procedures for budget scorekeeping, opened the way for a major reduction in domestic discretionary spending, and set the stage for a balanced budget.

While a chorus of naysayers continued to chant that the GOP is afraid to touch entitlements, Speaker Gingrich appeared before the first Ways and Means Committee hearing chaired by Bill Archer (R., Tex.) to say that Medicare is "a large, clunky, inefficient government system." He urged the panel to design a Medicare program "which gives senior citizens greater choice of better health care at lower cost." Meanwhile, both Medicaid and welfare will come under the budget-cutting microscope, and an emerging GOP consensus of governors, senators, and House members favors restrictions on eligibility and funding. If my hunch is right, even the untouchable Social Security system, the great symbol of the New Deal, will be significantly privatized during the next ten years. With more than fifty million Americans invested in the stock market through mutual funds and brokerage accounts, enough voters will finally realize how wasteful it is to turn over 15 percent of their earnings to Uncle Sam for a return of less than 1 percent a year, given that John Templeton, the Fidelity Magellan Fund, and a host of other investment managers have generated annual returns of 15 percent or better for more than thirty years.

Downplaying the coming changes, the Washington Post reported that the House Republicans were giving up on the tax-limitation version of the balanced-budget amendment. It isn't true. Assuming a few liberal GOP defections, but with 52 House Democratic votes in favor of the three-fifths supermajority rule for raising income-tax rates, Gingrich is about 15 votes short of the requisite two-thirds. But approval is within reach, and there is no leadership backsliding yet. Similarly for the rumor that the zero-deficit target has been abandoned. House Budget Chairman John Kasich assures me that "the downward glide path toward zero over five years is still in place. Then it moves to zero by 2002, the seventh year. I'd quit before abandoning the zero-deficit target."

On the spending side, House Appropriations Committee Chairman Robert Livingston (R., La.) has decided not to wait until fiscal year 1996 to make cuts. Instead, he has crafted a strategy to rescind about $10 billion of appropriated but unspent funds in FY 1995, yielding a lower expense level from which to cut another $40 to $50 billion from domestic discretionary accounts in FY 1996. "Next year is a whole new ballgame," Livingston says. "The President can veto rescissions, but he cannot veto a zero. And we are going to eliminate as many programs as possible, putting up plenty of zeros."

Sweeping deregulation is another key part of the new economic policy. President Clinton has already said he will not sign a 100-day moratorium on new regulations, but the House will pass one anyway in early February. Then, working through the new Government Reform Committee (a restructured Government Operations Committee with new powers over the Commerce and Labor Departments), the GOP intends to pass legislation that requires risk assessment and cost-benefit analysis for new and existing regulations, allows citizens to challenge unfair regulations, and establishes a regulatory budget.

The man behind the deregulatory push is Representative Tom Delay (R., Tex.), the new House majority whip. A former Houston entrepreneur who built a successful pest-control business, Delay spent six years pulling together an unofficial $500-billion-a-year tally of federal regulatory costs. Now he is training his sights on the Environmental Protection Agency, the Occupational Safety and Health Administration, the Equal Employment Opportunity Commission, the Clean Air and Water Acts, and the Americans with Disabilities Act. "It's what got me into politics," he says. "It's what I'm here for."

The final piece of the new economic policy is a series of tax cuts to boost high-risk capital investment, liberalize corporate depreciation allowances, and provide relief for middle-class families. The Gingrich Contract also calls for expanded IRAs, a rollback of the Social Security benefits tax, and elimination of the goofy marriage penalty set up by the 1993 tax-hike bill. All of these measures are favorable to growth and capital formation. Only the $500 child tax credit is misdirected. It would have a greater impact on marginal rates if it were turned into a personal allowance or deduction, as recommended by Senate Majority Leader Phil Gramm.

Much more will be done in the tax area during the next Congress, beginning in 1997, if the GOP majority is re-elected. In general, the party wants to provide greater incentives for saving, investment, capital formation, and work effort by reducing marginal tax penalties to the lowest possible levels. Along with accounting simplification and base broadening, Dick Armey's 17 percent flat tax will get a strong hearing, as will the Nunn-Domenici consumption-tax proposal. Down the line, when the GOP turns to Social Security reform, it will need to focus on reducing the FICA payroll tax, the most formidable barrier to job and small-business creation.

The proposed tax cuts, especially the 50 percent capital-gains exclusion with inflation indexing thereafter, would certainly boost the economy's long-run potential to grow. Today's unindexed 28 percent nominal capital-gains tax rate turns into a 56 percent effective tax rate, given a 3 percent inflation rate and a 3 percent real return. Under the Gingrich proposal, this would drop to 20 percent.

Instead of keeping 44 cents on the real dollar gained, investors would keep 80 cents. For someone in the 15 percent tax bracket, the plan would allow 92.5 cents to be retained. If the Republican economic plan boosts long-term growth back to its 3 percent historical rate, tax collections by the year 2002 would be $85 billion higher than the Congressional Budget Office now predicts, and spending would be $35 billion lower, meaning a $120-billion reduction in the deficit. Furthermore, Federal Reserve Chairman Alan Greenspan recently argued that the government's consumer price index exaggerates inflation by 0.5 percent to 1 percent annually. Correcting this problem could reduce federal spending on Social Security and other pensions by $150 billion over five years.

Pro-growth policies will render the existing stock of money less, not more, inflationary. Efforts to shrink government, deregulate business, and improve incentives will increase the output of goods and services, so the same amount of money will be chasing more goods, thereby reducing the inflation rate. Since the November elections the price of gold has dropped to around $375, not far from the $350 or so that implies price stability. With higher expected economic returns, the U.S. dollar exchange rate has started to recover. Even long-term bond yields in the Treasury market have declined a bit.

In 1995 the stock market and economy may face an interest-rate wall, slowing growth to a trickle, perhaps raising inflation for a while, and pushing down share prices. But this need only be a temporary obstacle. The dramatic changes in fiscal policy scheduled for enactment by the new Congress—combined with the rise of cultural conservatism and traditional values among the citizenry—amount to a powerful prescription for twenty-first-century America: strong, competitive, productive, and responsible.

In the twentieth century, often called the American century, the Dow Jones stock-market index, a good proxy for wealth creation and social progress, started at 70.4 on January 2, 1901. Today it stands above 3800, a 5,474 percent gain. Why can't the twenty-first century be ours as well? At that rate, the stock market in a hundred years would reach a Dow Jones level of 211,073. Think of it. Buy America.

1.6 CROSSROADS

May 20, 1996

A re we at a major market juncture? All the signs indicate that we are—and in no small part because we are also at a major political juncture.

What a difference an era can make. When free-market entrepreneurial economics were revived during the Age of Reagan, and classical thinkers such as Friedrich Hayek, Milton Friedman, and Joseph Schumpeter replaced John Maynard Keynes, John Kenneth Galbraith, and Paul Samuelson, the American economy flourished on a grand scale.

From 1982 to 1995, the Dow Jones industrial average increased 300 percent (adjusted for inflation), or 11 percent per year. All told, a phenomenal performance. Along the way, roughly 100 million Americans who own stocks and bonds (through brokerage accounts, mutual funds, IRAs, and other retirement plans) saw their net worth go up by an extraordinary $10 trillion, a 176 percent gain, which annualizes to 8.1 percent. From this rising wealth base, the U.S. economy created 29 million new jobs and produced a whopping 43 percent gain in real disposable income. No other G-7 industrial nation has come close to this performance. It's a fact. You can look it up.

During the prior Age of Inflation, which I mark as 1965 to 1982, Democratic and Republican Presidents alike practiced Keynesian fine-tuning, de-linked the dollar from gold, inflated the money supply, raised taxes, imposed wage and price controls, and maintained tight government regulation over key economic sectors such as banking, transportation, and energy. Meanwhile, the U.S. stock market declined by 67 percent (adjusted for inflation), dropping by an average of 6.5 percent per year.

Of course, in recent years Reagan's tax-cut policies have been compromised, first by George Bush and then by Bill Clinton. But the damage so far has been manageable, and the tide has not yet turned back out to sea. The top income-tax rate, which stood at 70 percent during the Age of Inflation, is now holding at 40 percent. The 28 percent capital-gains tax rate is much lower than the 45 percent during the 1970s. Corporate-income-tax rates are in the low 30s, compared to their hefty earlier perch of the mid 40s. The inflation rate in recent years has hovered near 2 percent; it was 10 to 15 percent during the last years of the Age of Inflation. Interest rates today run from roughly 5 to 7 percent; they were 15 to 20 percent 15 years ago.

Just as important, although Reagan himself has departed from the public square, his spirit lingers on, especially among the new generation of business leaders that was spawned during the Eighties. These men and women came to live by the Schumpeterian growth model of innovation and risk-taking. They started new businesses on a massive scale, they modernized business practices through downsizing and consolidation, and they instituted sophisticated financial-management techniques every step of the way. Their footprints are found throughout the economy, in computer tech, telephone tech, information processing, autos, utilities, transportation, steel, textiles, and electronics.

And they went global. For it was Reagan who first opened free trade in Latin and Central America, then negotiated throughout the Pacific Rim, including China, and it was Reagan's political economy that caused Soviet Communism to implode, thus re-opening Central and Eastern Europe, then South Asia, and even kindling hope in the Middle East. In short, American—not German, not British, not Japanese, but American—business has provided the leadership and cutting-edge management infrastructure for the worldwide spread of democratic capitalism.

All that said, there is however a growing sense, at least in stock-market circles, that the best of our story may have passed. In recent months the market has stalled, interest rates have again started to rise, and inflation risk is in the air. A year ago, buoyed by the Republican capture of both houses of Congress, many believed that 1995 would bring a new installment of Reagan's agenda: another round of pro-growth tax cuts, serious entitlement reform, more deregulation, and substantially smaller government.

Yet none of this came to pass. Speaker Gingrich showed himself to be a shrill, uncompromising, and unpopular figure, unable to grow into the job. As a unit, the House Republicans were obsessed with dreary numerical budget formulas and the politics of austerity and sacrifice. Gone was Reagan's message of optimism and growth. By early 1996 the Contract with America was dead in the water, and its underlying policy agenda of tax cuts, smaller government, and cultural reformation had been tattered and muddled.

What's more, politicians ranging from Pat Buchanan to Dick Gephardt have emphasized the darker side of the economic story. Real median family income, they have been pointing out, has slumped in recent years after recovering nicely during the 1980s. And Social Security and Medicare payroll-tax increases have eroded take-home pay.

Of course, when measured properly, the worker wage story over the past twenty years is quite a bit more respectable. Wage data exclude a sizable chunk of the modern worker's real compensation: health care, retirement, vacations, holidays, sick leave, and so on. When those generally untaxed benefits are added in per-worker annual income has been rising at a rate of 1.4 percent. And, as the wealth numbers suggest, somebody has made good money. Even going back to the early 1970s, real per-capita consumption has averaged 1.7 percent yearly increases.

Whatever the correct data, though, today's political reality reflects a cranky attitude of restlessness, irritability, and discontent among a major population segment. Many middle-income workers—one might think of them as Reagan Democrats—simply do not believe they have the financial resources to take care of their businesses or their families. In social and cultural terms the deck is stacked against them: racial quotas, illegal immigration, liberal courts, no-fault divorce, generation X dress codes, rampant welfarism, schools without prayer (or education), and government opposition to moral standards. To defend against moral slippage—by putting their kids into private or parochial schools, for example—middle-class folk need financial resources.

For this group, President Clinton's tired old big-government nostrums just won't work. Nostalgic for the social-insurance welfarism of Germany, France, and Sweden, Clintonites such as Robert Reich, Laura Tyson, Jeff Bingaman, and Byron Dorgan have come up with a program of higher minimum wages, more health care, more federal education money, more union power, more caps on executive pay, more community investment schemes financed by corporate pensions, and more limits on layoffs and restructuring.

Fact is, nearly everyone in America knows this stuff won't work. It never has. Just look at Europe, where a social-democratic model has maintained double-digit unemployment and blocked private job creation. More to the point, American politics has never favored class warfare or zero-sum economic pessimism. A few months ago a Reader's Digest poll showed that "Americans in nearly every group—across racial, economic, age, ideological, religious, educational, and sexual lines—had the same median response: A family of four with an income of $200,000 should pay no more than 25 percent in all its taxes combined." Polltaker Everett Ladd called it "the single most extraordinary finding in the history of domestic-policy polling in the U.S. . . . America is probably the only country in the world where there are no significant differences by party or class in the 'ideal' fair tax." In other words, class warfare doesn't work.

But you cannot beat something with nothing. At this point, future economic policy and the stock market both stand at the crossroads. It is up to Senator Dole to renew and reinvigorate the optimistic economics of Ronald Reagan. This presidential election will not be fought over income inequality and redistribution, or over austere numerical balanced-budget plans, unless Republicans allow it to happen. And if they allow it to happen, they will lose.

To regain the political and economic high ground, the GOP should hark back to the 1993 gubernatorial campaign of underdog candidate Christine Todd Whitman. During the final weeks of her uphill quest, Mrs. Whitman hammered home one simple, clear message to the voters of New Jersey: "You will spend your money more wisely than the government will." On this impeccable premise, her plan to slash income taxes across the board catapulted her to victory over incumbent Jim Florio, who had enacted the largest tax increase in New Jersey history. And it was Mrs. Whitman's plucky adherence to a bold economic growth plan that started the national Republican Party on the road to political resuscitation in the aftermath of George Bush's devastating defeat.

For Senator Dole, who campaigned hard for Mrs. Whitman, the lessons are very clear. Across-the-board income-tax cuts generate a powerful message of traditional family values because they show trust in ordinary people, who will spend their own money more wisely than government will. American families are more than willing to accept the risk and responsibility of making personal choices with regard to education (vouchers), health care (portability and medical savings accounts), and retirement (unlimited IRAs invested in private markets).

Add to the merits of personal responsibility the related demand for governmental accountability. Taxpayers insist that large-scale entitlements such as welfare and Medicaid be turned over to the states, where legislatures and governors will be more responsive to voter preferences than far-away Washington. People are increasingly convinced that generational welfare dependency, alcohol and drug addiction, family break-up, unlimited abortion on demand, and recidivist criminal pathologies are more closely related to soul-sickness than to the absence of material benefits. Ordinary people intuitively know that working together, through local churches, synagogues, schools, charities, fellowships, and self-help groups, is the only lasting solution to our nation's social and cultural problems.

Of course, across-the-board income-tax-rate relief is not only a values issue: it is also an economics issue because of the favorable impact on incentives. Tax credits are more manna from Washington, part of the old model that elites know best. Bill Clinton is at home with his own scheme for tax credits because it preserves the centrality of governmental planning, prioritizing, and allocation. The Clinton Administration simply does not trust the populace. Because of this, it will never agree to income-tax-rate cuts. Senator Dole, however, is in a position to—and must—acknowledge that those who work harder, save more, and are willing to invest must be rewarded through the incentive structure of lower marginal income-tax rates.

Today, a family-owned business that grosses $50,000 per year pays income tax at a 28 percent rate and Social Security/Medicare payroll taxes at a 16 percent rate. In most of the twenty largest population centers, state and local taxes take another 5 percent. So, right off the top, the combined marginal tax rate takes away nearly 50 cents of every middle-class dollar earned. Senator Dole must champion the forgotten middle class with a bold across-the-board income-tax cut. Lower tax rates, higher tax-bracket thresholds, and a payroll tax deduction are far more powerful instruments of growth than government-given tax credits. After-tax take-home pay will go up; fresh incentives to earn, work, save, and invest will rejuvenate overall economic growth. And people will have much greater opportunity to form their own priorities, run their own businesses, and care for their own children.

Income-tax relief can be seen as a down payment on future, more radical tax reform. Right now the Republican Party and the nation are split over which system would be better: a single flat-rate income tax or a national sales tax that replaces the income tax altogether. And after tax hikes in 1990 and 1993, a majority of taxpayers seem unwilling to give up large deductions for mortgages, charitable contributions, and state and local taxes in return for yet another politician's promise. Once the White House is returned to safe hands, presumably with a Republican Congress, there'll be plenty of time to thrash out the most workable plan.

Meanwhile, income-tax cuts will keep the focus on the individual. Right now the biggest tax burdens hit individuals, not businesses. The GOP is too quick to emphasize full depreciation expensing, or eliminating the capital-gains tax altogether, and not quick enough to address the combined burden of high payroll- and income-tax rates. On capital gains, for now, indexing would be just fine. But as Reagan understood full well, cutting income taxes is a populist issue, whereas cutting business taxes looks like and often is an elitist approach.

In Washington today economists are beginning to sense the middle-class public's growing desire for expanded economic growth. Thanks to back-to-back large-scale tax hikes in 1990 and 1993, this recovery cycle has produced yearly growth of less than 3 percent, compared to a normal rate of better than 4 percent. As a result, the nation has forgone nearly $2 trillion in income and nearly 6 million jobs.

But the solution is not to force the Federal Reserve into inflating the money supply. Already this year, fears of inflation have driven up interest rates. Investors are worried that government policies will shift toward easy money rather than tax cuts, lower budget spending, and deregulation.

The Dole campaign should learn something else from Reagan's policy notebook: Inflation is caused by too much money chasing too few goods, not by growth. If across-the-board income-tax-rate cuts, along with higher-bracket thresholds, freshen economic growth incentives to produce more goods and services, then the larger volume of output would render the existing money supply less inflationary. Of course, when Paul Krugman and Larry Summers briefly worked on the staff of the Council of Economic Advisors during Reagan's first term, they argued that tax cuts would increase inflation. They were dead wrong. Smart men, wrong theory. Reagan had the story right. Now, Dole must draw from Reagan, not the Washington economic establishment.

The populist approach resonates with voters. It worked for Reagan, Whitman, Engler, Thompson, Symington, and Pataki, and it will work for Dole. Real simple: He raised them, I'm going to cut them. Across the board. For everyone. I led the fight in 1993, losing by only a few votes. Please give me a chance to finish the fight and win the war. People will spend their money more wisely than government will. The economy can grow by 3 percent or more, with a steady dollar and no inflation. And folks will be freer to set their own moral standards in communities across the nation. I am optimistic about the ability of individual men and women to make our nation grow and prosper, and to supply jobs, income, and financial power well into the next century.

1.7 A DOLE AGENDA: CUT TAXES, RESTORE ECONOMIC GROWTH

June 2, 1996

In a dramatic move designed to boost his presidential election prospects, Sen. Robert Dole recently reshuffled the political cards by resigning from the Senate and reinventing himself as Citizen Dole. Still, Dole is trailing President Clinton by 17 to 20 percentage points in most major opinion polls.

What next? Dole must formulate a bold economic growth plan centered on an income tax rate reduction for all Americans. With this across-the-board plan he can articulate a visionary and passionate message of future economic optimism. He can exhort people never to accept second-best. No one must be left behind. Working together in the spirit of virtue, with the right economic incentives, our nation's potential is unlimited.

Of course this policy approach harks back to the successful two-term presidency of Ronald Reagan, who reintroduced free-market entrepreneurial economics in the early 1980s. By cutting taxes, calming inflation, curbing domestic budget growth and lowering regulatory barriers, Reagan unleashed a decade of wealth creation, inventiveness and job creation. Not even tax increases under Republican George Bush and Democrat Bill Clinton have completely blunted the effects of Reaganomics, though growth has predictably slowed in recent years.

Nevertheless, the U.S. stock market, a bellwether of national wealth and well-being, increased an extraordinary 300 percent (adjusted for inflation), or 11 percent a year, since 1982. Cynics may scoff that only rich people benefited from the stock market surge. But they are wrong. Over 100 million Americans own stocks (and bonds) through brokerage accounts, mutual funds, Individual Retirement Accounts, 401(k)s, Keough accounts and other forms of defined contribution retirement savings programs.

What is more, data show that it is those of modest means who have garnered the lion's share of the new wealth creation in the stock market. Since the mid 1980s equity ownership by those with incomes above $250,000 as a percentage of total stock market ownership fell from 43 percent to 23 percent. Picking up the slack, those with incomes of $75,000 to $100,000 expanded their ownership share from 7 percent to 12 percent. Below them, the $50,000 group more than doubled its share from 8 percent to 18 percent. And get this: those with earnings under $25,000 also more than doubled their ownership share from 3 percent to 7 percent. This is democratic capitalism at its finest.

From this rising wealth base, since the inception of Reaganomics the U.S. economy has created 29 million jobs and produced a whopping 43 percent gain in real disposable income, the best measure of living standards. No other G-7 industrial nation has come close to this performance. Actually, the incremental gain in U.S. output exceeded the total size of any of the continental European economies.

And what a contrast to the prior 15 years, when both Republican and Democratic presidents practiced Keynesian fine-tuning by inflating the money supply, de-linking the dollar from gold, raising taxes, imposing wage and price controls, and maintaining tight government regulation over key sectors such as banking, transportation and energy. In those days inflation routinely reached double-digit levels, interest rates peaked at between 15 and 20 percent and unemployment rose above 10 percent. Meanwhile, the U.S. stock market from 1965 to 1982 declined by 67 percent (adjusted for inflation), dropping by an average of 6.5 percent per year.

It was Reagan's supply-side model that turned the tide. He understood that inflation, the primary devil, is caused by too much money chasing too few goods. So, at the Federal Reserve he directed Paul Volcker and Alan Greenspan to restrain the money supply, giving them the sound money ground to stand on. Then, he persuaded Congress to reduce the marginal rate on personal income taxes by 25 percent for all income earners. With greater after-tax incentives to work, invest and save (especially through the stock and bond markets), the economy produced more goods with less money growth.

Spurred by revitalized free-enterprise, innovative men and women spawned fabulous world class companies in computer technology, telecommunications, information processing, autos, utilities, transportation, steel, textiles, and electronics. In every nook and cranny of the economy, business was made more productive and efficient through the use of sophisticated financial and information management. As a result, the economy expanded by nearly 4 percent a year for seven years, while inflation declined from an annual rate of 12 percent to around 3 percent. Orthodox Washington politicians and Wall Street pundits were proven wrong. Tax cuts boosted economic growth. And stronger growth helped to lower inflation.

Meanwhile, despite a defense investment of roughly $1.5 trillion that ultimately brought the collapse of Soviet communism, and the huge drop in inflation that boosted the economy but starved the federal budget for inflated revenues, by 1989 the combined federal, state and local budget deficit had fallen to only $18 billion. After Japan, this was the lowest general government deficit in the G-7.

Despite an across-the-board income tax cut of 25 percent, federal income tax receipts from individuals increased by 50 percent, or 5.8 percent per year, from 1982 to 1989. Overall, federal, state and local tax revenues jumped 69 percent or 7.6 percent per year. By the way, this data comes from the 1996 annual report of President Clinton's Council of Economic Advisers.

Citizen Dole must borrow a page from the Gipper's supply-side playbook. Dole must point out that while the economy under President Clinton has muddled along at an annual rate of 2.4 percent, the growth at a comparable point in the business expansion cycle of the last five economic recoveries, under three Democrats and four Republicans, averaged 4.4 percent per year. Indeed, for 45 years after World War II, between 1947 and 1992, growth in the U.S. economy averaged 3.3 percent per year through recessions and recoveries.

Had Clinton not engineered a massive across-the-board tax hike in 1993, the historical U.S. growth rate would have resulted in $300 billion more in income, or about $3,000 more per household in 1996 alone. Actually, after back-to-back tax hikes under Bush and Clinton, a prolonged period of subpar 2 percent growth since 1989 has cost the U.S. economy about $2.5 trillion in cumulative income losses and roughly 6 million fewer jobs from what should have been the case.

And it is precisely this growth deficit that has caused a cranky attitude of restlessness, irritability and discontent among the middle class. Between 1982 and 1989 the average income of the middle 20 percent of families rose by 12.6 percent in constant dollars, reaching a high of $40,882 in 1989, according to Census Bureau data. However, the average income of this middle class group has declined by 5 percent since then.

What is worse, the Census Bureau reports that the number of people below the official poverty income level reached 38.1 million in 1994, 5.7 million more than at the end of the Reagan years. By 1994 the poverty rate reached 14.5 percent of the population, well above the 12.5 percent of 1989. It is also worth noting that the jobless rate among young blacks, which rose sharply after the minimum wage was raised in 1990 and 1991, is now more than 33 percent.

In this year's campaign Robert Dole must talk about the human toll caused by America's prolonged growth deficit. Candidate Dole must talk about the need for income tax cuts.

By lowering the marginal tax rate on each new dollar earned from work or investment, every person in the economy derives new economic rewards. In other words, on the margin, it will pay to work and invest more. One simple way to lower income tax rates is to flatten the combined tax rate on personal income and FICA (Social Security and Medicare) at 30 percent. The FICA tax rate must be left alone for now so that leaves the adjustment to income tax rates.

For middle class Americans earning $29,150 to $61,500, the combined tax rate is now 43.3 percent (28 percent on income, 15.3 percent FICA). This is higher than the combined 31 percent for the next bracket of $61,500 to $121,400. (Remember, FICA taxes currently are not paid on wages above $61,200 so persons in a higher income tax bracket actually can pay a lower combined percentage.) Middle class Americans also pay more than those earning $121,400 to $256,400 (36 percent) or those taking in above $256,400 (39.6 percent). To get to a flat and fair combined tax rate of 30 percent for all brackets, the middle class bracket, for example, would be lowered about 13 percentage points.

Everyone would get a big boost in after-tax take-home pay. And the middle class would get the largest tax cut.

Today, the middle class takes home only 57 cents on each dollar earned. Under the new plan it would take home 70 cents. Additionally, unlimited IRA's that are front-loaded (pay taxes up front with no future taxes after that) would be a natural complement to promote additional saving.

Income tax cuts are much more efficient economic growth instruments than the $500 per child tax credit that comprises a centerpiece of the Contract With America. Tax credits are temporary and targeted government subsidies, with income eligibility thresholds ($75,000 presently) designed to meet class warfare arguments rather than to create economic growth incentives. Tax credits are a clumsy attempt to use the tax code for social policy. Passage of a child tax credit would open a Pandora's box with lobbyists proposing hundreds of new special purpose credits. Also, families and individuals without children would get no tax relief.

Beyond the economic advantages, income tax cuts are always a big political winner. President Reagan proved that with two landslide victories. When George Bush moved his lips and broke his no-tax-raise promise in 1992, he proved it in reverse.

Only a year after Bush's defeat, New Jersey Gov. Christine Todd Whitman's plan to slash state income taxes catapulted her to victory over high-tax incumbent Jim Florio. And a year later, in revolt against

President Clinton's massive tax hike, voters elected a Republican Congress for the first time in 40 years. Indeed, in recent years Republican governors such as John Engler in Michigan, Tommy Thompson in Wisconsin, William Weld in Massachusetts, George Pataki in New York, and Fife Symington in Arizona have successfully campaigned on across-the-board income tax cuts.

To maintain the GOP's electoral momentum, Robert Dole need only substitute income tax cuts for tax credits in the Republican congressional plan to shrink government and balance the budget. But the true fiscal objective is faster economic growth and a more financially secure future for all people, not the green-eyeshade austerity message that has become the Contract's principal focus.

Republicans must regain the high ground of tax cuts and economic growth that was abdicated by George Bush. The party must reinstate Reagan's message that as the economic pie grows larger, everyone benefits.

Citizen Dole must look America straight in the eye and state: "I trust you, but President Clinton trusts government. You will spend your money more wisely than government will." If Dole formulates this tax-cutting economic growth message then the "comeback adult" can snatch victory from the jaws of defeat. And the sunlight of the spirit will shine brightly on all Americans.

1.8 THANKFUL

November 26, 1996

The single most significant, inter-galactic, extra-celestial, interplanetary, and spiritual force behind the global stock market rally is the decline of inflation to rates not seen in over thirty years. While many industrial nations, including the U.S., have imposed anti-growth and anti-saving tax increases in recent years, fiscal drag has been offset by a steady decline of inflation. Inflation is a tax on money, wealth creation, income, and work effort. Inflation is a devastating tax on savings. But low inflation is a tax-cut. By enhancing the value of financial assets, price stability rewards patient savers and investors. It is a stimulant to capital formation, new business start-ups and growth. Growth does not cause inflation; low inflation causes growth. Low inflation is the primary determinant of historically low interest rates. Low inflation is the cause of relatively steady exchange rates. Low inflation has improved business confidence and the animal spirits of risk-taking. Low inflation has helped to *re*-moralize the social and cultural spheres.

In the U.S. since 1980, steadily declining inflation has been the key factor (along with earlier supply-side tax relief, de-regulation, and free-trade) behind a stock market that has appreciated by an 11% yearly average (inflation-adjusted), generating roughly $12 trillion in new financial wealth (including bonds). Since 1994, under a Republican Congress and a born again conservative President, stocks have appreciated another 68%, creating about $5 trillion in new wealth. Post-election 1996 share prices have jumped another 400 Dow points, expressing new confidence over the same conservative political line-up and the likelihood that hard-money Treasury Secretary Rubin will stay on to work with hard-money Fed Chairman Greenspan to promote price stability, with no new taxes. Maybe even some modest tax cuts (cap-gains indexing), and more tariff-cutting free-trade, according to Mr. Clinton's excellent Asia-Pacific Rim speech this week in Manila. Another good event: California's frivolous lawsuit Prop 211 was defeated, opening the way for a rally in small-cap stocks.

And what's good for America is good for the rest-of-the-world. U.S. economic policy, its markets, its economy, and its currency, all stand at the epicenter of the global economy. So do our free-market and pro-democracy values. When the U.S. errs, as it did in the late Sixties and Seventies, the global economy suffers. When the U.S.

recovers, as it has during the Eighties (helped by Britain's Mrs. Thatcher) and Nineties, so has the wealth of virtually all of the other nations.

Worldwide financial markets are applauding central bankers who have kept the money they supply in balance with money demanded by financial markets and the economy. That is why the U.S. dollar gold price is now about $375, suggesting that U.S. inflation may even fall below 2% in the year ahead, and why U.S. bond yields may make another run at 6%. And as goes U.S. inflation, so goes global inflation. It is reminiscent of the low-inflation Bretton Woods period, when from 1945 to 1970 the dollar was linked to gold, and international currencies were connected to the dollar.

While the U.S. stock market has appreciated 25% over the past year, Europe has rallied 17% and Asia Pacific (except Japan which is too heavily taxed and regulated) has increased by 22%. Meanwhile, ten-year government note yields are breathtakingly low: 6.10% in the U.S., 5.90% in France and Germany, 7.10% in Britain, 7% in Australia, 6.10% in Canada, 6.70% in Ireland, 7.10% in Sweden, 2.60% in Japan. And short-term rates are unusually stable. Currencies bob up and down in a narrow range. The trade-weighted G-10 dollar has been rock steady.

At the Fed's annual monetary conference held in Jackson Hole, Wyoming last summer, where the topic was global price stability, central bankers worldwide pledged to maintain tight inflation control. For the industrial G-7 nations, and the IMF, there was agreement on a 1% to 3% inflation range, centering on 2%. Seven nations, including New Zealand, Canada, United Kingdom, Sweden, Finland, Australia and Spain, have published inflation targets centered mostly around 2%. Japan's representative defended his nation's zero-inflation policy. Central bankers from Israel, the Czech Republic, Argentina, Brazil, Bulgaria and elsewhere subscribed to the need for low inflation targets. Alan Greenspan argued in favor of price *level* stability, but he is waiting for a better price index (he mentioned the new chain-weighted indexes). And Greenspan has always kept a clear eye on gold as the mother of all inflation barometers.

So, the low-inflation recent past is likely to be prologue to the future. Central bankers have become considerably *more* independent from political interference and hence *more* reliable in meeting their low-inflation targets. And just in case of slippage, global financial markets have become *more* punishing in their rapacious high interest rate response to nations that even temporarily stray off course.

INDUSTRIAL COUNTRY INFLATION
(GDP deflators, % ch)

	1996 (e)	1978–87
U.S.	2.1	5.9
JAPAN	0.5	2.7
GERMANY	1.4	3.4
FRANCE	1.7	8.5
ITALY	3.8	13.4
U.K.	2.4	8.7
CANADA	1.0	6.4
NETHERLANDS	2.7	3.0
SWEDEN	1.9	8.2
SPAIN	3.3	12.4
IRELAND	2.0	10.1
AUSTRALIA	2.6	8.3
NEW ZEALAND	2.8	15.5
G-7	1.9	6.5
EUROPEAN UNION	2.4	8.4

Source: IMF, Oct. 1996

DEVELOPING COUNTRY INFLATION
(CPI, % ch)

	1995	1978–87
ARGENTINA	3.2	210.9
MEXICO	35.0	55.2
CHILE	8.2	25.2
BRAZIL	14.8	127.1
PERU	11.1	84.9
VENEZUELA	60.0	13.5
KOREA	4.5	10.0
SINGAPORE	1.7	3.3
HONG KONG	9.0	8.6
MALAYSIA	3.4	3.9
TAIWAN	3.7	5.4
PHILLIPPINES	8.1	14.8
THAILAND	5.8	6.5
VIETNAM	12.8	86.9
ISRAEL	10.0	118.5
KUWAIT	1.0	4.0
EGYPT	9.4	16.0
JORDAN	2.4	5.8
SAUDIA ARABIA	5.0	1.4
SOUTH AFRICA	8.7	14.5

Source: IMF, Oct. 1996

In fiscal terms the G-7 is still top-heavy with high tax-rates and burdensome social insurance systems. Europe suffers from excessive labor market regulation, and Japan must unshackle and empower its entrepreneurs. All these nations must shift toward flat-tax reform and privatized Social Security and healthcare systems. Governments must be thoroughly downsized. If not, then global capital will continue to march toward Asia, where economic returns exceed those available in the West.

But good things are happening almost everywhere. Russia just tapped the global credit market in a successful bond sale. Communists were recently defeated in elections held in Bulgaria, Romania, the Czech Republic, Lithuania, and Nicaragua. The German Deutch Telekom privatization IPO was a success. Italy is getting ready to privatize its Eni oil company. Across Europe, governments are getting ready to privatize natural gas companies. The Pope's forthcoming Cuban trip may be as liberating there as when he returned to Poland 16 years ago. Free enterprise is hot, government engineering is not. Keynes is out, Schumpeter and Hayek are in. Free markets, free trade, sound money, individual creativity and personal responsibility are alive and well. We have much to be thankful for. Faith is the Spirit.

1.9 WITH CLINTON AND A REPUBLICAN CONGRESS, NATIONAL ECONOMY MAY BE IN GOOD SHAPE

December 1996

The Stock market jumped more than 200 points during the week after the election. Bond yields were dropping toward 6.5 percent. Gold remained under $380. The dollar slipped a bit—reacting to erroneous rumors that Robert Rubin might vacate the Treasury for the State Department, and a very unlikely Japanese interest-rate hike—but the currency still occupies the high ground. Foreign stock markets continue to rally. What are those markets telling us? What are they celebrating?

Well, perhaps it's a reach, but a case can be made that conservatives now hold the balance of power in the Senate, the House and 1600 Pennsylvania Ave. The upper chamber has become more conservative, an already conservative lower body will be a bit kinder and gentler and conservatism's most recent convert still occupies the White House.

After successfully running a Reaganesque "Morning in America" campaign, Bill Clinton is now trying to construct a "vital center." In the campaign, it was Clinton who took credit for the moderate 1950s-type expansion, accompanied by low inflation and declining interest rates. It was Clinton who spoke the spiritual language of the heart to soccer moms and their kids. It was Clinton who argued for a balanced budget with small doses of targeted tax relief for homeowners, college education, families with children and people coming off welfare. It was Clinton who somehow intends to "protect" health-care, education and the environment. It was Clinton who argued for an internationalist foreign policy.

In short, Clinton's campaign message could have easily passed for the old-style Republican centrism practiced by Eisenhower, Nixon, Ford and Bush. Include in that list Howard Baker, Bob Michel, Charlie Halleck, even a younger Bob Dole. In 1996, Clinton dished the Republicans. Big time. He played Disraeli, who in 1897 stole Gladstone's issues to finally become prime minister. He played Grover Cleveland, who in 1892 ran on a conservative zero-inflation pro-business gold plank to defeat lackluster Republican William Harrison.

46

DOLE RAN LISTLESS CAMPAIGN

Dole never really had a chance. Even if he had run a pluperfect campaign, which he most certainly did not, the economic cards were stacked against him. When the economy rebounded in the first half, ending the 1995 growth recession, Dole was sunk, provided that Clinton remained non-incarcerated on Election Day. A few facts tell the story. Over the 12 months ending election day, real economic growth rose 2.7 percent, real take-home pay increased 3.2 percent and inflation advanced only 2 percent, the pace since early 1965. The stock market bull gained another 25 percent. Actually, since 1992, stock market wealth has increased by a staggering $5.2 trillion.

When Dole failed to answer Clinton's charge that across-the-board tax cuts would blow a hole in the deficit, a matter of concern to most Americans, even if not to national Republicans, tens of millions of people worried that a hole would be blown in the stock market. Through IRAs, 401(k)s, Keoughs, mutual funds, variable annuities and other savings plans, working moms now own a piece of the rock. To them, abstract arguments about growth and capital gains were virtually unintelligible.

Dole should have talked about tax cuts to improve take-home pay, aiming this message directly at middle-income independents, but he never did. Dole should have talked about family values and spiritual principles, but he did not. Dole should have explained the merits of education choice, but he did not. Dole should have argued for a plan to privatize Social Security and Medicare, but he doesn't believe in it. Dole should have argued against partial-birth abortion and for voluntary school prayer, but he only whispered it. Dole should have aggressively opposed racial quotas and preferences, but it was too late when he finally did. Dole should have developed a strong foreign policy, but the GOP doesn't have one. It all cost him dearly.

Ironically, it was Ross Perot's blistering last-minute attacks on Clinton's campaign finance abuses that finally drew blood and narrowed the gap to 49 percent to 41 percent, perhaps in the process saving the Republican House, and sparing the nation a left-wing tax-and-spend assault from Gephardt, Waxman, Rangel, Conyers, Dellums, et al. According to exit polls, Dole won a plurality of votes only from married white males earning over $75,000 a year. He lost all age groups. He lost independents. He lost Catholics. He lost Webheads. He even lost smokers and gun-owners. Despite a string of tax-cutting Republicans gubernatorial victories in 1993–94, Dole was slaughtered in the Northeast, Midwest and the West Coast, sometimes by margins of 30 percentage points.

VITAL CENTER THERE FOR THE TAKING

With all this in mind, it is no wonder that Clinton is talking about the vital center. Right now, it's there for the taking. Crabby Republicans still believe that legal and ethical problems will bring down Clinton's second term. Maybe so, maybe not. To be sure, freshly-reelected Tennessee Senator Fred Thompson—a year-2000 presidential wannabe who was Howard Baker's Watergate counsel and now is chairman of the Senate Government Affairs committee that will oversee campaign finance reform will be a far more effective investigator than Al D'Amato. But until that story develops, Clinton is shedding the liberal skin of his first term, almost to the bone. Look at the list of departures: Christopher, Panetta, Stephanopoulos, O'Leary, Tyson, Reich, Cantor, Pena, Cisneros. Meanwhile, as this is written, Clinton has still not appeared publicly with liberal Democratic leaders Gephardt and Daschle.

And former Spingali Dick Morris is advising the president to replace some of them with Republicans such as Warren Rudman, Colin Powell, Bill Cohen and Richard Lugar, or perhaps conservative Democrats such as investment banker Erskine Bowles, or New York businessman Richard Ravitch, or CIA director John Deutch, or UN Ambassador Madeleine Albright, or pro-business Chicago Mayor Richard Daley, or pro-defense retiring Senator Sam Nunn. Morris told *USA Today* that Clinton " . . . has to reach out and craft a truly national government, including them in this Cabinet and embracing their ideas in his legislative program."

So national government is filling the vital center. Very shrewd. Besides the president, two others are likely to stand in the center of this vital center: Treasury Secretary Robert Rubin and Senate Majority Leader Trent Lott. Rubin has always been Clinton's master planner for the recovering economy, and he had a strong following on Wall Street and globally. Working closely with Fed Chairman Alan Greenspan, Rubin has given the central bank free rein to bring inflation down to its lowest pace in thirty years.

This reduction in the inflation tax has been the only stimulant to the economy and the driving force behind the phenomenal stock market surge, whose wealth creation power has provided added economic resiliency. At this year's Federal Reserve conference on global price stability, central bankers and financial officials agreed on a

2 percent worldwide inflation target. Rubin agrees with this goal. What's more, it was Rubin who engineered the G-7 dollar recovery effort that has bolstered financial market confidence and contributed to the steadiness of U.S. interest rates. As well, Rubin is a committed free trader who may push to expand NAFTA throughout Central and South America.

Regrettably, Rubin views tax policy through the lens of static-accounting deficit reduction rather than a dynamic growth model where lower tax-rate incentives will expand the supply of labor, capital and entrepreneurial risk-taking. So he is opposed to across-the-board tax reform. And his first-term tax hike plan placed an unnecessary drag on the economy. However, he supports Clinton's campaign pledge to eliminate the capital gains tax reform. And his first-term tax hike plan placed an unnecessary drag on the economy. However, he supports Clinton's campaign pledge to eliminate the capital gains tax on home sale profits up to $500,000, and the Treasury intends to offer inflation-indexed bonds to the public early next year. Hence Rubin may be amenable to a budget deal that included inflation indexing for all capital gains, including those from the sale of stocks and bonds. This would reduce the effective capital gains tax-rate from today's 47 percent to the statutory rate of 28 percent, create a massive unlocking of assets already owned, in the process reliquefying the economy without inflating the nation's money supply.

ECONOMY SHOULD REMAIN SOUND

Meanwhile, the economy and financial markets are basically sound and should remain so. With national income advancing at a 4.2 percent rate over the past year, and total labor compensation costs rising by 2.9 percent, business profits will continue to expand, albeit at a relatively slow pace. Job creation and personal incomes are holding up well, and consumers have slowed their spending in order to pay down debt. Against the backdrop of a strong stock market the value of household financial assets is twice that of consumer liabilities. Actually, consumer spending may pick up a bit during the next the next few quarters, thereby helping businesses to relieve a mild inventory overhang.

With a mildly upward-sloping Treasury yield curve, a stable Treasury-bill market holding around 5 percent and unusually narrow credit qualify yield spreads between high- and low-rate corporate bonds, there is no recession in sight. Relatively low gold, flat commodity indexes and a steady dollar all suggest that 2 percent inflation in sustainable. With the broad M2 money aggregate rising about 4 percent over the past year, nominal GNP growth should trend along a 4.5 percent path with real GNP bumping slightly above or below a 2.5 percent trajectory. Long-term Treasury yields, which have eased down from 7.25 to 6.5 percent through the year ahead. The Federal Reserve will keep to its goal of price stability, while both the federal budget and deficit will be restrained. Longer term, U.S. tax reform will provide additional incentives to gradually raise real economic growth toward 3 percent. Stock market prices, which in real terms have appreciated by over 10 percent per year since 1980, should continue on this path. Post-election, the intellectual sweep of free markets, free enterprise, individual initiative and personal responsibility is alive and well at home and abroad.

1.10 MARKETS ARE TELLING US . . .

January 10, 1997

. . . that a growth revival is consistent with low inflation. More goods and services are being purchased with sound dollars. Real interest rate movements, which are driving the bond market, will continue to regulate economic swings without Federal Reserve fine-tuning. Everyone around the world wants dollars, including Bulgaria. Trent Lott, the titular Republican party leader, wants a broad-based capital gains tax-cut, probably with estate tax relief and liberalized IRA's. Ways and Means chief Bill Archer is on board with a similar growth policy. Regrettably, House budget leader John Kasich clings to tax credits, which have no growth impact, distort market prices and clutter the tax code. Hopefully this gooey, interest group-pleasing, subsidy approach will be short-lived and will give way to true tax reform. But the hand-writing is on the wall: for the first time since 1986, federal policies will be aimed at pro-growth tax cuts and smaller government, however much stumbling along the way. Joseph Schumpeter's economic growth model of entrepreneurship is winning—he's our favorite dead economist.

Meanwhile, the bond correction is probably four-fifths completed. As for the stock market, year-to-date the big-cap S&P 500 is up 1.9%, but the smaller cap NASDAQ has increased 2.7%. Autos are up over 6%, advertising and energy are up over 5%, as is communications tech and computer tech, basic materials have gained over 4%, construction and machinery over 3%, while precious metals have dropped 3.5% and utilities have slipped nearly 2%. So leadership continues to rotate toward growth. Keep the faith, a rising tide lifts all boats.

- *Bond yields up, gold down.* Growth is not inflationary. The rise in bond yields is being driven by a rise in the real interest component of the market rate, not the inflation premium component. If inflation risk was the problem, then gold would be rising. But gold has fallen. So it's higher capital investment returns, stemming from stronger growth, that are moving note and bond yields up. Thus far, two year notes have moved up about 45 basis points (5.60% to 6.05%) and 30 year bonds have kicked up about 60 basis points (6.30% to 6.88%). Business cycle-related shifts in real interest rates provide a self-regulating and self-correcting mechanism for the economy. Fine-tuning

51

measures from the Fed will only destabilize the economy. Markets are the most efficient resource allocators. This includes goods markets, labor markets, loan markets, commodity markets and financial markets. All the Fed should do is keep on eye on price stability—especially gold. Right now there's no need for Fed tightening or easing. Rising real rates will keep the economy on a 3% growth path in 1997, after perhaps a 4% fourth quarter. President Reagan called it the magic of the marketplace. Milton Friedman abhorred fine-tuning. They were both right.

- *Oil up, gold down.* Bet on gold to forecast inflation, not oil. Oil is one price, but gold reflects the overall purchasing power of money. Oil price increases are not spreading because the Fed has not created excess money. In a price-rule monetary regime, some prices rise while other prices fall. Oil is up, but computing-related prices are down. Overall, broad commodity indexes are flat. Note today's chart du jour.

Commodity Indexes
(Yr/Tr % Change)

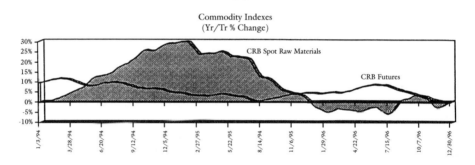

- *King Dollar.* The greenback has moved to 116 yen and 1.58 German marks on international exchange markets, and the dollar rally is not over yet. The U.S. is the best steadily performing economy among the G-7, and arguably the rest of the world. Improved economic growth is reflected in a rising *real exchange rate*, the near cousin to the rising real interest rate. U.S. capital returns are attracting worldwide money flows. What's more, a rising dollar and slumping gold shows that global investors are voting against inflation. That is, with very low inflation expectations, world investors prefer to buy dollars and park their money in high-yielding U.S. bonds. With a 2% inflation trend, inflation-adjusted bonds yield nearly 5%. With this attractive real rate, and a sound-money economic performance, U.S. financial assets are the place to be.

With prospects for pro-growth tax-cutting policies, including capgains relief, the U.S. will continue to magnetize world money flows. So the dollar will rise more. Who wants to invest in tax-heavy low-capital return Japan or Germany? Also, for those with a trade-deficit obsession, the U.S. Customs Service suggests that the reporting of international trade services may be 40% or $85 billion deficient. And the Census Bureau suggests that the Customs Service fails to count about 10% of the forms filed by exporters. That is a roughly $60 billion deficiency. Putting these figures together, $145 billion of actual U.S. exports may be missing. Which implies about a $40 billion some odd trade *surplus*. Think of it.

And there's more on the dollar. Just last week Bulgaria adopted a currency board approach to monetary policy that links to the dollar. The Russian economy has already been dollarized. So has the Central and Latin American economies. So has Hong Kong and PRC-China. So has the Phillipines. So basically have Australia, New Zealand, Canada, Indonesia, Thailand, Malaysia and Singapore. Treasury Secretary Rubin has linked to the dollar, talking it *up* on a daily basis. On the margin, private and official investors will prefer dollars to European Union Euros. Other than austerity-driven fiscal policies, no one really understands the Euro. But they understand dollars.

- *Supply-side in the U.S. Northeast.* Speaking of Schumpeterian improvements in after-tax returns to entrepreneurs and innovators, did you notice the State-of-the-State speeches by New York Governor George Pataki and Connecticut Governor John Rowland? Last year they both cut income tax-rates, as did Christine Whitman in New Jersey. This year Pataki wants to cut property taxes *and* gift and inheritance estate taxes. Rowland want to *eliminate* his state's income tax. And get this. In New York City, formerly Moscow on the Hudson, Mayor Guiliani and Assembly Speaker Silver want to *abolish* the clothing sales tax! Just listen to this quote from Mr. Silver: "It creates employment, because of greater sales volume." And the *New York Post* story went on: "Silver said that rather than lowering state and city tax revenues, the program may in fact increase revenues by creating an economic ripple effect." Now I ask you, is this a great country, or what?

1.11 The Case for Market-Based Forecasting

Spring/Summer 1992

My comments will begin with some of the themes that Jerry Jordan mentioned in his paper, especially the theme of government policy rules, which is, of course, crucial to Karl Brunner's work. Brunner was a great friend and teacher of mine, as is Jerry Jordan. So there is a little bit of a historical conspiracy. But the question of rules in government policy is irrevocably tied up in a very general point: the use or the utility of the markets and market prices, which is really the thrust of my comments.

I agree with the people who have mentioned how poor economic forecasts are. Markets strike me as really the best—the only reliable—forecasting tool. In the same respect, I think markets are the only reliable policy tool. And as Jordan noted in his distinction between government forecasting and private forecasting: Private forecasting is largely defensive in response to government events, which are frequently unpredictable and irrational.

MARKETS, INFORMATION, AND POLICY FORMATION

Inside government, the use of markets—not only to discipline policymakers but to provide information—can be an awesome tool in helping policymakers chart the right course. When I served in the Reagan administration, I thought we made a much greater use of markets than others had—not only in the sense of letting markets tell us what was right and wrong, but also in the sense of deregulating them to increase their efficiency. To the extent that we enjoyed a much better economic success in the 1980s than was the case in the 1970s—not perfect but substantially better—I think my point of view is vindicated. In particular, I have argued, written, and defended the view that gold prices and, to a lesser extent, the equally important sensitive commodity indexes, are the only way to capture the mix or the balance between the money supplied by the Fed and the money demanded by the private economy. It is a question of the interaction of money supply and money demand. We cannot focus on the only the supply of money, because, after all, the ultimate game is to get inflation as close to zero as possible. I believe we can achieve zero inflation by raising the domestic purchasing power, or value, of our money, which is largely a function of the demand for money. I do not mean the demand for credit; I am not talking about commercial loans. I mean the willingness of people to hold financial balances or financial assets such as stocks and bonds. If people are willing to hold those monetary balances, then the price or value of money goes up. Hence, money buys more goods and services, and inflation goes down. In my judgment, the price of gold is the ultimate indicator of the purchasing power or value of money. The market value of gold tells us whether the demand for money is in line with the supply of money created by the Federal Reserve.

I am not dismissing the argument to use the quantity of money as an indicator of monetary policy, but I think using monetary aggregates is a tricky business. Even the most rigorous and consistent students of money are still confused about which monetary aggregate—the base, M1, M2, M3—is the right indicator to gauge monetary policy.

In choosing a measure of the quantity of money, there is a tendency to select the one that tells the story you want to tell rather than the one that is actually the "correct one," which is almost unknowable. We have all played the game—whether it is M2; whether is ought to be the monetary base; whether it ought to be the unadjusted base or Federal Reserve credit, which comes off the balance sheet of the Fed; or whether it would be bank reserves or other things. For example, if the growth of M2 is below the Fed's target range while the monetary base is exploding, which is the right aggregate? If I distrust the monetary base because currency is flowing abroad or because I know the Fed has reduced reserve requirements on some of the institutional deposit accounts, and the so-called reserve adjustment formula might not yet have gotten it right, then I do not want to use the base as an indicator of monetary policy. Instead, I might look at the Fed's balance sheet and use adjusted or unadjusted Federal Reserve credit. But even that indicator may not be correct. The domestic banking system may not be using the Fed's high-powered credit.

On the margin, the last announced piece of information is always going to be in an open market, and free markets will always know more than the most complex and comprehensive econometric model or the 500 some odd Ph.Ds at the Federal Reserve Bond.

WHY FORECASTS FAIL

One of the reasons econometric models do not work, never have worked, and, in my view, never will work, is that economics itself is simply not a Newtonian physical science. Professionals, academics, and policymakers have tried to make it into a physical science for the past 40 or 50 years, particularly since the rise of Keynesianism and the decline of classical thinking. But the physical science approach does not work. So if we are now having a general rebirth of classical approach—because of the work of Friedrich Hayek, Milton Friedman, Karl Brunner, and many others—then we have to admit that economics is really not a physical science. It is not clockwork. Time never stands still.

We are dealing with human behavior, which is always changing, not mechanical constructs. And human behavior is always evolving and changing in response to events, both government and nongovernment. We have a historical continuum here. Because human behavior is always evolving, I believe that the evolution of economics and human behavior is a lot closer to biology than it is to physics. And it is a lot closer to Darwinian evolution theories because, after all, individuals compete, which was also the essence of the beginning of biology.

MARKETS AS FORECASTING DEVICES

My experience on government and the private sector has convinced me that markets are crucial for policymaking, for rule making, and for forecasting. Indeed, I now rely almost exclusively on using markets as forecasting devices. In forecasting inflation, for example, I pay little attention to the CPI, or to data from the Commerce Department, the Treasury Department, or the Federal Reserve. I certainly examine the data, and my clients expect me to comment on it; but I do not believe any of it. Gold and commodity prices tell me a much better story about inflation, because they are market prices.

MONETARY POLICY

With respect to monetary policy, I believe more and more strongly that market prices have more information than monetary aggregates.

No one really knows which quantity indicator is correct. My answer is "Why don't you just look at the price of gold or commodity indexes?" Although no Fed governor has said it and although the Fed chairman has never explicitly discussed it, I think we are actually operating on a de facto, Bretton Woods-style, *domestic price rule* whereby the value of the domestic dollar is linked to gold and whereby the supply of dollars created by the Fed is basically linked to a yardstick called gold. When the Fed operated in this Bretton Woods Fashion in 1989 and 1990, the money supply was, on average, well controlled.

M2 growth was about 4 percent, nominal GNP growth was about 5 percent, and gold stayed, on average, at around $375–$380. We had a terrific bond rally; long-term interest rates, which can stimulate corporate investment and housing, dropped from 9.5 percent to 8.5 percent in 1990. Short-term rates went down even more. There was virtually no inflation risk in the market. The Fed was operating exactly the right way.

When the Fed went off the Bretton Woods price rule in the middle 1980s and decided to increase the money supply, we paid heavily for it. Gold and interest rates skyrocketed, which led to the stock market crash of 1987. That crash was, among other factors, the precursor of the recession. Therefore, the stock market crash of 1987 turned out to be a better forecaster than some people thought.

If the Fed stays with the implicit price rule it is now using, we are going to be in better shape than we think. I like the price-rule approach because I think it captures not only the supply of money in the Fed's actions but also fiscal policy. Taxes and regulations count a lot in monetary value and in the inflation outlook. Taxing, spending, and regulating can affect inflation. If we increase taxes, if we raise government spending as a share of GNP, or if we regulate more heavily, we will reduce incentives, efficiency, and productivity in the economy (that is, we will reduce real economic growth).

If money growth is constant, but you shrink or reduce the growth of goods and services, you cause inflation from the supply side because you roll back incentives. Markets will respond. Look at the behavior of the Dow Jones in 1990. It rose to 3,000 in the late winter and early spring. At almost the moment President Bush moved his lips, the Dow's rally ended. As the shape of that budget deal, which was nothing but a high tax and spending package, became clearer and clearer to the markets—before Saddam Hussein and after Saddam Hussein—the Dow Jones dropped about 700 points. And the market was headed lower, until, in my judgment, (1) the Fed made it clear it was not going to monetize the oil price shock but was going to stay with the gold-price, Bretton Woods-type rule; and (2) it became obvious that the Bush administration was going to move back on the supply-side growth path. The combination of a steady, domestic Fed price rule and what looked like the return to growth economics moved the Dow from 2,300 in the fall of 1990 to 2,900 and higher by early 1991.

I am not attacking monetarism, which is, after all, the study of money. The Federal Reserve controls our money supply, however it is defined. But there is good monetarism and bad monetarism. Bad monetarism says we are going to fine-tune the monetary aggregates or some measure of the quantity of money to hit some artificial target. Bad monetarism also believes that the Fed can fine-tune nominal GDP growth over short time intervals. Some very bright people of great integrity whom I respect are now saying we should significantly increase the growth of M2. Such a policy, however, would undermine the price rule, drive the price of gold and interest rates—particularly long rates—sky high, and wreck whatever chances of recovery we have.

In contrast, good monetarism says the Fed should add or withdraw reserves while keeping a sharp eye on gold and commodities as the value-of-money yardstick. That kind of monetarism is really what the Fed is now engaged in and is the right way to go.

CONCLUSION

I want to end on an optimistic note, because of my dislike for the stagnation model. Why does everyone always assume the worst case? If the Fed continues with a domestic price rule, then interest rates of 3 to 4 percent for Treasury bills and 5 to 6 percent for Treasury bonds should result. The budget deficit would then be eliminated, because over the next five or six years we would save a couple of hundred billion dollars in net interest expense compared to the current services baseline. I think a global case can be made that countries are operating on domestic price rules everywhere, thereby punishing inflation. That is why we have a big bull market in bonds and stocks in almost every national currency, which, in turn, should move the exchange rates back into equilibrium.

Markets are made up of the decisions of millions of people who want prosperity, progress, and better living standards. When governments interfere, markets will punish right away and get policymakers back on the right track. The Malthusian notion, which is the stagnation view or the global capital-shortage view, can be rejected and discarded as long as we let markets operate freely and pay attention to them as private citizens and government policymakers. Population growth is a plus because of the potential creativity of individual men and women. Resources are not scarce; they are limitless—because technology is boundless. If we stay close to the free market, the 1990s can be another decade of strong growth.

Reference

Rothschild, Michael. *Bionomics: The Inevitability of Capitalism.* New York: Henry Holt, 1990.

1.12 IN SEARCH OF A RULE

February 27, 1997

Following Alan Greenspan's front-page testimony on the dangers of inflation, economic overheating, excess wage rates and the exuberant stock market, one key point must be kept firmly in mind: market-based price indicators are the best measures of future inflation expectations. Right now, flat gold and commodity price indexes strongly suggest that profit-maximizing investors all over the world do not anticipate higher U.S. inflation. In fact, the behavior of these inflation sensitive commodity indicators suggest that future inflation a year from now could actually come in lower than actual inflation reported over the past year. Our inflation forecasting model, which uses year-to-year changes in gold and precious metals to predict year-ahead inflation, points to a 1½% to 2% estimate for the chain-weighted GDP price index. The Golden Cone analytical model also points to a 1% handle on year ahead inflation.

The Golden Cone

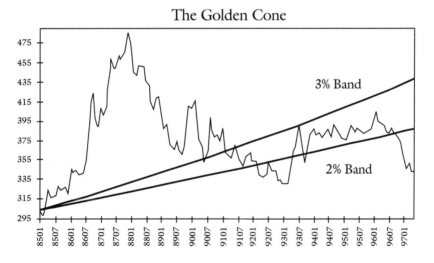

Elsewhere on the commodity front, the oil-heavy Goldman Sachs index has been slumping since November, primarily from a 22% year-to-date drop in the energy sector. In fact, the decline of crude oil from $26 to $21 is a good omen for reduced inflation and lower bond yields (see "Oil & Bonds", dated February 7, 1997), and oil could fall to $17 or $18 per barrel during the next year. Meanwhile, Goldman's sub-indexes show a 10% year-to-year decline in precious metals, a 13% fall in agriculture and a 1% industrial metals rise (up 10% year-to-date, suggesting no recession in sight). Elsewhere on the commodity front, the CRB futures index is off 2.6% over the past 52 weeks, while the Dow-Jones spot index remains flat. And in the real world of transactions pricing, let's not ignore the fast-food price war launched by McDonald's, or the big airline ticket discounting war triggered by American's labor dispute.

Goldman Sachs Commodity Index

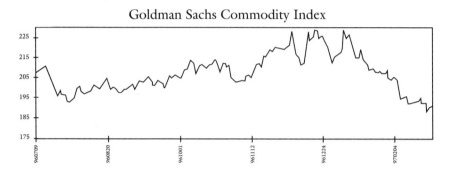

All this said, the primary significance of Greenspan's testimony is his desire to underscore the Fed's continued vigilance in the effort to maintain near-zero inflation price stability. This is very important. Greenspan warnings of the *possibility* of pre-emptive anti-inflation strikes are designed to bolster the central bank's credibility. Implicit in Greenspan's warning is a desire to maintain a 2% core CPI inflation target, which translates to about a $1\frac{1}{2}$% chain-weighted GDP price index rise. At present, there is no need to raise the federal funds rate. Greenspan knows this because he's an inveterate gold watcher. At $5\frac{1}{4}$%, the funds rate is in line with the 5.2% nominal GDP rise over the past four quarters, and much higher than the 2.1% GDP chain price index rise (implying a healthy 3% real Fed funds rate). Of course, $350 gold is the best indicator of Fed restraint. Unless gold rises to $400–$425, there's no threat of excess money or rising future inflation.

Actually, Greenspan's warnings have the effect of raising market interest rates without overt Fed action. Two-year note yields have increased 35 basis points recently to 6.05%, while 3-month Eurodollar rates have moved up about 20 bp's to 5.76%. This action causes banks to pay more for money, imparting a restraining influence on the economy. What's more, in a fundamental environment of price stability, market rate increases are really *real* interest rate increases. These real rate hikes dampen investment demand and cool the economy. It is a *self-regulating and self-correcting* process driven by market forces, not Federal Reserve fine-tuning. Since markets are better resource allocaters than government planners, and the Greenspan planners have mostly stayed away from fine-tuning actions, the current business cycle has been durable and long-lived. The bull market in stocks tells the story.

At a Manhattan Institute-sponsored dinner meeting last night hosted by *Wall Street Journal* editor Bob Bartley and Columbia economics professor Bob Mundell, nearly all the classically-oriented economists in attendance expected economic growth to continue, with muted inflation. Guest speaker John Taylor, a Stanford economics professor, former Dole-Kemp economic advisor and presently a consultant to the Congressional Budget Office, believes that Fed policy is just about right. The U.S. could do with a flatter and simpler income tax system, more limited government and less regulation, but the money story is basically sound. Amen to all this.

To be sure, Alan Greenspan is the man. He has piloted the U.S. economy toward better growth and lower inflation than most folks thought possible. But institutionalized rules are more lasting than individuals. *What if* something should happen to Mr. Greenspan? And, there are two open seats on the Fed board. The rumor-mill has former J.P. Morgan banker and deputy Comptroller of the Currency Doug Harris and left-of-center Brookings economist Susan Collins on the short list, along with senior Fed staffer Ted Truman. None of these candidates are hard-money thinkers.

To reduce uncertainty over future policy, the Congress should go forward with a plan to remove the full employment mandate from Humphrey-Hawkins oversight and institutionalize the primary goal of price stability. This reform is advocated by Senator Connie Mack of the Banking Committee. Preferably the Fed would target gold or precious metals as their standard of value. Second-best would be a publicly announced inflation target. This approach is supported by Congressmen Jim Saxton, chairman of the Joint Economic Committee. Numerous central banks around the world have successfully implemented inflation-targeting. It's time for the U.S. to go for it. The public has a right to know. Monetary uncertainty is a tax. A monetary rule would cut it.

1.13 SHOW US THE INFLATION

April 18, 1997

Instead of "show me the money," the now famous line from the movie *Jerry Maguire*, Americans should be asking Alan Greenspan to show us the inflation. For many months the Fed chairman and many of his top lieutenants have been publicly grumbling about the inflationary dangers of too much growth, or stock prices that are too exuberant, or unemployment that is too low, or wages that are too high. In the Fed's view too many people are working and prospering, and somehow this must be a bad thing. So, in the Fed's perversely pessimistic logic, interest-rate increases must be applied to stop the march of progress. Put another way, the Fed's self-defined mission is no different than other Federal regulatory agencies: free markets and free economies must never be left to their own devices. They cannot function efficiently without the controlling hand of government.

Nonsense. Free-market financial and commodity prices, always hyper-sensitive to the threat of currency devaluation and price-level increases, show there is not one whiff of inflation anywhere. Leading commodity indexes published by Goldman Sachs and the Commodity Research Bureau have fallen nearly 10% over the past year. Gold and precious metals have dropped more than 12%. Crude oil is down 25% from its recent peak. Industrial metals have lost 5% from year ago levels. The dollar has appreciated roughly 15% over the past year. Even the flawed consumer price index, which overstates inflation by 1% according to the recent report of the Boskin Commission, registered a mild 2.8% rise for the twelve months to March, 1997. The producer price index showed only a 1.6% rise over the same period. An earlier report on the GDP chain price index, which is more up-to-date than the CPI, indicated 2.1% inflation for all of 1996.

Gold & CPI

62

Despite the flood of new evidence that extraordinary innovations stemming from advances in high technology, now the driving force in the U.S. economy, have increased worker productivity and enlarged the economy's capacity to grow, senior Fed staffers Donald Kohn and Mike Prell, along with recent Clinton Board appointee Laurence Meyer, continue to promote the Phillips Curve, an old-world Keynesian approach that asserts a trade-off between unemployment and inflation. In this model the central bank must identify and target the non-accelerating rate of inflation, or NAIRU. When the actual unemployment rate falls below NAIRU, wages will be pushed up and inflation will rise. Actual GDP rises above potential GDP, creating "excess demand." It's like a computer virus that brings the system down when growth appears on the screen.

Trouble is, this model has never worked. Milton Friedman long ago reminded us that inflation is a monetary phenomenon: too much money chasing too few goods, leading to a decline in money's purchasing power value. What's more, the Fed has causality running from wages to inflation, when in fact history shows that rising inflation causes excessive wage hikes. Additionally, in the stagflationary 1970s we saw that rising inflation, which saps growth, *causes* unemployment to rise. In the 1980s, declining inflation sparked higher capital investment returns, improved the quality of corporate earnings and raised real incomes (and wages), thereby lowering the unemployment rate.

Unemployment and Inflation

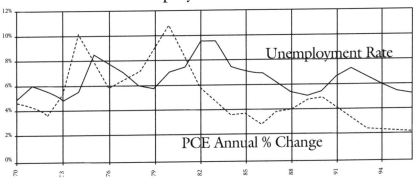

When President Reagan appointed hard-money commodity-watchers Manley Johnson, Wayne Angell and Robert Heller to work with Alan Greenspan, between 1985 and 1994 the Fed focused on free-market price-level indicators to gauge whether the money it supplied was excessive or scarce. In particular, emphasis was placed on the price movement of gold, broad commodity indexes, the dollar exchange rate and Treasury yield curve spreads. The "price rule" approach laid the groundwork for a healthy economy, stable financial markets and a low inflation rate. Over the past five years inflation has increased only 2.5% per year, while real GDP has advanced by 2.7% annually. When government statisticians learn to accurately measure the effects of the hi-tech transformation of the economy, the revised data will probably show about 3.5% trend growth and below 2% inflation for this period.

If the Republican Congress gets around to reforming the tax code with a lower, simpler and flatter tax-rate system, ending the double and triple taxation of capital, saving and investment, the same quantity of money will chase more goods and services, thereby creating *faster* economic growth accompanied by *lower* inflation. By pushing the supply curve outward, the frontier economic growth rate and the unemployment rate could be sustained in the 4% zone, with price stability. What we don't need now is a higher interest rate policy from the Fed. What we do need is a policy of smaller government and lower taxes that will unleash yet another hi-tech wave of innovation that will maintain U.S. leadership in the 21st century race for global capital and economic progress.

1.14 THIS BUDGET WON'T STOP GROWTH

May 9, 1997

While playing two decidedly mixed reviews among conservatives in Washington, the first act of this year's budget soap opera has met with rave reviews from the stock market. Despite Wednesday's respite, the major indexes have made heftly gains in the month or so since the broad outlines of the new budget became clear.

This approval is surely not linked to the spending side of the budget deal, for there are far too many domestic potholes and pork barrels in the deal. Nor is the market exclaiming over the Medicare piece of the budget, since Washington has again resorted to expenditure price controls on health care providers rather than free-market consumer choice through expanded medical savings accounts. These points of criticism have been forcefully made by Sen. Phil Gramm (R., Texas) and Cato Institute economist Steve Moore. And they are dead right. What's more, markets are sophisticated enough to dismiss five-year budget and economic projections, which aren't worth the paper they are printed on.

Instead, it is the across-the-board reduction in the capital-gains tax rate that has galvanized the stock market, and that is the saving grace of this budget. It will provide the first economywide tax cut in 10 years, and thus it wins the budget deal a passing grade, a gentlemen's C. (The last five or six high-tax austerity budgets earned F's.) This new budget also includes inheritance and death tax relief, and it may still include expanded IRAs if Delaware Sen. Bill Roth can work it out in his Finance Committee, and perhaps inflation indexing from Texas Rep. Bill Archer's Ways and Means Committee mark-up. Now that conservative angels, not liberal devils, control the committees' print, this may well be the first pro-growth fiscal package since 1986.

Warts and all, this is progress. The political game, like life itself, is about incremental progress, not perfection. At any rate, with a thin 10-seat GOP House majority it's probably the best deal Senate Majority Leader Trent Lott could get. This is what the stock market is telling us. Just as gold is the best barometer of inflation risk, stocks are the best indicator of tax and economic growth risk. Since Newt Gingrich returned from China and launched a tax-cut offensive, the Dow Jones Industrial Average has increased by nearly 9% and the Nasdaq

Composite Index has risen by 6.5%. So the revival of tax cuts sparked a comeback in the stock market. It's not happenstance.

Because a capital gains levy directly taxes innovation, risk-taking and human creativity, it is the most important tax in our system. It is human ingenuity that has created our bull market economic expansion, now in its 15th year, adding 35 million new jobs in this remarkable wave of high-tech prosperity. Not coincidentally, this expansion can be dated from the 1978 Steiger capital gains tax cut.

Since the late 1970s, the effective tax rate on capital gains (including fictitious inflation gains) has dropped from nearly 200% to a current rate of 47%. This has lowered the risk and raised the reward for all manner of high-tech entrepreneurship. Every nook and cranny of our lives has been improved by the high-tech wave of the past 20 years, from personal computers to VCRs to CDs to medical diagnostic and delivery services to automatic teller machines to the Internet and on and on. Housing, autos, transportation and financial services are just some of the sectors of our economy that have benefited enormously from their investments in computers and telecommunications.

This wave of high-tech innovation has produced a stronger and more efficient economy, at lower inflation, than suggested by mismeasured government statistical reports. Leonard Nakamura, an economist at the Federal Reserve Bank of Philadelphia, reports that since 1978 the U.S. economy has expanded by 4.5% per year, with productivity rising by 3% and inflation of only 2%. This contrasts with the Commerce Department's reported data of 2.3% growth, 0.9% productivity growth and 5% inflation. Similarly, Dallas Fed economic adviser Michael Cox believes that information-age improvements in product quality, variety and customization have been largely ignored by government statisticians.

In recent years high-tech production and investment have contributed nearly four of every 10 additional dollars of reported real gross domestic product. Since 1980 the Commerce Department's high-tech price index, measuring the costs of computers and related equipment, has deflated by nearly 100%. Here, too, prices are probably overstated, but even the reported data are startling.

Joseph Schumpeter would call this a gale of creative destruction. In his opus, "Business Cycles," he clearly stated that innovation leads to higher productivity and lower prices. His long-wave cycles were focused on industrial innovation: shipbuilding, cotton milling, iron making and power machinery from 1787 to 1842; steam, steel and railroads from 1842 to 1897; and electricity, chemistry and autos from

1898. Just as in past cycles of innovation, today's high-tech production is higher and prices are lower than virtually anyone recognizes.

The Congressional Budget Office's recent $225 billion in increased revenue projection is de facto recognition of the power of our high-tech economy. And now the Treasury predicts only a $75 billion budget deficit for fiscal 1997, after retiring $65 billion of federal debt. A good chunk of this revenue abundance comes from corporate profits, which are outstripping the growth of real GDP. As a result, during this recovery cycle profits as a share of the economy have moved up to nearly 9% from roughly 6.5%, which is only possible through a burst of high-tech-related productivity improvement.

What's more, a spate of recent economic reports put unemployment at 4.9%, while the GDP price deflator registered only 1.8% over the past year, with real GDP rising 4%. These results drive another stake into the heart of the Phillips Curve. In the early 1980s demand-siders told us inflation would rise when unemployment dropped below 7%; they were wrong. Then they told us inflation would rise when unemployment dropped below 6%. Wrong again. More recently the low-inflation Phillips Curve unemployment rate was said to be 5%. Today the latest low inflation data prove they're still wrong.

Despite all this evidence, economic agencies such as the Congressional Budget Office, the Office of Management and Budget and the Federal Reserve continue to understate the economy's potential growth rate. At some point their theory must give way to real-world results. Instead of revering their 2% to 2.5% theoretical economic speed limit, why don't they come out of denial and recognize that since 1982 reported real economic growth has averaged a solid 3% per year even with the government's mismeasurement problems? Then the CBO would stop crowding out tax cuts by overestimating the deficit each year, and the Fed would stop its premature credit tightening. Even more to the point, the stock market already knows that high-tech innovation has significantly expanded the economy's potential to grow, gradually pushing the noninflationary frontier growth rate to at least 4%, with a no more than 4% unemployment.

The budget's lower capital gains tax rate will help maintain U.S. global economic leadership in the 21st century. This is especially important in relation to the fast-growing economies of the Pacific Rim, with China looming not far behind. Most of the Asian tigers have lower tax burden on capital formation than the U.S.

Capital gains tax relief will also throw off an unexpected dividend at home: The federal budget could be balanced next year. Here's the logic: Net of corporate stock buybacks, the capitalized asset value of

U.S. stocks has increased more than $3 trillion since 1994. Should only 15% of investors decide to realize their gains at a new 20% rate, then the Treasury could reap a conservatively estimated $90 billion in windfall revenues, more than enough to cover the projected deficit.

Following that, capital gains tax relief will continue to produce a steady stream of increasing economic returns from high-tech innovations that will generate a permanently higher rate of economic growth. This is much different from the old theory of one-time diminishing returns. In other words, a true growth dynamic creates self-sustaining momentum.

Good things beget still more good things. Perhaps once real growth takes hold, the Congress will become sufficiently emboldened to pursue a next-generation policy of tax simplification that would end the double and triple taxation of saving and investment, raise tax-bracket thresholds for middle-income earners, and let more people spend their own money more wisely than government will. It may be the dawning of a new era.

1.15 THE GREENSPAN STANDARD

June 27, 1997

One of the interesting developments in 1997's first half is the near universal consensus that U.S. inflation and interest rates must rise, the only questions being how far and how quickly. Turns out, however, that inflation has *declined* significantly, and interest rates are gradually trending lower rather than higher. So, the forecasting consensus not only missed the magnitude, but more importantly entirely missed the *direction* of the inflation story.

Why is this? Well, if you track the wrong indicators, and hold to the wrong model, even the smartest chaps will get the wrong results. By following the unemployment rate, or wage rates, or real GDP growth rates, Phillips curve—NAIRU (non-accelerating inflation rate of unemployment) approach believers expected at least 4% inflation. And from this view they predicted that the Fed funds rate would rise to 6% or even higher, with 30 year Treasury bonds yielding 7½% or higher.

But interest rates are trending down, not up, and various government inflation reports suggest 2% or even a bit lower. Keynesians didn't get it, but the classical commodity price rule model did. Using gold, the mother of all leading inflation indicators, generated a declining inflation forecast. Gold prices have dropped more than $60 over the past year (over $400 to below $340). Black gold, sometimes called oil, has collapsed from $28 to $19. Broad commodity indexes such as the Goldman Sachs and the CRB have lost roughly 5% over the past year. Our golden cone forecasting model is now beginning to predict *a 1% inflation handle over the year ahead.*

Golden Cone

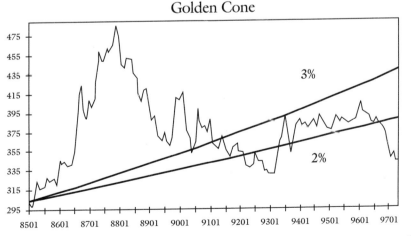

How's this model doing? Well, today's GDP report shows a 1.8% deflator over the past four quarters, along with a 2.2% yearly rise in the chain-price index. Last week the CPI registered a 2.2% gain, while the PPI only a 0.3% yearly rise. A year ago these inflation measures were around 3%. Now, however, we are closing in on zero inflation. The Greenspan Standard is working. While there are no clear rules, targets, or benchmarks, the fact is the best Federal Reserve chairman in my professional lifetime has succeeded in curbing inflation. *Importantly, 1997 has brought a new inflation downturn.* 3% is gone; 1% looms on the horizon. The Keynesian Phillips curve view is dead. The classical commodity price rule is alive. Market price indicators are better forecasters than Ivy League economists (including this one).

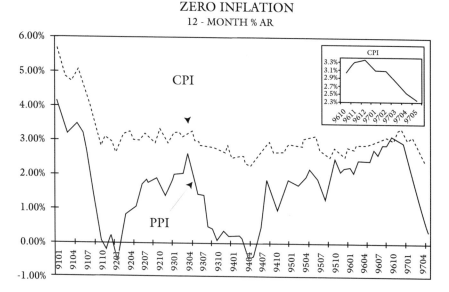

ZERO INFLATION
12 - MONTH % AR

And let's not forget that inflation is the most pervasive economy-wide tax. So, declining inflation is a huge economy wide *tax cut*, stimulating real capital investment returns, real wages and real incomes. Put differently, falling inflation stimulates economic growth. Keynesians have it bass akward. Growth does not cause inflation. Low inflation causes growth.

One take on the inflation tax cut theme is the capital gains dynamic. Using the (mismeasured) CPI, a year ago its 3% inflation trend generated an effective tax rate on real capital gains of 56%. This is a good low rate, compared to 200% in the inflation prone 1970s, or even 75% in the inflationist late 1980s.

But, a 2% inflation rate drops the effective capgains burden down to 47%. This allows investors to take home 53 cents on the capital gain dollar, instead of 44 cents, a 20% improvement. Now, however, if Congress takes the statutory tax rate on capital gains to 20%, as we believe they will, and inflation over the next 12 to 18 months drops down to 1½%, then the effective tax on real capital gains falls to 30%, an interplanetary and extra-celestial historical low. This allows investors to take home 70 cents, not 53 cents. 70 is better than 53 by 32%. Even better, if Congressman Bill Archer succeeds in indexing capgains to inflation, then the effective tax rate drops to 20%.

Effective Capital Gains Tax Rate

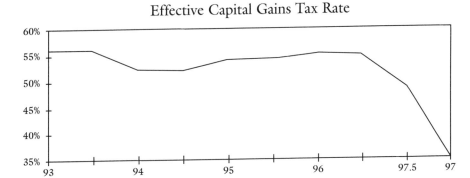

Do we think the stock market is discounting this gospel? (For the non-spiritual, gospel means good news.) You bet it is. Lower inflation is a tax cut. A lower capital gains tax is also a tax cut. We are talking about two tax cuts here. And here's another point: raising the after-tax reward on high risk capital will expand the supply of risk taking. In our information-age innovative high-tech economy, nothing is more important than investing in high risk next generation ideas. More risk taking will lead to more innovation, which will generate more economic growth. With a solid gold-backed value of money, more goods and services will generate even lower inflation. Schumpeter is our guide: more innovative output coexists with falling prices.

Alan Greenspan understands all this. Sometimes he talks the language of Phillips curve austerity, but more often than not he lectures on the importance of free markets and high technology in our dynamic post cold war new world economy. He knows the score, even if he refuses to be bound by numerical policy targets. Perhaps even that story will improve. For the here and now, the inside Fed grapevine is chattering about a shift of chairmanesque priorities. Namely, A-G is downplaying NAIRU and upgrading actual inflation reports as well as commodity price indicators. So the Fed will not be tightening policy.

Welcome home Alan. We greet you with open arms. And, even if the Japanese Prime Minister doesn't like our bonds, we do. The way this zero inflation story is progressing, long-term bond yields could drop to 6% before long. Keep the faith. Faith is the spirit.

1.16 NEW PARADIGM

July 9, 1997

Even as the Congress and President struggle to complete a very mediocre FY '98 budget, the U.S. economy and stock market are already enjoying the considerable benefits of a very substantial tax cut and a budget that is essentially balanced. Prosperity is making Washington seem less and less important.

The tax cut results from a big downturn of inflation, where producer prices have actually declined over the past five months (following a 2.6% rise in 1996) and consumer prices have advanced by only 1.4% at an annual rate (compared to 2.9% in 1996). Lower inflation provides a powerful economywide tax cut. It boosts real investment returns on capital and risk taking, raises real incomes and wages, lifts real corporate profits and increases real economic growth. And it is solid growth which has reduced the federal budget deficit to less than $50 billion, actually a combined $100 billion surplus for federal, state, and local government. The inflation tax cut is the single biggest financial market story this year. It has proven the forecasting consensus to be very wrong. But it has made 125 million American investors very wealthy.

Two market price indicators have been signaling this tax cut effect for quite some time: gold and stocks. If only economists would put more faith in the message of market prices. Gold prices have been steadily falling for nearly 18 months, from over $400 in early 1996 to around $320 recently. This centuries old barometer of monetary purchasing power has once again proven to be a reliable inflation forecasting tool. The decline of gold has been signaling that the money supplied by the Federal Reserve has moved steadily into balance with the volume of money demanded by financial markets and the economy. There is no excess liquidity, which is the ultimate cause of inflation. Weak gold means hard money, hard money means more purchasing power and more purchasing power, leads to zero inflation.

Still, the Fed seems baffled by this year's inflation decline. The minutes of their May 20 open market committee meeting reveal that " . . . members found it very difficult to account for this surprisingly benign behavior of inflation in an economy that had been operating at a level approximating full employment. . . . " But it's really not so difficult to understand. People working, producing, and prospering never cause inflation. More to the point, Greenspan and Co. have returned to an inflation targeting approach which amounts to a domestic price rule. In the event, Fed actions have kept the dollar-gold exchange rate floating narrowly around $350. This is good. In effect, the Fed has recreated a 1950s/early 60s-style Bretton Woods gold standard of monetary value. The longer this standard is maintained, the more global investors come to believe it. As more people believe in it, pricing decisions and inflation expectations become steadier and steadier. Call it *price stability.*

The most recent gold decline shows that powerful disinflationary forces are still at work. No wonder the Australian central bank is selling gold. The metal yields no interest rate and there's no inflation to hedge against. What's more, memories of the 1966–1980 Age of Inflation are gradually receding, replaced by new confidence in the Greenspan Standard, which has apparently adopted gold as its monetary policy lodestar. At the very least, Greenspan has rejected unemployment, NAIRU (so-called non-accelerating inflation rate of unemployment), and real economic growth as primary policy guides. Instead, he is beginning to recognize a new Information Age paradigm. Hi-tech innovation raises productivity and lowers costs. As our favorite dead economist Joseph Schumpeter predicted, innovation increases output and lowers prices. Growth is now to be praised not criticized. Greenspan himself is now telling insiders that the March tightening was a mistake.

Fortunately, a pleased President Clinton agrees with this logic according to *Business Week*'s recent cover story, hinting that Greenspan could be re-appointed to another four-year term when this one expires in June of 2000. If that means seven more years of U.S. price stability, then it's no wonder that long bonds are mounting a powerful rally. Ten-year Treasury yields have fallen to 6.25%, while 30-year issues are marching toward 6.5%; both have rallied by nearly 75 basis points. Continued zero-inflation implies that long-term interest rates could fall *another 100 basis points* before this rally has run its course.

Of course the stock market thrives on lower bond rates. The yield on long-term Treasury bonds represents the discounting factor for future company earnings. With declining yields, the net present value of future profits goes up and up. The combination of reduced inflation (tax cut) and lower bond yields (lower discount factor) is enough to drive share prices right through the roof. That is exactly what is happening. That is why the Dow has risen by 1700 points to nearly 8000 in just over three months.

But lower inflation and declining interest rates are not simply a one-time happening, as pessimistic Wall Street gurus such as Barton Biggs and George Soros would have us believe. They are trapped by the old Keynesian paradigm of the law of diminishing returns. Actually, information age hi-tech breakthroughs have undreamed of spillovers that impact every nook and cranny of the new economy. At the same time, declining inflation will, in unpredictable fits and starts, reduce interest rates to levels lower than virtually any economist is now willing to predict.

Therefore the new paradigm is about *increasing returns,* where the positive effects of high-tech innovation and price stability release economic forces that *feed on themselves.* All this suggests even higher stock prices and even more economic growth as far as the eye can see. Just as gold is the best barometer of future inflation, the stock market value of U.S. business firms is the best gauge of future growth, wealth and progress. Can it be purely a coincidence that crime, welfare, teenage pregnancies and other social problems are waning while stock markets are rising? I think not. Fin de siecle America is becoming a much healthier place. Keep the faith. Faith is the spirit.

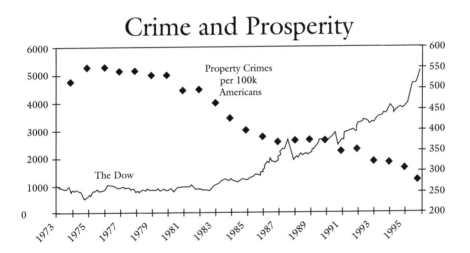

Crime and Prosperity

75

1.17 GOP and Clinton II

August 6, 1997

In the week or so after final signoff on the Federal budget and tax deal, both the NASDAQ and the Russell 2000 high tech stock market indexes outperformed the Dow, which itself increased nearly 140 points. This follows the tremendous July performance, where the Dow soared 500 points (6.5%), and the high tech indexes had their best percentage gain in a year. What's the link between the new budget plan and the stock market? Stocks love lower taxes. In classical economics the stock market value of all business firms is the best barometer of future economic growth and wealth creation. So the hot market is signaling strong approval of the new direction for U.S. fiscal policy.

Direction is the key. Take taxes. Warts and all, taxes are (mostly) going down, not up. In particular, the basic capital gains tax rate will drop from 28% to 20%. This means that for each dollar of successful investment risk the taxpayer reward rises to 80 cents from 72 cents, an 11 percentage point improvement. Adjusted for a 2% inflation horizon (indexing never made it into the bill), the effective return on *real* capital gains increases by roughly 25 percentage points. This is big stuff. Prospects of better after-tax returns (including corporate profits and economic growth) are already being capitalized into higher market valuations.

Regrettably, the capgains story was made more complex by the last minute inclusion of multiple holding periods associated with different tax rates. For assets held under a year, the 39.6% ordinary income tax rate still applies. The old 28% capgains rate now kicks in between 12 and 18 months. A new 20% capgains tax rate will apply to holding periods of 18 months or longer. And in 2001 an asset held more than 5 years will be eligible for an 18% tax rate. So now there are four tax rates for four holding periods. So it goes. Score it as another win for lawyers and accountants. Most regrettable. But, even Washington's convoluted thinking (mainly from Treasury big wigs Robert Rubin and Lawrence Summers) does not diminish the pro-growth significance of a sizable reduction in the capgains tax rate. Especially in today's more stable near-zero inflation environment, where investor horizons have been steadily lengthened, 18 month holding periods are not a big deal. Risk taking *is* more patient. Some supply-siders have been very grumpy about this. But the good should never be the enemy of the perfect.

Also underrated by many conservatives is the advent of universal IRAs. Sponsored by Senate finance chairman William Roth, these "back-ended" savings plans (after tax deposits are allowed to accumulate as tax deferred investments with tax free withdrawals) constitute a huge camel's nose under the tent of Social Security privatization, Medicare privatization, and education choice vouchers. This is pro-competition, pro-saving and pro-growth. Future tax bills undoubtedly will raise allowable investment amounts and family income limits. Another pro-growth idea is the $500k capgains exclusion from the sale of homes, which is bound to increase the real estate turnover rate. Most people will be able to take out tax-free cash, while the interest expense carrying cost is still tax deductible, and home equity borrowing could generate even more cash. All this will free up a sizable chunk of new investment resources that could flow into new business start-ups or technology innovations that require high risk financing.

Of course the dark side of the tax bill is the anti-growth kiddie tax credits. Motives were pure, but results will be poor. With strict income eligibility limits, successful working families will forfeit the credit if they get a salary raise. So the incentive is to work less, not more. This is why social engineering, including conservative social engineering, always backfires. An across the board income tax rate reduction would have been much more efficient and far reaching. Why not reward *everyone's* added work effort and productivity. Alas, in this tax bill if you have no children, or no dependent children living at home, or you're not in college, or planning to attend a community college, or if you fly a lot, or (heaven forbid) if you smoke, then you lose big-time!

But after all, sometimes the sum is greater than the parts. In this particular case it's important to keep an eye on the whole forest rather than the lesser trees. The key point is this: in 1990 and 1993 taxes were raised big-time. This year taxes are mostly being cut. Nationalized health care is gone. Privatized retirement and health care prospects are on the rise. Let's give the Republican Congress and the born-again President some credit. Call it the GOP and Clinton II. Gingrich & Co. saved Clinton from himself. And then Dick Morris morphed Clinton into a moderate Republican.

This budget deal is really the culmination of a story that began in November 1994. The Republican take-over of Congress signified the end of austere tax hikes and the resumption of Reaganesque policies aimed at diminished government and greater free enterprise. Not only capgains relief, expanded IRAs and reduced inheritance taxes, reforms that were unthinkable during Clinton I and the Democratic Congress, but on the spending side what is essentially a flexible budget freeze

77

could reduce the government's share of the economy to only 18%, Uncle Sam's lowest take since the mid Sixties.

November 1994 is the key date. The election generated a tax cut psychology. Once again markets tell the story. In the year following the 1993 tax hike the stock market went nowhere and Treasury bond rates skyrocketed from less than 6% to over 8%. But the 1994 mid-term elections changed everything. Stock and bond prices soared. Especially stocks, representing an enhanced economic growth outlook from the change in fiscal direction. Only two and a half years later the Dow Jones has more than doubled, moving from under 4000 to over 8000. This is extraordinary. And it is not a coincidence. Free market economics are winning. And the best is yet to come.

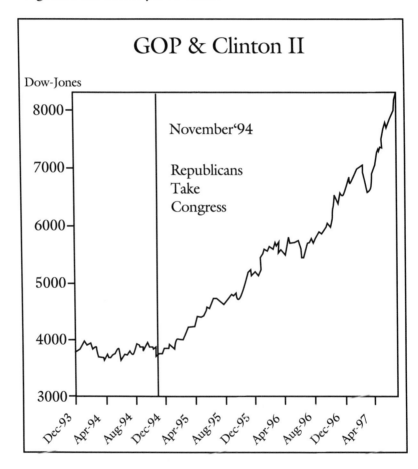

1.18 VAT ATTACKS

BILL CLINTON'S PROPOSED VALUE-ADDED TAX

May 24, 1993

Bill Clinton promised to help small business, create new jobs, and reduce the deficit, all while reducing the burden on the middle class. The real agenda seems rather different.

Perhaps it's a clever ruse, a breathtaking ploy whereby President Clinton gave all the remaining liberal-left policy people in the United States jobs in his Administration just so he could keep a careful eye on them. Then, crafty politician that he is, the President permitted them to pull together the most liberal economic program since World War II, knowing full well that Congress—not to speak of the American taxpayers—would never support it.

Or then again, perhaps President Clinton actually believes in his program to increase taxes, re-regulate business, enlarge domestic spending, and extend international trade sanctions. In this more likely scenario, Clinton spent last year's election campaign spinning the most elaborate web of cognitive dissonance in recent political history.

At its center, this web was held together by a series of little white lies and policy deceptions. It seduced just enough marginal voters—especially Reagan Democrats—into believing that Clinton's refreshing activism would replace Bush's standpat austerity with a new wave of small-business expansion, job growth, and deficit reduction, without burdensome tax increases on middle-class families.

But, as it turns out, Clinton's new economic plan follows a very different script: rising domestic spending, very high taxes, and across-the-board re-regulation. The number of broken campaign promises and policy reversals continues to mount. After the proposed $75-billion energy tax, which will fall most heavily on small businesses and middle-income families, nothing illustrates Clinton's commitment to big government better than the recently resurfaced Value-Added Tax, which like a bad penny, keeps popping up in high-level Administration planning discussions.

ONCE AND FUTURE TAX

Clinton insiders refer to the VAT as a "future" policy that would be used for deficit reduction (read: higher spending) as well as health-care finance. And make no mistake about it, government activism must be financed.

All during the campaign both Clinton and Gore asserted over and over that government-sponsored and directed universal health care would cost Americans less, not more, than the present system. Seasoned political observers wondered aloud about the validity of the much-used phrase "government cost control," surely one of the great oxymorons of our time. Practical budget hands wondered how expanding benefit eligibility to cover roughly 35 million additional people could possibly result in lower spending, especially given the 25-year history of Medicare and Medicaid spending overruns.

Gradually during Clinton's first hundred days the white lie was exposed. Health-care planners inside the Administration quietly leaked that universal coverage might add spending of some $30 to $100 billion after all. More recently the range has been vamped up to $100 to $150 billion. The problem, of course, is how to pay for it.

This is particularly the case in the context of the overall public disappointment with Clinton's budget package, in which taxes are raised roughly three times more than spending is reduced, domestic spending actually rises, and the projected deficit averages $240 billion in the next four years, barely lower than Bush's $260-billion average and nearly $100 billion above Ronald Reagan's last deficit in fiscal year 1989.

A second white lie relates to the financing issue, since, in an effort to attract Main Street shopkeepers and owners of small family businesses from the Republican Party, Clinton repeatedly promised not to increase payroll taxes. Then again, promises are made to be broken.

That said, the Clintonites now find themselves wedged between a rock and a hard place. To finance their government-engineering social agenda and still take care of traditional Democratic interest groups, the new Administration has already proposed steep income-tax hikes on individuals and businesses, a Social Security tax increase, and a large-scale energy levy. It has used up its sources of funding even before it has got to its health-care reform.

Enter the VAT, a favorite fiscal tool of European industrial planners and state collectivists. Fashionable among Clinton advisors is the notion that latter-day Germany and Jacques Delors's technocratic vision of European unity is a far more intelligent organization of economic resources than was ever created in the relatively free-market economy of the United States.

The problem with this "new Europe" is that it simply doesn't work. Far from the free-market entrepreneurial capitalism of Adenauer's

Ludwig Erhard and de Gaulle's Jacques Rueff, today's Europe increasingly drifts toward larger government, higher taxes, and slower growth.

Take the four largest economies of Europe—Britain, France, Germany, and Italy—with a combined population of 250 million and GDP of roughly $5 trillion. Together these countries created a combined total of only 5 million new jobs in the past 12 years, with an average unemployment rate which today is just short of 10 percent. Directing these sluggish economies, the average government budget share of GDP comes to slightly less than 50 percent. Financing this massive government influence is a VAT system that averages 17 percent.

What's more, the VAT rate has a habit of rising. This is because it is something of a stealth tax, not scored on yearly tax-date calculations nor appearing on sales-tax receipts at most stages of production. Because it is far less visible than income taxes, the VAT is more easily raised over time to finance the ever-rising tide of government expenditure.

In Britain, for example, the VAT, first imposed in 1973 at a 10 percent rate, has grown to its present 17.5 percent rate. Italy's started in 1973 at 12 percent, and today is at 19 percent. A smaller nation like Denmark moved the VAT from 10 to 22 percent, while the Netherlands moved it from 12 to 20 percent. Undoubtedly these trends are not lost on the Clintonites.

Yet the economically burdensome VAT has never solved the Europeans' chronic budget-deficit problems. Currently, the highest deficits among the big four are the United Kingdom, with a deficit of 7.6 percent of GDP and a 17.5 percent VAT, and Italy, with a 10.2 percent deficit share of GDP and a 19 percent VAT. Over the past decade, the E-4 generated an average 4.3 percent deficit share of GDP with a 17 percent average VAT, while the U.S. ran a 3 percent deficit share with no VAT.

THE VAT-LESS U.S.

Not only does the U.S. show a lower deficit with no VAT, American economic performance has been well ahead of Europe's. During the past 12 years, including President Bush's dismal period, the U.S. economy generated 20 million new jobs, four times the number generated by Europe's largest economies. The U.S. unemployment rate today is 7 percent and falling, 3 percent below Europe's, and our VAT-less government share of GDP stands at 38 percent, nearly a third smaller than Europe's. Hence there is no evidence to support the academy's fashionable view, propagated by Laura Tyson, Robert Reich, and Lester Thurow, that spend-and-VAT policies direct resources toward better economic performance.

The explanation for this is simple. People produce in order to consume. But the VAT drives a wedge between what they produce and what they consume. While a VAT is different from an income tax, the burden is just as damaging to the overall economy. The VAT is a tax on labor and production and, at the end, also a tax on consumption.

The very notion of taxing the "value added" should be seen clearly for what it is: a tax on business profits and individual wealth. Moreover, by fueling the growth of government, the VAT leaves a considerably smaller remaining share of the economy that works for profit and prosperity. This is why high-VAT nations in Europe have low economic performance.

What's more, an American VAT would be piled on top of current tax burdens—in addition to Clinton Administration proposals to raise income and energy and other sales taxes by $300 billion over the next five years. For some reason, most journalists keep repeating the mantra that a value-added tax will reduce consumption and raise investment. Nothing could be further from the truth.

A 5 percent VAT applied at each stage of production and sales would generate an estimated $500 billion by 1998, according to the Congressional Budget Office. No tax relief on capital gains or business depreciation or IRA-type savings is contemplated in the Clinton plan. Individual and corporate income-tax rates will rise to a range of 36 to 40.2 percent, along with the $75-billion energy tax, itself an add-on to the VAT.

A combined tax increase projected at $800 billion, or roughly 10 percent of estimated 1998 GDP, couldn't possibly promote saving and investment, though it surely would impoverish consumers. Business costs will rise sharply, rendering the American firms far less profitable at home and much less competitive in the global market-place.

Alongside higher tax rates on those families with the highest propensity to save and invest, Clinton's tax package will substantially dampen wealth creation, capital formation, and the economy's long-run potential to grow. Assuming that the Federal Reserve continues to take price stability as its goal, Clinton's scheme of both permanent and one-time tax increases will raise inflation and reduce output by roughly 2 percent, reducing real economic growth to something like 1 to 2 percent and raising inflation to 4 to 5 percent, with a budget deficit that will rise at least $50 billion above Mr. Clinton's projections. For example, when Britain and Canada recently raised the VAT and other taxes, both found themselves with a witches' brew of simultaneous prolonged recession and higher inflation. In Canada, where the central bank leaned hard to offset tax-induced fiscal inflation, Prime Minister Brian Mulroney saw his approval rating drop to under 10 percent. He was eventually forced to announce that he will resign in June. Both nations experienced much higher budget deficits.

Meanwhile, in another of his little white lies, President Clinton strenuously denied that a VAT was under consideration when his planners first leaked the idea last February. When Laura Tyson and Donna Shalala surfaced the idea again a few weeks ago, both Clinton and Gore promptly issued a series of non-denial denials. Just to rub salt into the wounds, the Clintonites managed to revive the VAT issue on the April 15 tax-payment day, thus putting a relatively obscure policy leak on the front pages of every newspaper in the country.

In Washington, where there's smoke there's usually fire. Breaking yet another campaign pledge, Clinton's national-health-care package will cost more money, and lots of it. As a result, tax burdens will in fact rise across the board, including on the middle class, thus breaking his second campaign promise a second time (the first middle-class tax promise had gone up in flames with the energy tax).

But the issues here are larger than health care and the Value-Added Tax. The Clinton Administration is driven by a philosophy and a set of values which strongly favor enlarged government and a sweeping use of its powers: government as investor; government as banker; government as industrial planner, as commercial regulator, as trade protector; government as doctor, as teacher, as parent. The size and scope of government will be expanded incomparably more than at any time since the 1930s. Unsurprisingly, President Clinton frequently cites Franklin Roosevelt's government activism as his favorite model.

Originally billing himself as a "new" Democrat, Mr. Clinton has veered sharply left in his first hundred days. His economic package was first advertised as a means to boost economic growth and lower the deficit. It will achieve neither. Instead, it is a grandiose plan of social engineering and income redistribution. Unless Senator Dole and others can stop it, Clintonism's leftward bent suggests that U.S. health care and tax policy will come more and more to resemble Europe's, and thence so will our economic performance.

1.19 ON THE SUPPLY SIDE

FAILURE OF CLINTON ADMINISTRATION
WELFARE REFORM POLICIES

May 16, 1994

Wouldn't it make sense to the average taxpaying voter if the current Washington effort to "end welfare as we know it" actually produced less, rather than more, federal spending for welfare? Not a chance. Instead, the Clinton Administration is about to propose a plan that will cost at least $35 billion more than current plans and by 2000 may total $60 billion above current plans. Despite New Democrat rhetoric about "two years and you're out," the social engineers in HHS and the White House are coming up with a massive bureaucratized entitlement for daycare spending, along with expanded job training, with only a small percentage of welfare recipients actually subject to workfare provisions.

Unfortunately, an early plan from House Republicans, authored by Pennsylvania Senate hopeful Rick Santorum and Connecticut Representative Nancy Johnston, is far too timid: five years and you're still not really out. This proposal creates a new entitlement of $6,000 for each person moving from welfare to workfare. Its off-budget scoring mechanism will result in huge out-year spending increases. And though it does provide for a 2-percent-plus-inflation cap on five welfare programs (AFDC, SSI, EITC, food stamps, and housing allowances), the cap is not legally binding.

What is more, the Santorum-Johnston proposal deals very lightly with spiraling out-of-wedlock births. It requires mothers under 18 to live at home, has inadequately enforced paternity requirements, and gives states the option of limiting AFDC for mothers under 18. But most illegitimate births occur to women between the ages of 19 to 21. And would states ever deny themselves federal funding by exercising the AFDC option?

None of this generates the "more deterrents, greater social stigma, and more economic penalties" advocated by William Bennett. Nor does it meet the criteria set out by Charles Murray, who argues that welfare will never truly be reformed until it is extinguished. Following their lead, Empower America (where Bennett, Jack Kemp, and Vin Weber perch in opposition) sharply criticized the House GOP proposal and urged a "bold, principled, and fundamentally different alternative."

The Empower America approach emphasizes much tougher limitations for welfare assistance to unwed mothers, stronger workfare provisions, and stiff spending caps. Additionally, at the urging of Jack Kemp, the organization's plan contains strong economic-growth provisions for blighted urban and rural areas, including the elimination of capital-gains and payroll taxes and the encouragement of commercial bank lending to minority entrepreneurs in those areas.

Republicans will ultimately come up with a tough alternative to the Clinton proposal, for it is hard to overstate the failure of the U.S. welfare system. Since the mid-1960s, federal, state, and local government spending on welfare, measured in 1992 dollars, has increased nearly eight-fold, from $37 billion in 1965 to $305 billion in 1992. All told, spending on "greater welfare" (to borrow columnist Ben Wattenberg's term) has cumulatively totaled a staggering $4.9 trillion. Welfare has grown from 1.5 percent of gross domestic product in 1965 to 4 percent currently.

Looking ahead, according to the Congressional Budget Office's January 1994 baseline projections, mandatory spending on means-tested programs is expected to rise by $114 billion between now and 1999—9.2 percent annually, or three times the expected inflation rate. All this after an "end welfare as we know it" bill in 1988, and two budget "deals of the century" in 1990 and 1993.

What have Americans gotten for this? More welfare recipients (Robert Rector of the Heritage Foundation estimates that the total welfare population may be something like 60 million people) and rising social pathologies, including drug abuse, crime, and violence. For instance, the out-of-wedlock birth-rate had increased from 5.3 percent in 1960 to 29.5 percent in 1991, including a 67.9 percent rate among blacks; and the number of violent crimes has risen from 288,000 in 1960 to nearly two million in 1992.

It is time to spend less, while creating both incentives for traditional two-parent families and penalties for unwed mothers. This is exactly the approach taken in a new proposal sponsored by Republicans Lauch Faircloth, Charles Grassley, and Hank Brown in the Senate, and Representatives James Talent, Tim Hutchinson, and Charles Canady in the House. On illegitimacy, the Faircloth-Talent bill stipulates that one year after enactment unwed mothers age 21 and younger would receive no direct welfare payments except Medicaid: no AFDC, no food stamps, no public-housing assistance. Four years after the bill passes, the cut-off age would be raised to 26.

The budget savings from this reform would be allocated to the states in the form of a block grant designed to provide help to orphanages, adoption, or group homes. However, these federal funds could not be spent for abortions or conventional welfare subsidies. For any unwed mothers currently on welfare, if they had additional children they would be ineligible for welfare increases. What's more, the bill would create a $1,000 partially refundable tax credit for working married couples with children.

On the budget side, Faircloth-Talent would create an enforceable aggregate cap of 3/2 percent per year for a new block grant of 76 different federal means-tested programs that currently total $170 billion. That would achieve an estimated cost savings of $90 billion over five years, which would then be turned over to the states. For workfare, the bill proposes that one parent in every two-parent family receiving AFDC must work. All single able-bodied individuals receiving food stamps must work, and all absent fathers who fail to pay child support for kids on welfare would have to perform community-service work. Finally, single mothers currently on AFDC whose children are over age five (about half of all AFDC single mothers) would have to do community-service work by 1996. All told, 4.4 million welfare recipients would have to participate in work programs by 1996.

One additional point never properly addressed by welfare reformers is the desperate need to teach children, especially those in inner cities, the traditional moral values necessary to carry them through successful daily living—personal responsibility, discipline, abstinence, thrift, hard work, respect for others, and spiritual faith.

One of the most innovative approaches is used by the Darrell Green Learning Center in Washington, D.C. Founded by the Washington Redskins all-pro cornerback, the center is an after-school program that teaches behavior and moral character, as well as the academic skills of reading, writing, and math. It is exactly the sort of local self-help program that should be eligible for public funding under flexible block grants, or vouchers, or even tax credits for private contributors.

Indeed, some combination of the Faircloth-Talent bill and the Empower America proposals, plus the Green self-help moral and academic program, should be stitched together by the Republican Party as its own version of welfare reform. Halfway measures such as the Santorum plan, though better than nothing and much better than Clinton's reform, are simply insufficient.

Democrats will never sign off on such a major redirection of policy—not even Senator Moynihan, arguably the most important welfare-reform player in Washington. Mr. Moynihan's analysis of social issues is frequently prescient, but his voting record speaks differently: against workfare in 1988, 1992, and 1993; against learnfare in 1992;

against drug-testing and rehabilitation in 1993. Indeed, referring to the views of Charles Murray and Empower America, Mr. Moynihan recently told the *New York Times*, "This kind of thing is simply not going to happen."

Indeed, the Republicans should sharpen, not blur, their differences with Democrats on welfare reform—and on health care, crime, and job training with, as Dan Rostenkowski has indiscreetly confirmed, the Clinton Democrats view as opportunities for new open-ended entitlements funded by huge tax increases. Though Republicans will lose in this congressional session, they may be able to filibuster or defeat an expansion of the status quo. The electorate, still awaiting an alternative vision from the GOP, is more than willing to wait another year until a new Congress provides a real solution.

1.20 MIDDLE-CLASS TAX HIKE

THE PRICE OF MAJOR GOVERNMENT PROGRAMS IN
HEALTH CARE, WELFARE REFORM AND CRIME PREVENTION

June 13, 1994

Ironically, the closest thing to a truth-teller these days in Washington is Ways and Means Chairman Dan Rostenkowski. No matter that he may soon come under indictment for converting postage stamps to cash. On the question of how to pay for health-care reform, as well as other new or enlarged entitlement plans surfacing in Congress, Rosty has been brutally honest in calling for broad-based increases in taxation.

Equally surprising is the general silence emanating from the alleged anti-tax party, a.k.a. the Republicans. Should there be passage of major bills on health care, welfare, job training, and crime, then Americans will for the third time in the last four years be burdened by another "largest tax increase in peacetime history." What's more, to finance these massive expansions of government intrusion, the middle class is being set up for a tremendous pummeling through higher payroll-tax burdens.

Few policy-makers may realize it, but as a result of repeated payroll-tax increases in the 1970s and 1980s, middle-class wage-earners shoulder a higher tax burden today than they did in the 1960s. The overall marginal tax rate (income, FICA, earned income tax credit) for the $30,000 earner measured in constant 1991 dollars, has increased from 20 percent in 1985 to 30.3 percent by 1994. For a $50,000 earner, the tax rate moved from 25 percent to 43.3 percent. That means that instead of taking home 75 cents on the added dollar earned, the earner keeps only 57 cents, a whopping 24 percent cutback in after-tax purchasing power.

Meanwhile, a successful upper-end earner making $200,000 (also 1991 dollars) saw a decline in his or her marginal tax-rate from 50 percent in 1965 to 43 percent in 1994, which increased after-tax incentives to work, save, and invest by 14 percent. These tax changes are a function not of income-tax policies, where rates were slashed by President Reagan in 1981 and 1986, but of payroll-tax policies. In 1977, President Carter signed a bill that raised Social Security taxes by $227 billion, proclaiming that the system would be made sound through 2030. By 1983, however, in order to keep the program solvent (supposedly until 2065) President Reagan had to raise Social Security taxes another $165 billion.

Now, the latest trustee reports suggest that Social Security will go bankrupt in 2029, the Medicare trust fund will run dry by 2001, and a fund to pay benefits to disabled workers will be exhausted next year. That is why Mr. Rostenkowski has proposed another set of payroll-tax increases to shore it up, along with paying for Clinton's health-care package and Labor Secretary Reich's job-training package. Rosty's truth-telling also includes lower benefits for new retirees and a cutback in cost-of-living adjustments.

In short, we keep raising payroll taxes to fund entitlements that keep going bankrupt. Perhaps this is the ultimate defiance by the professional political class of economic and political sense. For the middle class is growing increasingly cantankerous.

A study done by former Treasury economists Gary and Aldona Robbins, now at Fiscal Associates in Arlington, Virginia, shows that the average tax rate on labor—including the federal income tax, state and local income taxes, and the OASDHI tax—has moved upward from about 20 percent in the mid-sixties to about 34 percent currently. Primarily driven higher by rising payroll-tax rates, which have moved from 6 percent to over 15 percent, while income subject to payroll taxes has risen from $4,800 to $60,600, the Robbinses' calculation of the economy-wide weighted-average tax burden implies an average wage of roughly $28,000 in current dollars, surely the middle-class zone.

Not only has the middle class suffered; businesses have as well. Remember, a good many U.S. firms are small family-owned enterprises that are not taxed at corporate rates. IRS statistics show that 45 percent of all business income was reported by unincorporated firms earning between $20,000 and $60,000 annually. When their employees are taken into account, according to Wall Street economist John Ryding, 44 million middle-class returns were affected by the average marginal tax-rate hike from 20 percent to 34 percent over the past thirty years.

By raising the cost of employment and lowering the return to labor, rising payroll taxes have steadily blunted job opportunities. Mainstream economists nowadays suggest that a 6 percent unemployment rate is the "natural" rate. Yet in the 1960s, at much lower payroll-tax rates, unemployment averaged 4.6 percent while yearly inflation averaged only 2 percent. A recent article by Columbia University economist Edmund Phelps argues that a study of 17 OECD countries suggests that "big increases in payroll and personal income taxes in most countries have been mass jobkillers."

The middle class deserted George Bush, flirted with Ross Perot, and settled for Bill Clinton in 1992 out of a desire to change all this. Where's the change? In effect, the Clinton Democrats are set to give the middle class something it doesn't want and the economy desperately doesn't need: more government mandates, more controls, more bureaucracy, more welfare, and more payroll taxes.

Polls show that 60 percent of voters do not want a health package this year. Alas, Republicans seem to imagine that they have to produce some kind of health package or perish, attacked by the Democrats as, well—"nattering nabobs of negativism."

The Republicans are fighting yesterday's war—a sure-fire way to become yesterday's men. The Reagan Democrats and others who make up the middle-class swing vote are now deeply suspicious of the formula of more entitlements and higher taxation. On social issues they want traditional values such as individual responsibility, thrift, hard work, abstinence, virtue, and faith. On the economy they want reduced entitlement spending and lower tax burdens. Not heeding the call, the Clinton Democrats are poised to walk off the cliff. Will the Republicans follow them?

1.21 PHYSICIANS HEAL THEMSELVES

THE GOOD NEWS FOR CONSUMERS—DECLINING HEALTH-CARE INFLATION—IS BAD NEWS FOR THE WHITE HOUSE

September 26, 1994

Last October President Clinton kicked off the health-care debate by insisting that "only comprehensive reform will slow the frightening rate of increase in health-care costs." From day one even those who rejected his remedies agreed on the nature of the problem: soaring costs, which led in turn to a growing share of national output consumed by health care, to huge federal budget deficits, and to large numbers of Americans going uninsured.

The latest numbers on inflation in health-care costs could not have arrived at a more inconvenient time for the White House. Statistics collected by the U.S. Department of Labor show that health-care inflation is slowing dramatically. This collides squarely with the premise underlying the push for a radical overhaul of our current health-care system.

The Labor Department reports that in the first six months of 1994 health-care costs grew at an annual rate of just 4.5 percent, the smallest rise in twenty years. Even the real rate of increase in health-care costs has dipped from 4.4 percent in 1990 and 1991 to a predicted 1.9 percent this year.

Virtually every component of health-care inflation is on a downward path—hospital costs, physician services, drug prices. Employers are starting to report that increases in their medical-insurance costs are slowing down. The real rate of increase in employer-health-plan costs was 5 percent last year. That's nothing to celebrate, but it is half the rate of increase in the late 1980s and early 1990s, according to the Employee Benefit Research Institute. The Chamber of Commerce reports in its most recent member survey that medical-insurance premiums were up by only 1 percent in 1992.

Some of the reduction in health-care inflation is a dividend from lower overall inflation. But that's not the whole story. Although health-care costs continue to outpace consumer prices in general, in the last few years the difference between health-care inflation and overall inflation has been chopped in half.

Some say that it is jawboning by the Clintons and the mere threat of price controls that have driven down prices. There probably is some truth to the notion that just the specter of the economically muddle-headed Clinton and Clinton Lite plans have accelerated self-reform in medicine. But health-care inflation started tumbling in late 1990, long before Bill and Hillary came to Washington.

Competitive forces, not government controls, are the key. "Markets self-correct, and this one is well into that process," says Mitchell Daniels, vice president of Eli Lilly. "As usual, the politicians are miles behind the market." A recent analysis of the medical marketplace by business writer James Glassman of the *Washington Post* concurs. Glassman writes that "the free play of supply and demand is already working. . . . Private firms are putting intense pressure on insurance companies to freeze or cut premiums, and the insurance companies are putting pressure on hospitals and doctors and pharmaceutical manufacturers." Other factors contributing to the slowdown in cost increases include the move toward generic drugs and greater reliance on health-insurance policies that require patient cost sharing.

THE MEDICAID NIGHTMARE

There is one sector of the health-care industry where "rampant inflation" can still be labeled a crisis, and that is government programs. Even with overall health-care inflation declining, Medicaid remains a nightmare of stampeding costs. In 1989 the program's costs increased by 13 percent, in 1990 by 18 percent, in 1991 by 30 percent, in 1992 by 21 percent, and in 1993 by 20 percent. Since 1989 Medicaid has grown at five times the rate of the CPI. Even the *Washington Post*'s recent feature on the history of Medicaid notes wistfully: "It seems clear the Federal Government has lost control of this program."

The person most responsible for this fiscal black hole is Representative Henry Waxman (D., Calif.), nicknamed the Trillion-Dollar Man to signify the long-term impact of his Medicaid expansions. Waxman openly boasts that he has spent the past 15 years converting Medicaid into a de facto national health-insurance program. Twenty-four separate Medicaid expansions were instituted in the 1980s, thanks mostly to him. They have added nearly $20 billion to Medicaid's price tag for this year alone. The program is now so generous that in some states a family of four can have an income of up to $40,000 and still qualify. The history of Medicaid expansions, concedes Ron Wyden (D., Ore.), a member of Waxman's Subcommittee on Health and the Environment, is that "costs were always greater than anticipated." It's not surprising that most Americans are reluctant to give people like Waxman and Wyden the responsibility for cost containment under a Clinton Lite health-care system.

Although both Bill and Hillary Clinton have at various times blamed the health-care inflation crisis on 'greedy' drug companies, insurance companies, and private hospitals, the truth is that government programs, principally Medicare and Medicaid, have been the engine of health-care inflation for more than a quarter-century. From 1950 to 1965—the 15 years before Medicare and Medicaid— health-care costs grew at 3.5 percent a year. But since 1966, the health-care inflation rate has more than doubled, to 7.8 percent.

This is not just coincidental. Since 1966 private-sector health costs have grown by about 7 percent a year, while government programs have grown by roughly 15 percent a year—despite a series of laws passed by Congress in the 1980s and early 1990s to "control government costs" through price controls and other measures.

The performance of Medicare and Medicaid makes one thing clear: any health-care legislation that expands government programs will almost certainly fuel inflation. "Over the last quarter-century," admits Senate Finance Committee Chairman Daniel Patrick Moynihan (D., N.Y.), "we have all been wrong on the costs of entitlements." This is a vast understatement. The Hospital Insurance program was supposed to cost $9 billion in 1990. Instead it cost $67 billion—a 600 percent forecasting error. The propensity to underestimate the cost of new entitlements is not something unique to Medicare. A recent Citizens for a Sound Economy report shows that Social Security now costs six times as much as was projected as recently as 1965; federal disability insurance costs nine times as much as originally predicted.

Even with overall health-care inflation slowing, reform of government health programs is necessary. Medicare is already teetering on the brink of bankruptcy. By 1998 the program's expenditures will begin to outpace payroll-tax revenues, and the deficit will widen rapidly. For the program to remain financially viable, the payroll tax would have to rise from 2 percent of taxable payroll today to a staggering 24 percent by 2020, according to calculations by Haeworth Robertson, former chief actuary of the Social Security Administration.

These numbers underscore the absurdity of the current reform proposals. House Majority Leader Richard Gephardt's bill would create "Medicare Part C," almost doubling the number of Americans on this nearly insolvent program. If there are truly 37 million uninsured Americans, and even if it takes only $2,000 a year to cover each one, this would cost taxpayers about $75 billion a year.

The Clinton Lite plans do not solve the essence of the health-care problem, which is that the vast majority of Americans are overinsured, not underinsured. As economist Stan Liebowitz of the University of Texas at Dallas writes in a new Cato Institute study: "The major culprit in the seemingly endless rise in health-care costs is the removal of the patient as a major participant in the financial and medical choices that are currently being made by others." Since 1960 the share of medical bills paid by patients has dropped from 58 to 20 percent, while the share paid by government has risen from 22 to 42 percent; 95 percent of hospital bills are now paid through government or private insurance. Not surprisingly, hospital fees have long been the fastest growing component of health-care costs.

The quick and simple way to fix the system, slow inflation further, and make health insurance more affordable is through Medical Savings Accounts. These accounts would essentially force patients to be cost-conscious consumers. Each American could put $3,000 a year into a personal health account similar to an IRA. Any unused money would eventually be rolled over into a personal IRA to be spent at retirement. This approach not only cuts out the insurance and government middlemen for minor expenses but gives consumers an incentive to seek low-cost care.

If Congress continues to resist these sensible changes, it should at least follow the Hippocratic injunction: "First, do no harm." The self-reforms transforming the medical marketplace are far more promising than the proposals moving through Congress. The real looming crisis in health care today is the possibility that Congress will manage to pass "broad-based reform" after all.

PART TWO

KUDLOW ON FINANCIAL AND ECONOMIC INDICATORS

2.1 THE ERA OF SURPLUS POLITICS

FROM A SPEECH DELIVERED AT A
CITIZENS FOR A SOUND ECONOMY "POLICYWATCH" BREAKFAST

July 30, 1997

I'm going to speak primarily against the National Debt Repayment Act, H.R. 2191, introduced by Representative Mark Neumann (R-WI), which proposes to somehow cap federal spending a percentage point below revenues. It also specifies that roughly one-third of expected surpluses will go to tax reduction and two-thirds to debt retirement. Within that mix there's some replenishment of Social Security and the Highway Trust Fund, but essentially it's a two-thirds/one-third split.

I am much opposed to this bill, and I am much opposed to the thinking behind the bill. I want to lay out for you some of my thoughts and analysis, some historical views, and then some suggestions as to what I believe is a better economic policy for the nation.

Static formulas. First, in general, I have always been opposed to static formulas, such as the one in the Neumann bill, where you somehow take snapshots and keep spending below revenues. I don't think such formulas ever work in a dynamic economy.

Hysterical debt obsession. Second, and probably much more important, I believe this hysterical obsession over the federal debt is entirely misplaced. It's misplaced in economic terms, and it's fraught with danger in political terms. The focus on debt really removes the focus from controlling federal spending, broad-based tax reform, and the privatization of Social Security. Spending control and tax reform are where we should be. Focusing on the debt confuses causes with effects.

Deficit politics to surplus politics. All of that said, I do believe this is a new era. I would characterize the first half of the 1980s as the politics of growth. The next 10 years I would characterize as deficit politics. And now I believe we are entering a new period, which I will characterize as "surplus politics."

Consider the following charts (Figures 1 and 2 on the next page). Having run the numbers at the Office of Management and Budget (OMB) for three years, I've admired their specificity and accuracy. But I've done some reestimating of my own, and that's where I want to start the analysis.

My reestimation of the budget deal shows a surplus of 1.4 billion by 2002. In fact, I think there's still a very decent chance that the FY

1997 budget will come in flat or even slightly in surplus. But all I have done here is use the budget deal as quantified in various releases from the Senate Budget Committee.

Figure 1

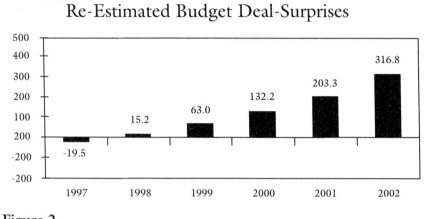

Re-Estimated Budget Deal-Surprises

Figure 2

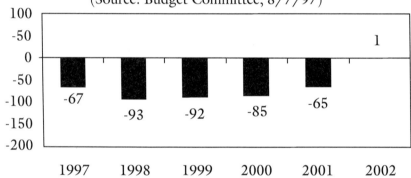

Budget Deal-Deficits
(Source: Budget Committee, 8/7/97)

I think that the 3 percent growth path for total spending, beginning in 1998 and extending to 2002, is probably close to the truth. Accordingly, I left the spending side alone.

What is not close to the truth, however, is the lowball revenue path. Revenue flows will be much greater than the deal would suggest. For the five years ending 1996, to show you my methodology, total federal revenues grew at a 6.6 percent annual rate. In FY 1997, through the first nine months of the fiscal year, revenues are rising at slightly better than 10 percent.

There's a lot going on in that mix, including some capital gains stuff, which is a function of the bull market in stocks but also a function of the transition to a lower and retroactive capital gains tax rate. But I used 10 percent for 1997. For 1998 through 2002, I go back to the trend line of 6.6 percent revenues. I made this judgment on historical grounds. I'm just saying the revenue path was close to 7 percent for five years to 1996. Those were not particularly good years for the economy. The average growth was only about 2.5 or 2.6 percent at an annual rate, but that's what we got. And I extrapolated that 7 percent revenue growth into the five years after 1997.

FY 2002 surplus at $317 billion. Just on that basis, I get a complete reestimate with a $16 billion surplus next year, rising to a $317 billion surplus in FY 2002. Furthermore, I believe that I'm underestimating the surpluses, because we are going to yield plenty of revenues from the capital gains tax cut. As sloppy as that tax cut is, with goofy holding periods and so forth, it's going to help. Moreover, the capitalized asset value of the stock market has expanded by a cool $4 trillion since December 1994, which is pretty good. So, I believe the combination of the bull market and the reduction in the capital gains rate will probably yield at least $50 billion a year in capital gains-related receipts. It might prove as high as $100 billion a year. Either way, we're going to get a bigger surplus path.

This is one reason why I believe we are going into an era of what I would call "surplus politics," and leaving the era of deficit politics which has characterized so much of Washington policy for so long.

The economy ain't perfect, but it's pretty good. Let me also quickly relay my own views on the economy. As I have argued in various publications and talking-head shows, it ain't perfect, but it's pretty good. And you-all in Washington are too pessimistic about what's happening. We have seen a combination of zero inflation—not 3 percent, not even 2 percent, but zero inflation, which itself is a huge economy-wide tax cut—along with the general trends of deregulation and free trade. And all three of these, inflation, deregulation, and free trade, were started during the Reagan years, interrupted during the Bush years, and, frankly, at least with respect to free trade and zero inflation, continued during the Clinton years.

I will give Mr. Clinton considerable credit for his trade policy and cooperation with the Federal Reserve. We lost a little ground on tax rates in the tax hikes of 1990 and 1993, but it didn't do significant damage, in my opinion, to the trend of lower tax rates. And fortunately, the tax hikes left the capital gains tax alone. Lower inflation leveraged through the unindexed capital gains tax led to another tax cut. In effect,

99

we've had two tax cuts, an inflation tax cut and an effective capital gains tax cut. These have saved the president from his own tax increase—that, I think, and a GOP Congress which has held his feet to the fire.

So, you've got pretty good free-market policy trends on inflation, deregulation, trade, and taxes. Furthermore, the advances of our information-age, high-technology economy, with their spillover effects that have transformed virtually every nook and cranny of the economy, have had an extraordinarily positive impact on risk-taking, innovation, entrepreneurship, new business start-ups, and job creation.

The tragedy is the Commerce Department doesn't know how to measure this. I think if we eventually reconcile all this real economic growth we'll be at least a percentage point higher than reported in productivity, but I don't need to wait for that since it shows up in the revenue flow.

Unfortunately, because this rise in growth and productivity isn't official, the Congressional Budget Office and the OMB don't acknowledge it. A lot of conservatives don't acknowledge it because they don't like Clinton. But they should, because it helps our case. These are the policy ideas that we promoted 15 years ago. If President Clinton goes along with them half the time, that's okay.

Talking about debt. Now, let's talk about debt, because some people, Mr. Neumann and others, want to use surpluses to pay down debt and leave only a trickle for tax reduction. Here's my basic point on debt: Debt finance is nothing more than a means of payment, a means of finance. It has no intrinsic economic meaning. It isn't necessarily good, and it isn't necessarily bad. It is a means of finance. That's the first overriding point. For centuries, governments that have spent more than they took in have been faced with the options of either financing the shortfall through higher taxes or higher inflation, or, more recently, selling interest-bearing obligations called "debt."

We learned, in the 20th century particularly, that raising taxes and inflation have severe economic consequences. But debt finance is really a neutral technique. It is not to be praised or railed at, it just is. It's a financing method. Basically, its value depends on what it is you're financing. If the government program or the government investment is good, then debt finance serves a very healthy purpose. If, on the other hand, the government financing plan or the government investment is bad, then the debt financing serves an unhealthy, unsound purpose. It depends what it is you're funding.

A look at junk bonds. It's no different than what we went through on Wall Street a few years ago. We had a hysteria in the late 1980s over the use of so-called high-yield finance techniques, sometimes uncharitably referred to as "junk bonds." Well, junk bonds brought a lot of new technologies to the marketplace. And then, because we hit a few bumps in the stock market road and a few bumps in the credit road, everybody jumped on junk bond financing without recognizing all the good it had done.

The curious thing is that in the last five or six years junk bonds have been the best return in the financial community. The highest total returns have accrued from junk bond ownership. That's because the new hi-tech companies that junk bonds were funding were good. If they had funded bad companies, you wouldn't have had any returns. It's the same thing for the United States government.

Three investments. My point here is very simple. I believe that the use of debt financing, particularly during the Reagan years, which is where the bulk of the debt story starts, was a constructive financing tool for three crucial investments.

Number one, debt finance underwrote the sharp reduction of inflation, which was an absolute, necessary starting point for any economic recovery or stabilization. Moving the inflation rate from roughly 15 percent in 1980, down to 2 percent in 1986, had a tremendous positive impact on the economy, in effect, a huge tax cut which restabilized monetary value. But we had to pay for that because the government had been living on inflated revenue financing for years. Nominal Gross Domestic Product (GDP) was growing at 10 or 12 percent. We cut it back to 5 percent, where it ought to be. In the short run, we created large deficits. Those deficits, however, were financing an end to inflation.

Second, debt finance, at least for a couple of years, was necessary to fund the tax rate cut program that President Reagan put into place. Frankly, I think this so-called short-term revenue problem has been vastly overemphasized by most of the critics. I doubt if the deficits accruing from these tax cuts came to more than $50 billion in the first three or four years. And, then, in the second half of the 1980s they more than paid for themselves. Even if there were short-run deficits accruing from the income tax rate cuts, deficit finance funding was a reasonable price to pay for the restoration of incentives to produce, take risks, start new companies, and ultimately rebuild the economy.

The third investment financed by debt was the defense build-up, which was necessary not only to restore the United States' place in world affairs, but ultimately to defeat Soviet Communism. We forget that today. In 1980, the position of the United States in world affairs was nothing short of precarious. The Soviet Union was a highly expansionist monster. Curiously enough, Reagan's vision on this was not so much to create an arsenal to beat them in war, but to create an arsenal so we wouldn't have to go to war. And that's exactly what happened at Reykjavik and after, culminating in the fall of the Berlin Wall.

What I am saying is that all this doom and gloom over the debt obscures the fact that it was a significant means of financing three vital American investments: the end of inflation, lower taxes, and the end of the Cold War. This is our bequest to children, grandchildren and future generations. When people talk about the intergenerational burden of the debt, I tell them that what we are leaving our heirs is the best functioning economy and the strongest international security power on the globe. Put another way, the investments made in the 1980s, which required debt funding, gave us more peace and prosperity than anybody in the Reagan administration dreamed possible, with the possible exception of the Gipper himself.

Figure 3

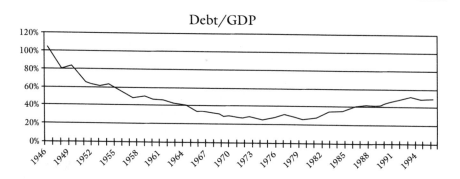

Debt/GDP

Debt doesn't affect growth. Now, as for the obsession over the debt by itself, a couple of quick points. Number one, I have never seen any discernible evidence that debt affects economic growth one way or the other. If you'll look at Figure 3, you can see that the debt-to-GDP ratio is now at the lower end of its 50-year range. We're running about 50 percent presently. The high end was 100.

Moreover, the level of the debt seems to have no particular link to the performance of the economy. Sometimes the economy is growing rapidly, sometimes it's growing slowly. But I can't find any particular link, and I defy anyone to show what the linkage is between economic growth and debt. I can find clear linkages between tax rates and economic growth, between government spending rates and economic growth, between inflation rates and economic growth, between regulatory horizons and economic growth, but not between debt and economic growth.

102

Debt doesn't increase interest rates. Let me say also the argument that rising debt creates higher interest rates and that falling debt creates lower interest rates is absolutely unproven by the evidence. In fact, Figure 4 shows the steady rise in debt and the steady decline in long-term bond rates. In 1980 the long bond was up close to 15 percent. Today it is challenging 6 percent.

Figure 4

Federal Debt & 30yr. T-bond Yield

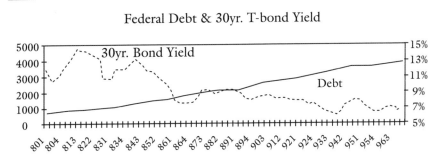

So there's no particular evidence that there's an interest rate link. Interest rates, by and large, are determined by the actual and expected inflation rate. From James Tobin to Milton Friedman to Bob Mundell, that is a given in economic literature. Since we've done quite well on inflation, long-term rates are closer to 6 percent than to the 15 percent they were at 15 years ago.

If you want to get the debt expense down the best thing you can do is to make the Federal Reserve toe the line with a publicly announced zero to 2 percent long-run inflation formal rule, and then try to get it to use gold and commodities and other market prices as a short-run gauge. If the Fed does this, and if Chairman Greenspan, who has done a great job in my view, says this publicly over and over, we can get long-term interest rates down to around 4.5 to 5 percent, where they have been for most of American history. That will take the net interest expense of the debt down from about its present $250 billion to probably less than $150 billion.

We're close. Greenspan is close. The rates are close. But that's Federal Reserve policy. Debt by itself or extinguishing or adding debt, does not have a discernable interest rate impact.

Two sides to the balance sheet. One other point I want to make on debt is this: One person's liability is another's asset. In other words, there are two sides to a balance sheet. There's the liability side and the asset side. This point is lost on Mr. Neumann, who I think is a good man, but we had a discussion of this at a New York meeting, and he didn't seem to grasp this point.

My point is that Treasury sells a liability called a bond, and John Q. Public buys the bond and it's his asset. Now, the Treasury Department has to service that bond. That's called the "interest payment" or the "interest expense." He gets the interest, and he just recycles it in the economy. He probably goes out and buys stock with it, which helps finance a company. Or he just spends it. We don't lose the money. It's not a tax. It's a flow. We pay; he pays. I sell; he buys. My debt; his asset.

Figure 5

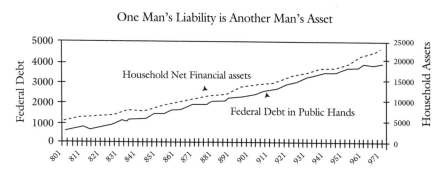

One Man's Liability is Another Man's Asset

The 15 percent coupon bonds sold in the early 1980s are just as good as a bond. If you bought $10,000 worth, they would be worth $94,000 today. They appreciated 840 percent, these awful bonds we were selling. And that's actually slightly better than the S&P 500, which has appreciated 750 percent.

Debt is crucial to world finance. Furthermore, the issuance of those bonds is extremely helpful to world finance. This is a vital point. We could never have a functioning balance-of-payments system in the international credit markets unless we had plenty of U.S. Treasury debt. The dollar is the world's reserve currency.

The recovery of the dollar has enhanced its value as the world's reserve currency. But when newspapers talk about dollars, they're really talking about debt—T-bills principally, sometimes two and three-year notes. So let's assume for the moment you have a balance-of trade deficit. Surplus dollars go overseas, but they're not buried in the sand. They don't wind up in the lunar machines in these space shots to Mars. They come right back to the United States. Foreign central banks and foreign institutions take the dollar surplus, which comes because we're growing faster than the rest of the world, and they reinvest it in our securities, our debt. That's why it's so important to have debt. If we extinguished all the debt, the value of the dollar would collapse, the

104

world trading system would collapse, and the world's economy would collapse because there would be no means of payment for foreign exchange circulating overseas.

It's a terribly important technical point. I guarantee you that if the idea of eliminating our debt entirely develops too far, you will hear the Treasury, the Federal Reserve and the International Monetary Fund put a halt to it because the world trading system needs these dollar-related securities in order to function.

Debt ownership. This is my last set of points on this whole issue of confusion over debt. Who owns the debt? Well, roughly 22 percent of the debt is owned by foreigners. In other words, there's $5.4 trillion of gross debt, of which about $1.2 trillion, or 22 percent, is owned by foreigners. And the rest, 78 percent, is owned domestically.

On the margin, the biggest foreign buyers right now are the Bank of Japan, the PRC Central Bank of China, and the Bank of Taiwan, with the United Kingdom and the German Bundesbank close behind—also, the Bank of Canada and the Bank of Australia. But big deal, they own it. They can't sell it. If they sell it, they lose their rear ends. They own it for a good reason. It's a good buy. We pay them interest. And then they recycle the interest back into our economy. Dollar interest flows have to be spent in the U.S., so as long as we don't go back to double-digit inflation or devalue our currency, we have complete command and control over those interest expense payments.

As far as who owns the debt at home, well, actually, individuals, who are supposed to be really under the burden of this debt according to Mr. Neumann, only own 12 percent, or $640 billion. About half of that is in savings bonds, which is a good thing, right? This is all a good thing.

As I mentioned earlier, had some of these debt-repressed individuals bought bonds 15 years ago, they would have made fortunes. Guess what? A lot of them did make fortunes. Of the rest, 24 percent are owned by mutual funds, banks, insurance companies, and various retirement funds.

The Federal Reserve owns about $400 billion, or roughly 7 percent of the debt. You're not going to redeem the Fed's debt. That's how they conduct open market operations.

Finally, the remainder, 28 percent or $1.5 trillion, is owned by the Social Security system and other government trust funds.

The point here is, not only has the debt been used to finance terrific investments, making America peaceful and prosperous, but the ownership of the debt is a) friendly and b) useful. The ownership is us. The liability called debt has become a valuable interest-earning, principal-accruing asset, and is, therefore, not to be feared. It helps expedite the whole international currency and trading system because of the dollar's status as the world's reserve currency.

Fine print arcana. If we want to do some debt buyouts in the next 10 or 20 years. I'm not against the whole concept of retiring some debt. I would, however, relegate this to the dimension of highly technical fine print and footnoted arcana. It shouldn't be a part of the national campaign of a major political party interested in economic growth and political coalition-building.

So what I call "fiscal tidying up" is okay. But the question is: How do we do it, and when do we do it?

Every now and then we do redeem debt. In fact, Robert Rubin just redeemed $65 billion worth of federal debt this spring. Treasury did that because the revenues were coming in with huge surpluses and because the Treasury's cash management balance was very high. So, instead of reissuing 30-year bonds, 10-year notes, 5-year notes, 3-year notes, 2-year notes, and even Treasury bills, it just redeemed them. It ran them down. And the people got no more paper, and they got their cash. The paper is worth more than the cash because the cash is taxed at a very high rate, so that's too bad, but that was part of the Treasury's debt management policies.

Periodically we could do that. Over the next 10 years, we can pay down $60-65 billion a year just through Treasury cash management practices and retire $650 billion. Or for 20 years, we could retire $1.3 trillion just by letting issues come due and not reopening the issues. But we *can't* go on the open market and use our scarce cash resources to buy up all the debt around the world. It's a minor point but probably an important tactical one.

Maximum freedom to choose. Finally, we need to make it possible for people to keep more of what they earn and give them maximum freedom-to-choose in retirement, health care, and education.

One of the things that continues to attract me to the study of economics is that it has moral, even spiritual, overtones. The issues of personal responsibility and accountability are very much part of economics. This goes back to Adam Smith's theory of moral sentiment. And I believe tax policy plays a role in this. Individuals should be free to choose to spend and invest their own money as they see fit.

Tax reform. So, instead of retiring the debt, my first policy priority is to streamline, reduce, and simplify the nation's tax code. I am a strong supporter of flat tax reform. Streamline, reduce, and simplify the tax code; push back the IRS; and give us more authority over our own funds.

I would suggest starting with small steps. I'd like to move back to the 15 and 28 percent tax brackets of 1986. That would be a step towards tax-flattening. I would also like to substantially raise the tax bracket threshold at the 15 and 28 percent brackets. Successful working people in the last 10 years have been moved up from the 15 percent bracket to the 28 percent bracket just because they've been successful. This is real income bracket-creep. I think we need to look at private retirement accounts and expansion of medical savings accounts. I think we need to look at capital gains rollovers. I think we need to look at cash-expensing for business depreciation. And, of course, in general, we need to reduce complexities, reduce compliance costs, and reduce the IRS' overt regulation.

Privatizing Social Security. Second, we need to privatize Social Security, which reinforces the exact same themes of personal responsibility and accountability and allows people maximum freedom to choose. Social Security privatization will do more to enhance national saving, will do more to enhance the financial confidence in the future, than anything else. Countries in Latin America and Asia that have tried it have done marvelously well. It's even popping up in the U.K. and parts of Northern Europe. We need to do it here.

I think tax reform and Social Security privatization in the economic sphere are the two hot-button issues that we have to pursue. These reforms will transform our economy, streamline it, make it more efficient, give power to people and take power from Washington. I don't think Washington is evil per se. I just think it's the kind of system that has to be completely changed, if even in small increments.

Streamlining and downsizing government. On the spending side, we must not give up the fight to streamline and downsize federal departments, agencies, and programs. We need to devolve to the local level, not aggrandize at the federal level. If more spending worked, then it would have worked already. It hasn't worked, and we know it's not going to. As a perpetual optimist, I believe Democrats are coming around to this view as well as Republicans.

Let's move towards a free-market vision, a free-to-choose vision, an economic growth vision that has as its central points tax streamlining, Social Security privatization, and governmental downsizing. Let's turn money back to the taxpayers. Let's grow the economy to its maximum potential, and let's really try to take this a new era of surplus politics and make sure it intersects squarely with growth politics. Because, as you know, when we practice growth politics, everybody wins. When we practice austerity politics, nobody does.

2.2 BACK TO BRETTON WOODS

December 31, 1991

What is truly remarkable about the 3½% Fed discount rate is the near $350 an ounce gold price that now accompanies it. In other words, after six discount rate cuts and a 575 basis point drop in the federal funds rate over the past three years, commodity prices are stable. Gold in particular is down by $86 from its 1988 price.

True, the dollar exchange rate has lost ground, but that is principally a function of overly tight money in Japan and in Europe, especially Germany. But more important, none of the dollar-based market price indicators are flashing signs of rising inflation expectations. Meanwhile the demand for U.S. money and financial assets remains strong, despite the decline in 10-year Treasury to 6.8%. The stock market is once again breaking records.

All of which raises some lovely thoughts about the serious possibility that Greenspan and Co. are in fact running a Bretton Woods style monetary policy anchored by a steady gold price of roughly 10 times the old $35 an ounce gold exchange rate.

Just to reminisce, the golden age of Bretton Woods, from 1950 to 1966, generated nominal gross domestic product growth of 6% and real growth of 3.6%. Three-month Treasury bills averaged 3% interest rates, and 10-year Treasury bonds averaged 4%. For comparison, over the past four years, nominal GDP growth has declined from roughly 8% to near 4%, the inflation rate has eased from around 5% to less than 3%, the interest rate on three-month Treasury bills has fallen from more than 9% to 3.7%, and the rate on 10-year Treasury bonds has slipped from 9.25% to 6.8%.

This cannot be a coincidence. It seems overwhelmingly likely that the Greenspan Federal Reserve is deliberately trying to bring about 1950s-style low inflation.

At 3.8%, three-month Treasury bills stand at 26-year lows. At 6.8%, 10-year Treasury notes are at their lowest point since 1973. Very possibly, if the Fed clearly announced to the public its commodity price-rule strategy, long-bond yields would be much lower today. Then again, the long end of the bond market probably wants to see more evidence that price stability is sustainable. But the evidence on gold and money strongly suggests that the Fed intends to stay the course. Two percent inflation, along with commodity price stability, is in effect a zero inflation rate. This argues that bond yields can decline significantly more over time.

The consequences of this revolution in monetary policy are enormously positive. Low inflation and declining interest rates are producing significantly reduced interest burdens. Residential housing and other fixed-asset values are stabilizing. Real household net worth is recovering.

The purchasing power of household and business income will be substantially improved. So will the quality of corporate earnings. The entire cost structure of the U.S. economy has been dramatically reduced, thereby increasing American competitiveness in the global marketplace.

In short, Greenspan and Co. have delivered the monetary equivalent of a sizeable tax cut, which not only improves prospects for next year, but for the long run as well. All this has been missed by the pessimistic chorus of economists, pundits and talking heads on television. But it's a key factor nonetheless. Actually, it's the invisible hand of the next economic recovery.

Governments and businesses should take great care to understand the full impact of 1950s-style money and inflation. It means, for example, that nominal income at all levels, for governments and businesses, is likely to grow at a pace closer to 5% and 6% than 8% and 10%.

Both private and public budget planners must recognize this. Topline corporate revenues will not be inflated to bail out high-cost enterprises. Recent restructuring announcements by the likes of IBM, General Motors and Citicorp probably reflect this. State and local budget officials must not assume that inflated tax-revenue growth will provide the resources to fund spending programs of questionable merit.

Under the Bretton Woods approach to money, 6% average growth in nominal GDP leads to around 4% real growth. Similarly, 6% growth in nominal corporate earnings leads to about 4% growth in real profits. All of this generates quite a respectable long-run performance. But only if expenses are held down and efficiencies maintained.

In response to the Federal Reserve, Washington's fiscal policymakers should accommodate the return to hard money by providing stronger incentives for new business starts, productive work effort, capital formation and economic growth. The golden age of Bretton Woods and the Reagan 1980s produced the best economic and stock market performance of the past 40 years. Why? Two reasons. First, low inflation and low interest rates. Second, a low effective tax rate on real (inflation-adjusted) capital gains, which is the key tax incentive required to promote the risk-taking, innovation and enterprise necessary for long-run economic expansion.

With a 25% average tax-rate on nominal capital gains, and a 44% average on real capital gains, the 1950–1966 Bretton Woods period produced 4.2% average annual real GDP growth, with 2.3% inflation and 10.2% annualized growth in the Standard & Poor's 500 stock-index after inflation. However, over the next 15 years major fiscal and monetary mistakes drove up the nominal capital gains tax-rate to an average of 37.6%, cheap money created 7% inflation, and the tax rate on real capital gains skyrocketed to 129%. As a result, the economy experienced prolonged stagflation and the S&P average declined by 7% per year after inflation.

Not until the supply-side reforms of the 1980s did economic growth, inflation and the stock market return to their old levels. By lowering tax rates on income and capital gains, along with movement toward a gold-backed dollar, 4% annual economic growth was restored, with 3% inflation and 20% annual real stock market gains.

But the 1986 tax bill began a new fiscal policy direction that halted this progress. Over the four years from 1987 to 1991, higher tax rates on capital investment, personal income and payroll wages, as well as longer depreciation schedules and increases in numerous business and real estate taxes, along with a host of new regulatory cost burdens, and a dose of mid-1980s cheap money flattened the stock market. The economy lapsed back into stagflation.

In particular, the effective tax rate on real capital gains jumped back up to average 65.5%, putting an end to the rise of national wealth creation, new business starts and new jobs. Since the end of 1988, when the full force of these tax changes took effect, annual real GDP growth has slumped to 0.6%, new business formation has fallen by 7.7% and employment growth has slowed to 0.2% per year. The after-inflation S&P 500 index has only just reattained its August 1987 level.

At this point, both Congress and the Bush administration would do well to heed the recent advice of Fed Chairman Alan Greenspan. From the man who has restored low inflation and declining interest rates through a gold-backed dollar comes this counsel: Reject quick-fixes such as temporary tax rebates. Instead, restore a low capital gains tax rate to generate improved economic growth, capital formation and productivity.

Mr. Greenspan grew up professionally at the height of the Bretton Woods period. That period has remained his basic economic yardstick. Normality should mean 4% real growth, 2% inflation and a strong

110

wealth-creating stock market. Normality should also include the lowest possible tax rates on capital and labor.

With an improved 1992 tax policy, the Bretton Woods baseline can be replicated and the U.S. economy can recapture its long-term potential to grow. With 10% yearly real gains, the Dow would be roughly 3400 in 1992, 3800 in 1993, 4300 in 1994 and 4800 in 1995. New business starts, jobs and wealth creation would explode. Budget deficits would evaporate. Think of it. And have a very happy New Year.

2.3 GOLDEN RULE
CAN PREVENT A CRASH

October 15, 1992

As Monday's fifth anniversary of the stock market crash approaches, Fedwatchers on Wall Street are clamoring for the Fed to ease. Perhaps there are reasons for a loosening of monetary policy. But deliberately pushing the Fed funds rate below the inflation rate is not one of them. In fact, the Fed-watchers' obsession with interest rates is in this case a misplaced one. Their real focus should be on the fiscal side-on, for example, lower tax rates or better treatment of capital gains and business depreciation.

Wall Street's nags might want to step back a bit and take a look at the context of their plea for lower rates. We have had 32 Fed interest rate cuts over the past three years. Ten-year government bonds currently yield only 6.5%. Today's 3% Fed funds rate is lower than any we have seen in 30 years. Surely, therefore, monetary policy is not what is standing in the way of a full-fledged recovery. There is evidence that might make the Fed want to ease: The fact that of late, gold and commodity prices have gotten a bit weaker. The Fed might want to protect against a European-style deflation with a 25-basis-point easing move. But for the U.S. economy, this is a trifle, not a major event.

A look at the history of the economy bears out my point. In fact, a healthy economy making productive use of both capital and labor, with ample returns for investment, is always associated with positive real interest rates. During the seven fat years of the Reagan growth there was a lot of bellyaching over high real interest rates. But at the same time the economy expanded at a 3.5% real rate. Real business investment rose to a record high of more than 12% of real gross domestic product. The market rose 270%, real household net worth increased by $4.3 trillion. Inflation averaged only 3.5%.

The so-called real Fed funds rate—the rate after inflation—during this long period of prosperity averaged about 4%. But this relatively high real rate did not prevent a growth performance stronger than any since the mid-1960s. Nor, interestingly, did the 4% rate prevent market interest rates from declining significantly. On balance, the nominal rate for both Fed funds and long-term Treasury bonds dropped by six percentage points.

Surely the Fed-watching community has not forgotten that the U.S. experimented with very low—sometimes negative—real interest rates in the 1970s and that the experience was not a happy one. From 1970 to 1981, a period in which the Fed funds rate averaged only 0.5% after subtracting for inflation, the economy saw four recessions and an average yearly growth rate of barely more than 2%.

This was the period that came after Richard Nixon closed the gold window and broke up the Bretton Woods world monetary system. The inflation rate averaged 8% a year, moving as high as 15%. The market value of stocks fell—in real terms, the Dow Jones Industrial Average lost 55%. Nominal interest rates skyrocketed. Then, the interaction of accelerating inflation with steeply progressive tax rates cut into profits and cut off capital formation and growth.

The whole debate about real interest rates now raging on Wall Street is nothing more than an unappetizing monetary stewpot which distracts from the main issue at hand: What is the best policy for long-term price stability and growth? Real interest rates aren't so important. Nor is the U.S. M-2, the German M-3, the British M-0 or the latest unemployment report. In today's globally integrated economy, with money flows that traverse continents in a nanosecond, commodity indicators linked to real production are the only reliable guide for central banks. They balance the creation of money with the availability of goods, essentially matching money supply with money demand. In fact, throughout economic history, gold and commodity prices have served as the only reliable indicators of monetary value.

On this point, Alan Greenspan and company have done very well. The Fed's use of the commodity price rule—which daily tells the Fed whether it is inflating or deflating—has proved sound. In its decision to choose domestic price stability over fixed exchange rates in the face of the Bundesbank's deflationary stubbornness, the Fed has shown true wisdom.

Going back a few years, the dollar exchange rate has sometimes appreciated and sometimes depreciated. But the only exchange rate that truly mattered was the volume of dollars necessary to buy an ounce of gold. The stability of the gold price—it has hovered around $350 an ounce —is no coincidence. Anchored by the Fed's commodity strategy, greenback purchasing power at home continues to improve. When properly measured, domestic inflation now ranges somewhere between 1% and 2%.

There's a real lesson in this for the crash-watchers. It is precisely this domestic monetary reform—the focus on the commodity rule—that has undergirded the steady recovery from the remarkable October

1987 crash. The gradual but steady rise in the market has paralleled a rise in the dollar's domestic value. We have moved from a low of 1750 in autumn 1987 to the present trading zone of 3200 to 3400. The recovery of money has walked arm in arm with the recovery of the stock market.

This is true for simple reasons. Weak money leads to higher inflation, which in turn raises taxes and removes incentives to work, produce and invest. The rising tax burden of inflation cuts at capital formation, since investment gains, depreciation schedules and business tax rates are not indexed. The inflation tax undermines corporate profits and blunts job creation, denying working families income.

Here is the way to look at the 1987 crash: The foolish 1986 tax bill significantly raised capital costs and lowered investment returns because it raised the capital gains tax, lengthened depreciation schedules, eliminated the investment tax credit and crushed real estate. By the spring of 1987, the stock market's underpinnings were weakened.

In the same period, the Fed ignored the message of gold. Gold rose to $450 an ounce by the spring of 1987. Treasury yields escalated to 9%. International exchange squabbles distracted both the Fed and Treasury that summer, and they took no remedial action on either the tax or the monetary front. By late August the warning signs were proliferating, and a dreadful momentum carried into the final October collapse.

If any of these lessons is learned properly, Wall Street will stop prattling about easy money to stimulate aggregate demand. Demand side economics didn't work in the 1970s, it didn't work in 1986 and 1987, and it won't work now. The stock market has recovered because Mr. Greenspan's golden rule is gaining credibility, not because the Fed wishes to abandon it.

Where is the economy now? The decline in inflation is stimulating the economy, generating the current 2% growth rate. (Declining inflation is the monetary equivalent of a tax cut, lowering the tax cost of capital and business depreciation, reducing expenses, and paving the way for a recovery of corporate profits.) With sound money, stable prices, low interest rates and rising profits, the economy isn't in such bad shape. It may be that the pundits in this wacky election year have underestimated its potential to recover.

In fact, the obstacle to a truly strong recovery comes from fiscal barriers. Investors are faced with numerous fiscal uncertainties. Proposals to launch massive public works and infrastructure programs—or other dubious and inefficient schemes to allocate government resources—carry with them the costs of higher tax rates on savers and investors. Massive fiscal projects can also mean larger tax and regulatory burdens on small-business payrolls. The nagging threat of higher future taxes is itself a strong deterrent to high-risk investing. It is a threat that has plagued and suppressed the economy for two years.

It is also possible that fiscal issues will be resolved favorably, and that the threat of higher taxes will recede. Luckily, there is serious talk in both political parties about improving treatment of capital gains and business depreciation. For at the end of the day, if economic history teaches us anything, it is certain that the unleashing of capital, creativity and inventiveness—along with sound money—will distance the market further and further from the unnecessary tragedy of another Black Monday.

2.4 BLINDER FAITH

September 26, 1994

Ivy League debutants usually come out in traditional towns like New York, Boston, or Philadelphia, but ex-Princeton economics professor Alan Blinder, recently appointed vice chairman of the Federal Reserve, chose instead to make his maiden speech in Jackson Hole, Wyoming, at a meeting sponsored by the Federal Reserve Bank of Kansas City. But nobody asked him to dance. In front of many of the world's leading central bankers, business people, and economists, Blinder argued that interest rate policies should be aimed at reducing unemployment rather than simply targeting price stability. In so doing, Blinder contradicted the views of his boss, Alan Greenspan, and offended Bundesbank head Hans Tietmeyer, both of whom were present.

As a devout Keynesian, Blinder has always favored a demand-management approach to economic policy. In numerous magazine columns and books, he describes himself as an "inflation dove" with boundless confidence in the efficacy of government; he believes that the U.S. public sector is "emaciated" and the country "undertaxed." During his confirmation hearings for the number-two job at the Fed, Blinder told Congress: "The older I get, the less respect I have for the signals emitted by our vaunted speculative markets."

Reminiscent of the Carter era, Blinder's policy prescription would have the Fed pour money into the economy to keep interest rates low and stimulate demand by consumers and businesses. This demand stimulus, in turn, is expected to create jobs and lower the unemployment rate. Bolstered by government taxing and spending, money manipulation by the Fed is supposed to give the government a near-complete ability to drive the economy by stepping on the gas during recessions or putting on the brakes should the economy overheat into inflation.

Demand-siders like Alan Blinder have never understood the crucial role of supply. People work, save, and invest only if after-tax returns are sufficient, payable in dollars that have real value. Higher tax rates on high-risk investment, personal income, or business payrolls blunt incentives and cause individuals to withhold their supply of capital and labor from the market. Risk-taking, entrepreneurship, good management practices, and plain old hard work are all discouraged by frequent government intervention. Cheap money de-linked from gold or other

116

real assets produced by the economy also causes people to withhold their supplies of capital and labor, since shrinking dollars further reduce the reward for work and risk-taking.

When both inflation and unemployment rose during the late Seventies, the Keynesian demand model imploded. Rather than stimulating demand, easy money drove inflation and interest rates sky high. Rather than holding down inflation, rising taxes weakened incentives and depressed the economy. Smart money and smart people boycotted the U.S. economy because it no longer paid to work and invest. Output and employment fell, while prices and interest rates rose.

Statistically, the demise of Keynesian demand-management policies is easy to chart. As the dollar was unhinged from gold, and as federal taxes and spending steadily moved up, aided respectively by inflation-driven bracket creep and by Great Society entitlements, the U.S. economy entered the stagflation period producing 7.2 percent average annual inflation and 2.1 percent real growth from 1968 to 1982. The average unemployment rate was 6.4 percent. During the end of this period, from 1978 through 1982, industrial production declined 3.2 percent, while the consumer price index rose 48 percent. By late 1982, unemployment had risen to 11 percent.

Contrast this with the early 1960s and most of the 1980s, when the dollar was more closely linked to gold and tax rates were brought down. From 1961 to 1967 real GDP growth averaged 4.9 percent, yearly inflation 2.4 percent, and unemployment 4.4 percent. From 1982 through 1988, as President Reagan ushered in a return to hard money and free-market risk-taking incentives, including across-the-board deregulation and tax cuts, real GDP increased by 3.9 percent a year, and inflation averaged 3.6 percent; by the end of the period unemployment had fallen to 5.4 percent. Under Kennedy and Reagan, the classical economic model of sound money and free enterprise produced strong growth with low inflation and unemployment. There was no Phillips Curve trade-off between inflation and unemployment. Under Johnson, Nixon, Ford, and Carter, the Keynesian model produced low growth with high inflation and unemployment. In all three periods, unemployment and inflation moved up and down together.

Have Blinder and his fellow Keynesians learned anything from the historical evidence? Says Arthur Laffer, one of the principal architects of President Reagan's successful growth policies: "There is no set of evidence that will ever shake their faith in the demandside Keynesian theory of the Phillips Curve."

I f this were merely an academic discussion, it would have little consequence. But Blinder is being touted by many as the next Federal
Reserve chairman, and even now he is in a position as vice chairman to
tilt the center of monetary gravity away from the relatively hard-money
policies that have prevailed until recently.

Blinder's monetary liberalism has strong support in Congress. This
year Democratic Senators Donald Riegle (Mich.), Paul Sarbanes
(Md.), and Jim Sasser (Tenn.)—all members of the Banking
Committee—have routinely trashed the Fed's belated interest-rate
moves to restrain inflation. "The Fed has launched another salvo of
friendly fire upon the economic recovery, despite overwhelming
evidence that inflation is no threat," said Budget Committee Chairman
Sasser after the Fed's latest rate hike.

At the Jackson Hole conference, however, the presidents and
research directors of the 12 regional Reserve Banks were furious at
Blinder's remarks, since they have spent years trying to focus Fed policy
exclusively on the goal of price stability and away from economic fine-
tuning. Indeed, virtually all participants agreed that chronic unemployment, especially in Europe, is a supply-side problem of excessive
social-insurance spending and rigid labor laws. With high benefits and
high payroll taxes to finance them, work incentives have disappeared,
and a reserve army of the unemployed has emerged. Fortunately, the
U.S. has not yet gone as far down this road as Europe. In any case,
central banks have no role to play in resolving this structural problem.

Yet Fed Chairman Greenspan is still sending mixed signals on the
central bank's policy targets. The interest-rate increase in August was
accompanied by a statement that the measures "were taken against the
backdrop of evidence of continuing strength in the economic
expansion and high levels of capacity utilization." In other words, too
much growth might cause inflation. Economic policy wonk Jude
Wanniski, who has worked hard to gain support for a gold price target,
disapprovingly noted that "Greenspan has not lifted a finger to alert
markets that the Phillips Curve is not an operative theory."

Greenspan occasionally pays lip service to the use of gold as an
early-warning inflation indicator, but he never follows through. Blinder
abhors the use of gold or commodities, or for that matter any price
signals from global auction markets. This is too bad, since both market
prices and government reports are showing an inflation upturn. The
widely followed Journal of Commerce industrial commodity index, for
example, has just hit a new high, rising at a 25 percent annual rate this
year. Gold is holding around $390, and the dollar remains low in terms
of the perennially hard Japanese yen and German mark.

These trends spell trouble for the economy, which is just beginning to suffer from the effects of easy money and higher taxes. The former will drive inflation higher, while the latter will depress growth. Blinder's Keynesian demand obsession will prevent him from understanding how prices and unemployment can rise simultaneously.

The solution can only be found on the supply side, where a dollar as good as gold could roll back inflation and interest rates, while permanent tax cuts on capital and labor (that is, capital-gains-tax and payroll-tax relief) would bring down unemployment. But having blinded himself to the past, the Fed's new man may be even blinder in the future.

2.5 THE DEFICIT OBSESSION

January 25, 1993

Clearly the deficit is taking center stage again for President Clinton and his economic team. At his inauguration, Mr. Clinton called for "sacrifice" to control the deficit. (Hence, apparently, the middle class must sacrifice its tax cut.) At their confirmation hearings, Lloyd Bentsen, the new Treasury secretary, and Leon Panetta, director of the Office of Management and Budget, spoke in a similar way. Unfortunately, Wall Street economists are following Mr. Clinton's lead, again linking deficit estimates with the interest rate and economic outlook.

The only trouble with this deficit obsession is that it confuses cause with effect. It is not the deficit per se that is the problem, but rather the taxing, spending, regulatory and monetary policies that help to determine interest rates, the economy's performance, and thus the deficit. Unless the true cause of the deficit is properly diagnosed, there will never be any permanent progress toward deficit reduction.

The single best measure of the budget's impact on the economy is not the deficit but the share of gross domestic product absorbed by federal spending. Since 1988 this ratio has increased to 23.5% from 21.7%, excluding deposit insurance. Indeed, since 1965, when it was 17.6%, this fraction has grown to a peak of 24.3% in 1983, dropped to a low of 21.7% in 1989 and then moved back up to the 23.5% level for 1992.

During this entire 28-year period, the revenue share of the economy has averaged 18.6%, never dropping below 17.4% or rising above 20.1%. During 1983–84, when President Reagan reduced marginal income tax rates, the average national tax rate held at 18.1%. In 1992, the revenue share of GDP registered 18.6%, exactly the average of the entire 1965–92 period.

What do these numbers mean? For one thing, that the deficit share of GDP, which stood at 0.2% in 1965 and rose to 4.9% in 1992, is entirely explained by the rise in federal spending. All the talk about "excessive" 1980s tax cuts causing the deficit is wrong.

But overspending is only part of the problem. By its very nature, government spending impedes economic growth. Unlike the private sector, the government is not disciplined by the marketplace, nor is it subject to bottom-line profit considerations. Government programs are driven by political decisions and bureaucratic incentives. As such, they too often are inefficient or redundant. And they develop a life of their own, continuing long after their reason for being has disappeared.

The South now has all the advanced electric utility and telephone services, yet rural electrification subsidies, started in the 1930s, live on. The Postal Service is being overtaken by fax machines and firms in the private sector, but federal assistance continues. There are many other examples: federal land acquisitions, agricultural subsidies, export enhancement programs, community development block grants, the Small Business Administration, and on and on.

Yet Mr. Clinton's team seems to be looking to taxes to fix the deficit, not spending cuts. At their confirmation hearings, Messrs. Panetta and Bentsen both testified strongly in support of the 1990 budget deal. Unfortunately, its higher taxes on personal income, business and so-called luxury sales did not reduce the deficit, which moved to 5% of GDP by 1992 from 3.1% in 1990. Nor did it revive economic growth or create jobs. Indeed, higher tax burdens on income and sales generated lower economic output and fewer jobs than would have otherwise been the case. Economic recovery did not truly materialize until 1992, after the private sector adjusted to the policy shocks of 1990. And even now the recovery rate remains below par.

Yet the policy options emanating from the Bentsen-Panetta confirmation hearings argued for still higher tax rates. The top income tax bracket would move up to 36%, along with a 10% surtax on millionaires, with only very narrow improvement for the treatment of capital gains and business investment. To this might be added corporate tax-rate hikes, value-added taxes and a gasoline tax. At the same time, there is very little talk of a truly rigorous budget scrub that would eliminate or substantially reduce unnecessary spending programs.

In other words, those who haven't learned the mistakes of the past are about to repeat them. The Clinton administration seems poised to embark on yet another high-tax austerity program that will neither move the economy toward 4% growth nor substantially narrow the deficit.

Throughout economic history this truth remains: When something is taxed more, we get less of it. When income, investment and sales are taxed more, we have less of them. When after-tax rewards are reduced, productivity and risk-taking diminish. When retail items are taxed more (including gasoline), fewer sales result. When the cost of doing business rises, profits decline, along with output and employment.

From 1985 through 1989, the four years preceding the 1990 debacle, the U.S. economy grew at an inflation-adjusted annual rate of 3.3%, which generated nominal budget revenue growth of 7.8% a year. If more constructive tax and regulatory policies had been applied over the next three years, even with the slowdown of inflation, a plausible path of 6½% annual revenue growth would have generated 1992 revenue of $1.275 trillion. The actual level was $183 billion less than that.

This stronger economic performance alone would have narrowed the budget deficit to $104 billion, or roughly 1.7% of re-estimated GDP. Meanwhile, lower countercyclical spending would have narrowed the deficit by an additional $20 billion or so—to 1.4% of GDP.

Such is the budgetary importance of economic growth. The lesson is simple: Without rising capital formation, output and employment, there will be no sustained deficit reduction. A 4% real growth rate, the proper target, can be achieved only through tax and regulatory policies that reduce capital and labor costs and raise investment and employment returns across the board.

What sorts of policies are necessary to achieve a 4% real growth target? At a bare minimum, both capital gains and business depreciation schedules should be immediately indexed to protect against inflation. Beyond this, Mr. Clinton's team should develop a multiyear phase-in of income-tax credits or a payroll tax-rate reduction; a reduction in the capital-gains tax rate for all assets (including Jack Kemp's proposed "enterprise zones"); accelerated depreciation schedules; and an end to the double taxation of corporate dividends. In short, national economic policies should reward risk-taking and economic achievement, not punish it.

At the same time, policy makers should undertake a thorough budget review from the bottom up. Every function, every account and every line item must be carefully examined. Hidden economic costs must be uncovered. Unnecessary and low-priority programs must be curtailed or eliminated. Entitlement programs must be reformed. Poorly managed assets should be sold to the highest bidder. Wasteful administrative overhead must be curbed through attrition. For more than 10 years nearly every private enterprise in the U.S. has undertaken this exercise. Now it is high time for the federal government to do exactly the same.

Economic growth will depend on a combination of policies: a redirection of tax and regulatory programs to promote lower costs and higher after-tax rewards, and a restructuring of government to eliminate wasteful spending. If we return to that all-important ratio of government spending to GDP, the trick is to undertake policies that will grow the denominator's supply (GDP) and lessen the numerator's demand (the budget). The Federal Reserve is doing its job by moving the economy toward price stability and low interest rates. Now it is time for the legislative and executive branches to embark on long overdue reforms.

Can the Clinton administration and the new Congress do it? One has one's doubts. Along with George Bush and his advisers, Messrs. Bentsen and Panetta were key architects of the failed economic policies of the past several years. Mr. Panetta has recently argued for higher taxes and easier money. But this notion of reducing the supply of goods through higher taxes, then substituting more money for the lost volume of goods, is a sure way to re-enact the stagflation of the 1970s.

At the end of the day, let us hope that Mr. Panetta and the rest of Mr. Clinton's team can quickly become students of history. A good deal of wisdom can be gleaned from the past, especially the recent past.

2.6 GROWTH RENAISSANCE?

January 2, 1997

A number of new year forecasting stories places the consensus bet on slow growth, low inflation and steady interest rates. Today's *Wall Street Journal* survey generated a 2% average real GDP growth estimate, coupled with 2.9% inflation, and a 5.10% T-bill with a 6.39% long bond by year end 1997. A *Barron's* story a week earlier had essentially the same view. But the forecasting fraternity may be too complacent. Big changes may be afoot in politics, policy and the economy. And those changes could generate an unexpected renaissance of economic growth, along with a new-look stock market rally.

For one, the economy is already showing signs of a faster pace. Recent reports on housing, production, consumer confidence and the manufacturing purchasing agents suggest 3% real growth in the fourth quarter of '96, likely continuing into 1997. Holiday sales may come in about 5% above last year, which would also translate into 3% real sales growth, assuming a 2% inflation rise as measured by the chain-weighted consumer expenditure price index.

Bond yields have already moved up from 6.35% to 6.75%, a good-sized correction that probably has not yet fully run its course. But inflation is not the culprit. Gold and commodity price indexes are flat. Instead, there's a *real interest rate* adjustment, where a strengthening in business cycle performance, including more productive returns from labor and capital, are reflected in higher real interest rates. Another indicator of a stronger economy, and the real interest effect, is the 12 percent rise in the *real* exchange rate of the dollar as measured as a blended rate versus the yen and the mark. With no inflation signs, the strengthening dollar is surely a function of stronger growth. Note today's charts du jour, which show a clear link between real growth, real bond yields and the real exchange rate.

And there is no need for Fed tightening or interventionist fine-tuning of any kind. In effect, with stable prices, the economy has become self-regulating, guided by swings in real rates. With gold below $370, a strong dollar, and a moderately upward-sloping yield curve, monetary policy looks to be consistent with price stability. The 5½% federal funds rate is over 300 basis points above the (chain weighted) inflation rate. Also, while the transactions demand for money is rising (sweep-adjusted M1 growth is 5.7% over the past 12 months), the volume of money supplied by the Fed remains in good balance (sweep-adjusted monetary base growth is 5.5%). With steady greenback purchasing power there is little or no future inflation risk.

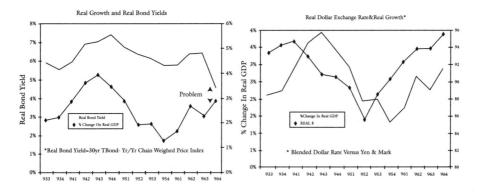

One reason for the improvement in the exchange rate and the economy is the recent free-trade tariff reduction on high-tech information processing. Trade negotiator Charlene Barshefsky called it a "global tax cut," and she is exactly right. While improved knowledge and information processing is a global development, the number #1 world-class U.S. position in this sector will benefit enormously, as will all U.S. industries that adopt and apply the new techniques. What's more, the ever-widening business use of high-tech information processing enhances the outlook for unexpectedly strong profits during the years ahead.

Another factor that may be fueling real economic returns is the growing likelihood of capital gain tax relief in this year's Federal budget. Whether or not Newt Gingrich hangs on to the Speakership, House Majority Leader Dick Armey, as well as Ways & Means chairman Bill Archer, are strong supporters of lower capgains with inflation indexing as well as broad-based tax reform. In fact, after Archer's private post-election meeting with President Clinton, Administration officials started hinting at a capgains compromise. And it was Archer last year who kept medical savings accounts in the compromise health bill deal struck with Senator Kennedy.

Senate Majority Leader Trent Lott and Senate Finance Committee chairman Bill Roth are equally strong in their support of capgains relief and overall tax reform. Actually, now that Robert Dole is out of the Senate, the *growth wing* of the GOP will gradually take command, shifting economic policy away from the establishment big-business— Fortune 500—Business Roundtable austerity wing of the GOP, formerly led by Richard Nixon, Gerald Ford, Howard Baker, George Bush and others who worshipped at the shrine of balanced budgets formulated at the Homestead or Greenbriar hotels. Good hotels, but bad policy.

Nowadays, GOP policy is likely to be more in sync with Joseph Schumpeter's waves of creative destruction (and downsizing), fostered by risk-taking and innovation by brand new business start-ups and small business entrepreneurs. This is the only reliable path to long-term wealth creation. Unfortunately, some Republicans, and President Clinton, are still stuck in the time-warp of inefficient demand-side tax credits, a form of government targeted social engineering rather than a bold tax reform vision that will lower and simplify the income tax-rate system to unleash entrepreneruial growth. But a capgains tax cut this year is at least a good place to start, and a way for the new GOP leadership (including Connie Mack, Spence Abraham, Chris Cox, Steve Forbes, Jack Kemp, Christine Whitman, Tommy Thompson, John Engler, George Pataki and others) to flex their muscles and shed the old skin of the Republican ancien regime. Balancing the budget is fine, but cutting tax-rates on high-return risk-taking is far better. Smaller government is important, but capital formation in the 21st century will be crucial.

Hopefully, the newly ascendant GOP growth wing will soon realize that Bill Clinton's vital center is more rhetorical than real. With some risk-taking of their own, the new GOP leadership can define the center. And President Clinton might well join a tax reform-based vital center once he sees that the train is leaving the station. Along with tax reform, the new GOP should sponsor a wave of creative destruction for the Federal sector, including department and agency closings, asset sales, and the gradual privatization of Social Security and healthcare. Instead of bridging to the Great Society 1960s, or the New Deal 1930s, the GOP must build a bridge to the free-market, rate-of-return, free-to-choose, personally responsible, spiritual growth 21st century.

Finally, as economic growth speeds up, the usual chorus of Keynesian pessimists will argue that growth causes inflation. This view is to be devoutly ignored. It has already been proven wrong. In coming years revisions to the national income accounts will show that inflation was overstated by at least a percentage point, and productivity, hence growth, has been understated by at least a half a percentage point, if not more. Despite the fiscal drag of two income tax hikes, economic performance in the 1990s has plausibily generated about 3% real growth with less than 2% inflation. That is one of the wealth-creating messages of the extraordinary stock market rise. Fortunately, the tax brake has been offset by a low inflation tax cut and another tax cut from tariff-cutting free trade (including, warts and all, NAFTA and WTO, along with the Information Technology Agreement). Were it not for the Bush-Clinton tax increases, the U.S. economy could have grown by 4% or better without inflation.

Forecasters may be surprised at the coming growth revival, but the stock market has seen it all along. Watch for a new rally led by small-cap and other companies benefitting from speedier growth and greater entrepreneurship; bonds and blue chips will underperform. This I believe is the real meaning of the so-called market correction. Trust, but verify. It looks like the real thing.

2.7 KING DOLLAR

January 29, 1997

In President Clinton's inaugural words, the U.S. economy is "the strongest on earth." He may well be right. Interrupted only briefly by a shallow recession in the early nineties, the American economy during the past fourteen years has averaged 3% growth per year, creating 35 million new jobs along the way. Today's unemployment rate stands at 5.3%, with a record 67% participation rate. Yet inflation, as measured by the GDP chain price index, has increased only 2.4% per year over the past five years, contradicting the Keynesian view that low inflation and low unemployment cannot peacefully co-exist. Interest rates are at twenty-five year lows. The stock market has soared during this period, rising by nearly 750%, or 10% per year in real terms. Household wealth creation has risen by over $16 trillion.

But when President Clinton last week told the Democratic National Committee that "we ended the illusion of supply-side economics . . . early enough to stop it from causing permanent disaster . . . " he went back on the wrong track. Economic policies put in place by the Reagan administration to reduce inflation, strengthen the dollar, lower tax-rates, curb regulatory excesses and expand world free-trade were the major factors in halting the U.S. economic decline of the 1970s and generating the long economic upturn of the 1980s and 1990s. Even today, despite some recent backsliding in the tax and regulatory areas, Reagan policies first put in place fifteen years ago provide the entrepreneurial backbone of an economy that continues to perform beyond all expectations.

And this is the key to understanding the amazing resurgence of the U.S. dollar. Paralleling the stronger than expected economy, the dollar has appreciated by over 20% versus the German mark and 40% against the Japanese yen since early 1995. At 1.64 marks and 119 yen, the dollar stands at levels not even remotely considered by experts a year or two ago. Call it King Dollar.

Even today a perpetually pessimistic forecasting fraternity (including government budget agencies such as CBO and OMB) continue to underestimate the economy. Yet the dollar's strength is principally a real exchange rate phenomenon based on stronger than predicted real economic growth and higher than reported productivity, coupled with domestic price stability. Importantly, the explosion of hi-tech information, communication and computing innovations, as well as the commercial application of these innovations throughout the economy, has created a more durable, efficient and productive private sector than most experts realize. And a stronger dollar.

Actually, hi-tech may now account for nearly 15% of GDP, compared to roughly 4% from the auto industry. And over the past year the price deflator for information processing and computing has fallen 15%. Some industry observers believe that total U.S. business costs have dropped roughly 50% over the past five years as a result of hi-tech. By some estimates hi-tech and electronics produced over 60% of the incremental increase in third quarter real GDP. With this push the overall economy in 1996 looks to have come in better than 3% measured on a fourth quarter to fourth quarter basis. Given the dollar's strength, which is an excellent gauge of economic health, along with the stock market rise and a relatively stable Treasury yield curve, another 3% growth year in 1997 looks increasingly possible.

As these facts begin to overtake the old expectations, razor-sharp financial markets adjust prices to reflect new realities. A more productive economy implies substantially stronger future corporate earnings flows. Hence stock market prices are recapitalized higher. Higher earnings raise expected capital returns, which also drives up the real exchange rate. Capital returns are far more important than trade flows in determining currency value. Greater productivity and increased investment returns raise the demand for money, which drives up the real interest rate component of bonds. Since financial assets and the economy are more productive, there's no need to hold gold or other inflation hedges. Hence precious metals prices slump.

This is all part of a growth dynamic that is fueling the dollar's appreciation. Another productivity-related factor boosting the dollar is the recent completion of the Information Technology Agreement. Trade Negotiator Charlene Barshefsky called it a "global tax cut" and she is exactly right. International barriers will be reduced for all manner of hi-tech information processing. The world economy will benefit enormously, especially the leading technology producer and exporter, namely the U.S. So the dollar strengthens further. Money flows to the highest economic returns. Right now, the race for capital is being won by the U.S.

Treasury Secretary Robert Rubin is riding the wave of hi-tech growth and unexpected economic performance, cleverly piloting the dollar upward through repeated public statements of support, knowing that a strong dollar will feed back into even more economic improvement through reduced inflation and ultimately a lower interest rate structure. Rubin is the first strong dollar man at Treasury since

Donald T. Regan in President Reagan's first term. Here too, the Clintonites are following a Reagan policy.

Hardly a day goes by that Rubin doesn't talk up the dollar. Just last week Rubin told a group of reporters in his office that "A strong dollar is in our national economic self-interest." Dismissing all manner of Keynesian devaluationist trade deficit theory, Rubin told the group: "The key to reducing the U.S. trade deficit is our competitiveness, not the dollar." A month earlier, responding to the usual strong dollar complaints from car makers, Rubin told a Wall Street Journal reporter " . . . if they want to have low inflation, low interest rates and a strong economy, a piece of that is the strong dollar."

Rubin deserves much credit for rejecting depreciation as a trade-deficit antidote. If devaluation were the route to economic success, then Britain would have ruled in the 1970s and Argentina would have been the center of the world economy in the 1980's. Those failures noted, it is also the case that both of those countries have prospered of late with strong currency models. Rubin's strong dollar policy also makes sense from another standpoint: Japanese and German economic growth rates have stalled, while their productivity continues to slip.

Over the past five years annual real economic growth in Japan has averaged only 0.8%, and in Germany only 1.4%. German unemployment is holding around 11%, with an inefficient economy that is strangled by exorbitant social welfare costs and high tax-rates. The same can be said for virtually all of Europe. In Japan, recent tax hikes have taken their toll on growth, with more tax increases scheduled to take effect this year.

Meanwhile, the once productive Japanese economy has been weighted down by overregulation from arrogant finance and trade ministries that seek to deny basic consumer choice to the new Japanese generation. As a result of tall fiscal barriers to growth, real exchange rates in both Japan and Germany are destined to keep falling, in line with declining productivity and real capital returns. Unless Japan and Germany miraculously reverse their declining productivity trends, and perhaps Germany is about to embark on some modest tax reforms, it would not be surprising to see a dollar worth 135 yen and 1.80 German marks before long. In short, don't bet against the dollar.

But Mr. Rubin is doing more than merely harnessing market forces in support of a strong foreign exchange dollar. He is also working hand-in-glove with Fed Chairman Alan Greenspan to form a bipartisan vital center for monetary policy and domestic price stability. As such, Rubin is forging a crucial link between a sound international dollar and a stable domestic dollar. It represents a substantial break from the recent past, when GOP finance men James Baker and Nicholas Brady used their Treasury pulpits to talk down the dollar, believing incorrectly that somehow dollar depreciation overseas could be unhinged from domestic prices and interest rates.

But they were wrong. Indeed, it was Baker's devaluationist headline-grabbing currency arguments with Japan and Germany that led to the stock market crash of 1987, a major bump-up for interest rates, and the end of decade inflation that led to the 1990 recession. What's more, both Baker and Brady engaged in repeated sniping at Paul Volcher and Alan Greenspan, always in the direction of loose money. This also undermined financial market confidence, kept interest rates high and restrained economic growth.

During the Reagan's first term the dollar-yen exchange rate averaged 238, slightly above the 223 level during President Carter's last two years, and appropriately so following U.S. disinflation and tax-rate reduction. By the end of Reagan's second term, however, the dollar had slipped below 130, a 45% decline in only four years. What's more, the dollar price of gold soared from $300 in early 1986 to an average $475 in the late 1980's. The gold rise accurately foreshadowed rising inflation, and the yearly average rate for the GDP chain price index moved up from 2.5% in 1986 to 4.3% in 1988–89. Not surprisingly, long-term Treasury bond yields moved up from about $7\frac{1}{2}$% in 1986 to just below 9% in 1988–89. The Dow-Jones stock index, which hit a 2700 peak in 1987, did not regain that level until 1991. Between 1987 and 1992 the economy slowed to 2% growth, including a brief recession. Prior to that, from 1982 through 1987, real GDP had advanced at a 4.1% annual pace. So, while devaluationist policies may have temporarily helped a few economic sectors, the big picture shows that broken promises on money created a considerable drag on prosperity.

Baker and Brady were establishment Republicans who cared more for illusory benefits to big business than the pocketbooks and savings accounts of ordinary Americans. The former GOP Treasury men mistakenly subscribed to the views of the international currency elite, experts who insisted on fine-tuning the dollar to suit their unsound theories. Instead, the nation would have been better served by a populist approach that simply preserved the value of money. Money is a democratic commodity. Nearly everyone owns greenbacks in one form or another. Therefore nothing can be more popular than a sound money policy that keeps the value of tomorrow's dollar the same as today's.

When the government keeps its promise on the purchasing power of money, then people are more apt to take risks, start business and invest for the future. Current consumption becomes less urgent and longer-term savings more attractive. Real incomes rise for working families, while the quality of earnings improve for business. Steady money means a lower inflation rate, and the decline of inflation generates a massive economy-wide tax cut. Look at the unindexed capital gains tax. With a 28% tax-rate on nominal capital gains, the effective tax-rate on real capital gains jumped to 67% in 1988–90 as the inflation rate nearly doubled. However, as Greenspan's price stability policies slowly took hold the tax-rate on real capital gains dropped to 47%. It is precisely this pervasive tax cut that has stimulated the U.S. economy in recent years despite the upward drift of income tax-rates. And were it not for the latter, then U.S. economic growth might have averaged 4% instead of 3%.

Rubin, however, has taken a different monetary tack from his predecessors. As President Clinton's first term economic czar, Rubin uttered not one peep of dissent when Greenspan restrained money in 1994. Nor when he came to Treasury in 1995, did Rubin join the easy money chorus when the economy temporarily slowed that year. Surely Rubin recognizes that Greenspan is calibrating money supply flows with a sharp eye on commodity indexes, especially gold and precious metals, as well as other market price indicators such as the Treasury yield curve and the dollar exchange rate itself. And surely Rubin agrees with this approach.

Just recently, in Congressional testimony last week, Greenspan dismissed the supposed trade-off between inflation and unemployment. Instead, he knows that any inflation threat will first surface through a rising gold price and a weak dollar, not new job creation. Today, with gold around $350, there is no fear of inflation. A domestic dollar as good as gold benefits ordinary Americans *and* big business through price stability, low interest rates, rising stock prices and easily affordable financing costs. Just as Rubin is reforming currency policy, so is Greenspan reforming monetary policy. Together they have moved monetary policy from the Phillips Curve to the price rule. Together they have become America's best monetary team since William McChesney Martin and Douglas Dillon operated in the 1960s.

The work of these two men has moved the U.S. back on the principles of the post World War II Bretton Woods treaty that successfully governed world monetary arrangements from 1945 to 1970, a halcyon period of economic history. The dollar was tied to gold at $35 per ounce, and the rest of the world currencies were linked to the dollar. Prices were stable. Interest rates routinely ranged between 3% and 5%. It is nearly so today. $350 gold is ten times the old par value. At this point, to guard against overly rapid dollar appreciation of a sort that would invite destabilizing speculation, or even domestic deflation, policy makers must watch gold carefully. Ultimately, the dollar-gold exchange rate is the best arbiter of domestic price stability and international currency equilibrium. If Rubin and Greenspan stay the course, then interest rates in the late Nineties will look a lot like the middle Sixties.

Watching this new policy regime in action, international investors *by choice* are re-linking to the dollar. Two weeks ago Bulgaria adopted a currency board approach to money that links to the dollar. Obscure, perhaps, but apocryphal. The Russian economy has already been dollarized. So have the Central and Latin American economies. So has Hong Kong and PRC-China. So has the Phillipines. So basically, have Australia, New Zealand, Canada, Indonesia, Thailand, Malaysia and Singapore. On the margin, private and official investors prefer dollars to the European Union's Euro. Other than socially engineered and over-regulated tax and labor policies, no one really understands the prospective Euro. But people understand dollars.

Before we can declare total victory, however, two key issues remain. First, broad-based tax reform to achieve a flatter, simpler and lower tax-rate system will boost the dollar even more, raising the real exchange rate and the real economic growth rate. Taxes affect currency value and the economy. Before James Baker's misguided depreciation policies, tax-rate reduction under President Reagan was a crucial factor in appreciating the dollar and snuffing out inflation. Following Reagan's lead, Japan and Western Europe also reduced tax-rates for a while in the late 1980s, thereby appreciating *their* currencies, before the G-7 back-tracked in the Nineties. It should also be noted that the November 1994 election of a Republican Congress, which remains totally opposed to new tax increases, presaged the dollar's recovery in 1995. Now the U.S. should take the lead in raising after-tax returns to work effort and investment. And as part of tax reform unlimited IRA's would pave the way for a privatized Social Security system that would greatly enhance the nation's accumulation of savings flows. In this sense we should recall the teaching of classical economist Joseph Schumpeter, who argued that technological innovation is crucial to economic growth, and the entrepreneur, who must be amply rewarded for his out-on-a-limb personal and financial risks, stands at the center of this dynamic growth process. It must pay to take risks.

Regrettably, President Clinton and Treasury Secretary Rubin seem unwilling to take this next step on taxes. While current economic policies are providing sound money and free trade, tax policies must still be reformed to supply greater after-tax rewards to the heroic entre-preneur. With the retirement of establishment Senate Republicans such as Robert Dole and Robert Packwood, the GOP growth wing led by Trent Lott has a golden opportunity to implement a bold plan of significant government downsizing and across the board tax-rate relief. Perhaps passage of broad-based capital gains relief could be the camel's nose under the tent that energizes real tax overhaul. This would spark yet another Schumpeterian wave of entrepreneurship, innovation, creative destruction and economic growth. Including a strong dollar.

Finally, the Federal Reserve and the Treasury should adopt formal rules of monetary behavior in order to make price stability truly credible. In other words, the government must keep its promises, first by clearly stating them, then by implementing them. The public has a right to know. Investors worldwide must be reassured that what goes up won't abruptly come back down. So the time has come for a clear price rule announcement, in quantitative terms. I would prefer a link to gold, or a precious metals index. But adherence to a price index level, perhaps a reformed GDP chain-weighted index or even a satisfactorily reformed CPI, would be a decent second-best. The key point is that the government must accept accountability and keep its promise to ordinary folks. We must all live by a code of rules. Think of it as personal responsibility writ economywide. This would add a moral dimension to monetary policy, and that would lift the dollar as well as the spirit of all who hold them.

2.8 LET'S CAPITALIZE

March 5, 1997

Hardly a day goes by without a Congressional leader predicting passage of a lower capital gains tax-rate. GOP policymakers such as Trent Lott, Dick Armey and Bill Archer have kept up a steady pre-election drumbeat in favor of reducing the capgains tax-rate from 28% to 20% for all asset classes, with an inflation-indexing provision to apply to all future gains, and a reduction in the corporate capgains tax from 35% to 28%. Top Senate Democrats Tom Daschle and Wendell Ford have endorsed a slightly less broadbased plan. President Clinton, whose budget includes a capgains break for home sales, told reporters he is "not philosophically opposed" to broad capgains relief. So the stage is set for the first economywide tax cut in *over ten years*, a long time between haircuts.

What will this mean for the economy and the stock market? Across-the-board positive. The capital gains tax is a penalty on risk-taking, entrepreneurship, capital investment, new business formation, jobs and growth. When you tax something you get less of it. But lowering the tax will raise after-tax capital returns and enhance every nook and cranny of the economy. Years ago Austrian economist Joseph Schumpeter wrote that innovation is the key to economic growth. The heroic entrepreneur must be amply rewarded for risking personal and finanical life and limb. Capital gains are primarily a tax on innovation and must therefore be taxed minimally if at all.

The previously unindexed capital gains tax, and its influence on the stock market, have been an excellent barometer of U.S. wealth creation and economic growth during the post World War II period. Remember, without indexation, the inflation rate is just as important as the statutory tax-rate. So, when inflation hovered around 2% during the 1950s and 1960s, and the capgains tax rate stayed around 25%, the relatively low 40% *effective* tax-rate on real capital gains generated economic growth of better than 3% per year, while the inflation adjusted real S & P 500 increased by nearly 10% per year. Then, as the statutory capgain tax-rate rose to 45% during the 1970s, and inflation increased to more than 10%, the effective capgains tax averaged over 100%, sometimes rising as high as 200%, while share prices *fell* roughly 7% per year and the economy was overcome by stagflation.

The malaise was broken by capgains reductions in 1978 (to 28%) and 1981 (20%), and a new era of disinflation, both of which triggered

Real S&P 500

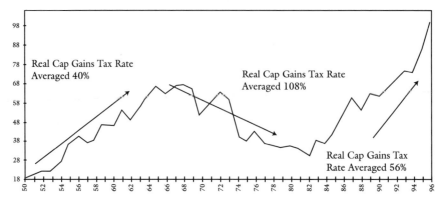

the bull market prosperity of the past fourteen years. Since 1982, real GDP growth has averaged 3% per year, while the real S & P 500 has averaged nearly 12% yearly gains (16% for the Dow-Jones). Parenthetically, two policy missteps caused the last mini-bear market correction of 1987–1990. The capgains tax-rate was raised to 28% in 1986, and the inflation rate rose to nearly 5% by 1990. As a result the effective capgains tax jumped to 75%, and the economy experienced a minor recession. However, steady disinflation since 1990 has brought inflation back to 2%, the real capgains burden has dropped to 47%, and share prices have soared since the early nineties. Presently, we are in the seventh year of the latest recovery cycle.

Reducing the effective tax burden on innovation and risk-taking in recent years has helped make the U.S. the global leader in all manner of hi-tech, including high-speed communications, information-processing and financial services. In 1996 alone, hi-tech produced 40% of the increase in U.S. economic growth. Expanding capacity and bolstering the supply-side of the economy, the hi-tech surge has driven business investment from 6% to 8½% of GDP. Waves of hi-tech creative destruction have raised productivity and economic growth well above reported government statistics, boosting King Dollar along the way.

With all the latest good news, however, we must not rest on our laurels. In the 21st century the race for global capital will be won by those nations with the highest returns and the lowest inflation. Smart money and smart people always seek the highest after-tax investment yield. Innovators and inventors can relocate almost anywhere. Today, for example, even with all its advantages, the U.S. is competing with lower effective capital gains tax-rates on corporations and individuals in Germany, Britain, Italy, Hong Kong, Singapore, and Japan, Argentina and Chile. On the margin, these tax differentials can make a big difference.

At home, the really good news is that a lower capgains tax could unlock as much as $10 trillion in unrealized gains. Most of this will be rolled over into the stock market, while some of it will be directly invested in the economy, thereby reliquifying the economy and prolonging the expansion without excess money creation from the Fed. The U.S. Treasury could net up to $50 billion in revenues per year as gains are realized and reinvested. Asset values, including stock prices, could initially rise as much as 20% just from capgains relief. Some of this has undoubtedly been discounted in the early year market rise. At continued 2% inflation, an indexed capgains tax-rate of 20% will reduce the effective tax-rate from 47% to 20%. Over a ten-year period, asset values could then rise cumulatively by 50%.

Look for small-cap stocks with little or no reliance on dividends to outperform big-cap blue chips, though a rising tide will lift all boats. After the 1978 capgain reduction, small stocks outperformed big stocks by a ratio of 5 to 1. Large stocks have paid out dividends at a 39% share of profits during this bull market, a much higher rate than newer small-cap companies. Since dividends are subject to the 40% income tax-rate, the next big rise in this group must await across-the-board income tax reduction as per the flat-tax proposals of Steve Forbes, Jack Kemp and Dick Armey.

So for now, investment strategy should focus on undervalued small companies that have lagged market performance over the past year. Sure, the stock market might sag a bit in the first month or two following capgains legislation, but this will be short-lived and should be ignored. Since Schumpeter's entrepreneur will be better rewarded for innovation and risk-taking, expect economic growth to improve, the dollar will rise and inflation will remain subdued. Bonds and commodities have relatively less to offer, stocks relatively more. If tax reform spreads overseas, then foreign markets will react positively. There's no zero-sum here; everyone will prosper and the U.S. will lead the global economy on the right path. This of course is just as it should be. We're talking about a 10,000 Dow. Let's capitalize on it.

2.9 GOOFY & DAFFY

March 21, 1997

O ne of the overlooked factors dragging down small-cap stocks in recent weeks is the goofy and daffy approach to tax policy taken by key Republican leaders this month. In mid-March third ranking House Republican Tom Delay (R, Tx.) announced that tax cut plans would be dropped until the budget is balanced. A day later Speaker Newt Gingrich (R, Ga.) supported this view by declaring a balanced budget to be a "moral imperative." Budgetmeisters Sen. Pete Domenici (R, N.M.) and John Kasich (R, Oh) also joined in.

Moral imperative? Nonsense. The purpose of fiscal policy should be limited government, reduced taxation, economic freedom, and wealth creation, not accounting gimmickry. Remember the bad old days of the Cold War? The former Soviet Union, and all of its East Block satellite states, always presented balanced budgets. But their command control statism caused economic decay, not growth, despite perpetually balanced budgets. The trouble today is that the GOP doesn't have a budget policy. A constitutional amendment to balance the budget is not a policy.

A real policy would eliminate unnecessary Federal departments, agencies, and programs, downsize the rest of government by 20% or more (as all American business has), sell financial loans and real estate assets, privatize Social Security, expand medical savings accounts, eliminate the capital gains tax, create unlimited IRA's and substantially flatten and simplify the income tax system. Budget estimates that reach balance five years from now have no meaning or credibility whatsoever. President Clinton's plan leaves 98% of deficit savings for 2001-02. Congressman Kasich's 1995 plan left 75% of the savings for the last two years. More nonsense. Any respectable budget green eyeshade will tell you that the only year that truly matters is the *next fiscal year.* After that it's a long day in the country. No one can predict the future.

Fortunately, a number of Republicans have risen in full revolt to prevent Gingrich's backsliding and muddle—headed vision from carrying the day. In the last forty-eight hours: Jack Kemp penned a three page letter blasting Newt; House Majority Leader Dick Armey (R, Tx) broke with Gingrich and told the *Washington Times* "there will be no budget without a significant tax reduction" this year; House backbenchers David McIntosh (R, Ind.) and Bill Paxton (R, N.Y.) attacked Gingrich face-to-face in a GOP House caucus meeting;

Finance Chairman Senator William Roth (R, Del) wrote his own budget that *included* tax cuts; and supply-side Senators Spence Abraham, (R, Mi) and Sam Brownback (R, Ks) organized a protest letter to Senator Majority Leader Lott signed by seventeen Republican Senate colleagues. So, as of this writing, the Republican program of a capital gains tax cut, inheritance gift tax relief and expanded IRA's *seems* to be back in place. Not surprisingly, NASDAQ stocks are up today even while the Dow continues to slip. Entrepreneurs, and their investors, need maximum after-tax returns in order to justify the risks and uncertainties that go along with innovative products and new business start-ups.

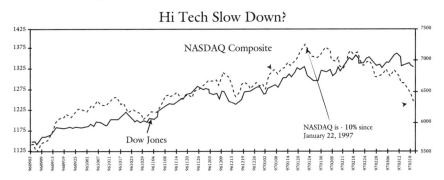

Hi Tech Slow Down?

More goofiness came yesterday from Alan Greenspan's testimony before the Joint Economic Committee. The estimable Fed chairman relied solely on Keynesian Phillips Curve arguments to intensify speculation on a federal funds rate increase at this Tuesday's meeting of the Open Market Committee. This is the old saw that too much prosperity causes inflation. Too bad we can't saw off the old saw. What's more, Greenspan hinted that "sustainable economic growth" is more important than price stability. This puts the cart before the horse. For it is low inflation (falling from 5% in 1990 to less than 2% currently) that has raised real capital investment returns, improved productivity and increased the real quality of profits (capitalized into higher stock prices) that has promoted economic growth in recent years. Call it an inflation tax cut.

Mr. Greenspan is correct to stand ready to preempt early warning signs of inflation, but he is watching the wrong indicators. Sensitive financial market prices are the best early warning indicators of future inflation risk. These market prices contain more information than most economic experts and their econometric computer models. Right now they are signaling price stability, not rising inflation. $350 gold is the best place to start looking, along with a precious metals index that is

139

over 10% below last year's level. Industrial metals are flat versus a year ago, as is the broad CRB futures commodity index. Energy commodities have fallen 20%. The dollar exchange rate continues to hold the high ground. The only possible glitch is the Treasury yield curve, which is averaging about 150 basis points. Historically, though, this is a moderate spread. Meanwhile, the GDP chain price index has increased only 1.8% over the past year. And the core PPI and CPI indexes have risen only 0.5% and 2.5%, respectively. At some point bond yields are going to gravitate toward the underlying 2% inflation rate.

Price Stability

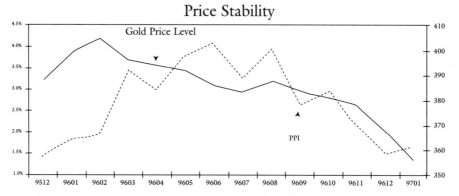

In truth, a quarter of a percent fed funds rate hike is small potatoes, nothing to fret about. Perhaps it could be justified as finally erasing the January 1996 fed funds rate cut, which was counterproductive at the time. But market-based price indicators suggest that Fed snugging today is not necessary. And a Fed snugging for the wrong reasons sends the wrong signals to the public. Why should anyone believe that growth is bad?

Ironically, the 10% to 20% year-to-date drop in small-cap hi-tech stocks is probably signaling a cooling off of the 35% growth of hi-tech investment. Rising real interest rates are tamping down this unsustainable boom, leading the way toward a slower future growth rate for the overall economy. But the key point here is our self-regulating economy. There is no need for Federal Reserve fine-tuning. A free-market economist like Alan Greenspan should appreciate this. So should a free-market politician like Newt Gingrich. Keep prices stable and remove government obstacles to entrepreneurship and innovation. Ronald Reagan, the most successful GOP politician of the century, abhorred economic fine-tuning and never obsessed over the budget deficit. So let's keep Goofy and Daffy in the Disney cartoons, where they belong. And let's keep Reagan's economic model front and center, where it belongs. Then the long wave bull market economy will continue.

140

2.10 CONNECTING DOTS

May 30, 1997

This is a short note that attempts to connect two dots. The first is Intel's announcement that sales and earnings are expected to soften. The second dot is the French elections. At first blush the two events seem distant. But they are not. The Intel press release mentioned that *European* sales were the big disappointment. And that brings us to the French elections.

The people of France are in a bad mood. Unemployment is hovering around 13%. Real GDP is barely rising. Industrial production is expanding at less than 2%. Retail sales are declining. Despite low inflation and interest rates, the French stock market over the past year is up only 9½%, compared to 42% in Finland, 39% in Spain, 35% in Denmark, 30% in Germany and the Netherlands, 28% in Sweden and 26% in the U.K.

French voters registered a strong protest at the Chirac administration austerity policies. He ran as a supply-sider, but he has not delivered. Within only a few weeks of forming a cabinet, Alain Madelin, the only free-market supply-sider, was tossed out of office. Prime Minister Juppe pursued a Hooveresque root-canal: government spending cuts without tax relief. Just as bad, the Juppe government frequently folded in the face of labor union protests. French conservatives have learned nothing from the Thatcher and Reagan experiences.

Watching all the French leaders campaigning this week (C-SPAN coverage has been terrific), all the candidates are talking growth but none of them has a pro-growth policy. My favorite was Giscard d'Estaing. The former president had a plan: *declare* that French growth will resume on July 1. No tax cut or deregulation plans. Just declare it. Fantastic.

It may be that Socialist Lionel Jospin, who advocates public job creation, cutting the work week from 39 hours to 35 hours, more generous pensions and no further privatization would do more harm than Philippe Seguin or Edouard Balladur, but it's a close call. Really, it's the evil of three lessers.

But let's not single out the French. Throughout the European Union, there are no growth policies. Tax rates run in the 50% to 60% zone, government spending routinely absorbs more than 50% of the continental economies, labor markets are inflexible and everything is over-regulated. Call it social democracy run amok.

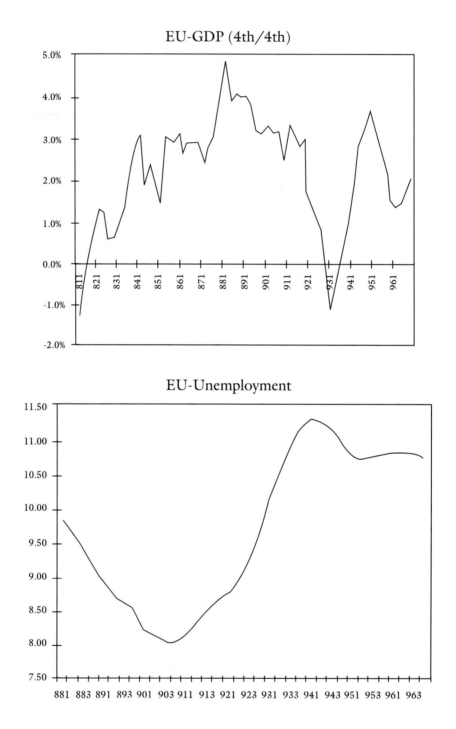

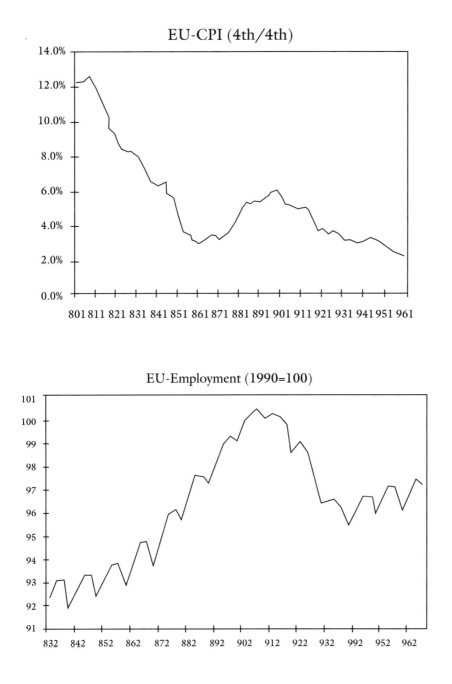

EU-CPI (4th/4th)

EU-Employment (1990=100)

143

The preceeding four charts tell the tale. Like the U.S., EU inflation is a low 2%. Unlike the U.S., the EU nations have *lost* jobs in the 1990s, with an 11% average unemployment rate and anemic 2% growth. With the same inflation rate, U.S. growth in the 1990s is running at 2.7% (with hi-tech productivity and output badly underreported), while about 12 million new jobs have been created (36 million since 1982) and our unemployment rate is 4.9%. The difference between the U.S. and the EU is *fiscal*. The U.S. has much lower tax rates, slower spending, flexible labor markets and across-the-board deregulation. Phillips Curvers take note: the same inflation rate is associated with vastly different unemployment rates.

A unified European currency may be a good idea (if only it were linked to gold or a commodity price rule anchor). Free trade and a single currency makes sense. What doesn't make any sense is the deficit targeting process mandated by Brussels. With 11% unemployment and continued recession deficits don't matter. Where's Maynard Keynes now that Europe needs him! What does matter is a series of across-the-board income tax rate reduction coupled with business, financial and labor market deregulation. But the deficit obsession has kept taxes high—and growth low. It's a goofy approach. And ordinary European people are increasingly fed up with it.

Longer term, I'd own Intel. It's a great company, on the cutting edge of next generation hi-tech breakthroughs. It's based in the U.S., which is gradually moving toward another round of flat tax reform and smaller government. As for Europe, it's very difficult to be optimistic. Perhaps, just perhaps, free people operating through free elections will force the politicians to liberate the continent. But right now it doesn't look good.

2.11 GOLDEN RULE:
ALAN GREENSPAN BELONGS
TO A LONG LINE OF GOLD BUGS

BUT HE MIGHT DO MORE TO SPREAD THE FAITH

April 21, 1997

"Gold is money, and nothing else." So J. P. Morgan testified
before the House of Representatives' Pugo Committee
(investigating the so-called money trusts) in 1913. A little more than
forty years later, in 1945, Cambridge don John Maynard Keynes and
U.S. Treasury official Harry Dexter White created a new world
monetary system that was based on a steady dollar linked to gold at $35
per ounce, thereby ushering in a 25-year period of postwar Western
prosperity. After Lyndon Johnson and Richard Nixon broke the
Bretton Woods monetary discipline, leading to 15 years of stagflation,
it was left to Ronald Reagan's advocacy of a gold-price rule (and tax
cuts) that provided Paul Volcker with the hard-money ground to stand
on in order to restore price stability and rebuild the U.S. economy.

Nearly 125 years before J. P. Morgan uttered his dictum, at the very
beginning of American economic history, Alexander Hamilton was able
to outflank Jefferson and Madison in 1791 and persuade President
George Washington to sign into law a bill to create a consolidated
national debt that would trade freely on the open market, along with a
national bank that would issue currency notes fully redeemable in gold
specie. By 1794 United States bonds had the highest credit rating in
Europe, according to John Steele Gordon's recent book *Hamilton's
Blessing*. Of course, looking as far back as the historical eye can see,
gold has always been endowed with a certain mysterious monetary
property, even a religious connotation. In ancient times the priest-kings
had the first gold coins minted in temples, suggesting that the gods,
not men, created money.

In today's world of high technology and global markets, it has
become fashionable to disbelieve in both God and gold. Too bad, for
continued application of old virtues would greatly assist the transition
to the next millennium. Belief in a higher spiritual power would surely
improve individual relationships and the general tone of discourse in
political life as well as civil society. In monetary terms, the gold price

remains the single best indicator of monetary value. Call it the mother of all inflation indicators.

Take a look at recent history. The $800 gold peak in 1980 predicted that year's 13.5 percent top in the consumer price index. By 1985 gold prices had fallen to $300 per ounce, and a year later the CPI troughed at 1.9 percent. Then, as James Baker took over the Treasury Department and embarked on a three-year quest to devalue the dollar on foreign exchanges and to pressure Volcker to create too many new dollars at home, gold gradually climbed to $475. Sure enough, in 1989 and 1990 the CPI averaged 5.1 percent, the stock market stagnated, and the economy briefly lapsed into recession.

During the 1990s, however, Federal Reserve chairman Alan Greenspan refocused monetary policy on the goal of price stability and near-zero inflation. In numerous testimonies on Capitol Hill, Greenspan invoked the use of gold (and broad commodity indexes) as a key advance-warning barometer of inflation fears. What's more, Greenspan has worked hand in glove with Clinton's economic-policy strongman, Robert Rubin, a canny former Wall Street bond trader and arbitrageur who recognized early on that price stability and a strong dollar were essential to maintaining low interest rates in the bond markets and steady economic growth.

The results of the Greenspan-Rubin hard-money collaboration are striking. Inflation, as measured by the new GDP chain price index (more accurate than the CPI), has averaged only 2.5 percent for the past five years, very close to the inflation rate of the Bretton Woods period, when the dollar was formally linked to gold. Reduced inflation has increased investment returns and enhanced capital formation (think of it as an economy-wide tax cut). Consequently the stock market has soared, as has household net worth. Recent polling data suggest that 43 percent of the adult population of this country are now invested in the stock market, nearly double the participation from seven years ago.

And guess what: the price of gold has averaged only $370 per ounce during this period, just a bit more than ten times the old Bretton Woods par value of $35 per ounce. Gold's critics argue that this proves gold is meaningless. No one's paying any attention to it. There's no investment interest. Good! It is precisely the low and stable gold price that has accurately signaled the decline of inflation and the emergence of price stability. If people were investing heavily in gold, as they did during the Seventies, it would be a very bad sign, an inflationist sign, probably auguring an end to the bull-market economy that has now lasted 14 years.

But, the anti-gold bugs say, gold is low because European central banks are selling the barbarous metal in order to meet deficit targets in advance of the European Union's single-currency plan. But a recent London-based study reports that daily gold trading has increased to nearly fifty million ounces, well more than double the entire gold holdings of all European central banks combined.

Then there are the monetarists, especially on Wall Street, who argue that elevated stock markets around the world are a function of overly rapid money-supply growth. According to this view, a new bout of higher inflation is lurking just around the corner. But hang on a minute. What's really happening is an unprecedented increase in the demand for money. With free-market economics spreading around the world, there are more opportunities to put more money to work more profitably than at any other time in history. And let's not forget the incredible high-tech boom, where fast information processing and communications breakthroughs, and the business application of these techniques, has created an unprecedented productivity boom that is expanding the supply side of the world economy. In the United States, numerous studies (including some by Federal Reserve staff) suggest that if the Commerce Department could figure out the proper accounting of the economic impact of high technology, we would see that inflation is actually less than 2 percent (as the gold price suggests), productivity nearly 3 percent, and real GDP growth between 4 and 5 percent. Think of it as the steam engine, the railroads, autos, the light bulb, and the telephone. Only more so. We are in a long-wave prosperity.

As long, that is, as entrepreneurs and inventors have the benefit of stable prices and sound money (and minimal taxation) to guarantee proper rewards for risking financial life and limb. Fortunately, Alan Greenspan recognizes this. He is following the lead of classical British economist John Stuart Mill, who wrote in 1848 that monetary value would be maintained by using the price of gold: "There is a clear and unequivocal indication by which to judge whether a currency is depreciated, and to what extent. That indication is the price of precious metals." So, from the priest-kings, to Hamilton, to Mill, to Morgan, to Keynes, to Reagan, and to Greenspan, the story line is linked to gold.

What remains is to institutionalize the gold-price rule formally. This would guarantee honest money well into the future. After all, Mr. Greenspan is 71 years old and mortal. Now is the time for the Fed chairman to cap his distinguished career by formally adopting a gold-point rule. Should the precious metal rise above about $375–$400, signaling excess money, the central bank would automatically raise the federal funds rate. Should gold fall below $300–$325, signaling deflationary money, the bank would ease by lowering the overnight funds rate.

This would ensure that tomorrow's dollar would have the same value as today's. In spiritual and monetary terms, it would be a new-millennium golden rule.

2.12 WINNING IDEALS

AN IMPROVING ECONOMY MARKS A CONSERVATIVE TRIUMPH

June 22, 1997

Conservatives are acting like disheartened losers recently. They complain that Bill Clinton outmaneuvers them at every turn and that the public isn't hearing their message.

What this blue funk ignores is historical context. In fact, and notwithstanding recent blunders by congressional Republicans, the conservative ideals of free markets, smaller government and lower taxes remain broadly ascendant.

For proof, examine both current developments and long-range trends.

Recent news on House Ways and Means Chairman Bill Archer's tax bill has provided even more stimulus to an already optimistic stock market. Few people expected an assault on the alternative minimum tax or a reduction in the corporate capgains tax, though markets have been discounting a 20 percent capgains rate for individuals. So far this year big cap stocks have appreciated by nearly 18 percent while smaller cap shares have improved by nearly 10 percent. By the way, since the Republicans took hold of Congress in late 1994, gradually pushing their economic agenda of smaller government and lower taxes, the major stock market indexes have increased by nearly 100 percent. This is serious wealth creation. It is also grounds for serious optimism about our nation's future.

Guess what? The much maligned 1997 budget deal is coming out better than nearly everyone expected. Take health care. Much greater free market consumer choice will be given to doctors, hospitals and other "provider-sponsored organizations" that form their own health plans to compete with HMOs in the Medicare market. What's more, another 500,000 tax-free medical savings accounts will be permitted.

Back to taxes. Capgains relief will spur yet another rough of high tech risk taking, innovation and entrepreneurial growth. And the Congressional Budget Office is reviewing the dynamic behavioral effects of capgains relief for an expanded growth and revenue impact. This may well balance the budget next year. Inflation indexing is still on the table. So are the enlarged deductions for inheritance taxes and expanded IRAs. These will be the first economywide tax cuts in ten years. The stock market loves it.

No, the Bush-Clinton income tax hikes will not be rolled back. Nor will any number of totally useless federal departments be abolished. Nor will the hundreds of unnecessary federal programs be zeroed out. Nor will Social Security be linked to stock market returns and privatized. But, the latest Senate Budget Committee bulletin informs us that non-defense discretionary spending is expected to rise by only one-half of one percent in each of the next five years, while overall budget outlays rise by an average of 3 percent per year. Not bad. Let's call it progress. As a result, the budget share of GDP could fall below 19 percent. Since the economy always outperforms the pessimistic experts, this "tax wedge" effect could even be weaker.

Now, let's conduct a thought experiment that puts a Republican in the White House. Then, let's assume that today's splendid economic landscape remains in place: 4 percent growth, 2 percent inflation, expanding global free trade, a budget nearly in balance, a strong dollar and a 7700 Dow. And a fiscal plan that modestly shrinks government and lowers tax burdens, following last year's triumphant disentitlement of welfare. Do we think this scenario would be wildly applauded by conservatives? Of course.

But it's not happening. Nearly all conservative thinkers and critics are cranky, angry, resentful, frustrated, dejected, pessimistic and declinist. Why is this? Take a guess. There's a Democrat in the White House. And he's taking credit for all that is good in our new Camelot. And conservatives don't like it one bit. Just like the 1996 election campaign. The economy is rolling along, politics and policies are center-right, and President Clinton is stealing the Right's best lines: smaller government, lower taxes, traditional family values. It's Disraeli dissing Gladstone. Post-election, most conservatives still haven't recovered.

Talk about anger, resentment and frustration. Nearly all the leading conservative journals have chosen to pile on the budget deal and blame the Republican leadership for its failure to achieve utopia in one giant step. My most recent favorite example of blaming and resentful literary expression is David Frum's sub-opus in *The Weekly Standard*. Frum, a card-carrying Clinton-hater and recent convert to Hooverism austerity economics, takes aim at House Speaker Newt Gingrich and Senate Majority Leader Trent Lott. He argues that this year's budget-balancing plan is "in many ways worse than the one the congressional Democrats enacted in 1993"—despite that year's record tax increase and ground laying for Clinton's misbegotten nationalized health plan. Hyperbole? Maybe. Frustration? Definitely. But Frum has more. He describes the GOP leadership performance as "crave" (read: cowardly and contemptibly fainthearted); and asserts "It's a truly desperate situation."

What's truly desperate? The strong economy? The 4.8 percent unemployment rate? The 7700 Dow? But Frum is not keen on economic growth and wealth-creating stock markets. He argues later in his critique that "since few Americans are in much of a position to benefit directly from estate tax relief or a capital gains tax cut, those cuts must be defended in terms of their economic effects. And, those arguments necessarily sound speculative to the voting public."

Speculative economic effects? Which planet is Frum describing? Is it the planet Earth, where the U.S. stock market has created over $16 trillion in new household net worth during this bull market, two and one-half times the combined European Union GDP? Where 43 percent of the American population, roughly 125 million people, comprising virtually the entire work force, a figure that has doubled in the last seven years, now owns shares? The bulk of whom are women and non-professional white and blue collar workers.

These are people who are very interested in capgains tax relief that could increase after-tax nest eggs for retirement, health care, insurance and children's education by as much as 50 percent. These are people who own their own (at home?) small businesses or who have invested in high risk ventures proposed by family members, in-laws, cousins, friends, co-workers, you name it. Ordinary Americans now have a piece of the rock. They own the means of production. This is how our 21st century economy now works. It's called free-market democratic capitalism. It's about risk and reward. After-tax. Actually, the capital gains tax cut is now a quintessentially middle class proposal. That is why Clinton and other new Democrats are supporting it.

Frum and other cranky conservatives should stop their grousing. Consumer confidence in the United States is at an all-time high. Socially, crime, family breakup and unwed mothering is down. Ordinary Americans know we are in a prosperous period. They didn't like the Dole-Kemp pessimism in the last election ("the worst economy in 100 years"!), and they won't vote for conservative declinist-pessimistic candidates in the next one either. Thoughtful and well-meaning conservatives should get real. Accept that Bill Clinton is president. It's a good place to start.

And then recognize, indeed argue, that it was Ronald Reagan who started all this over 15 years ago when he reversed 50 years of big government engineering. It was Reagan's tax cuts, deregulation, disinflation, free trade and spending restraint (believe it or not, a recent Urban Institute article shows that FDR and Reagan were the two stingiest government spenders in this century) that gave the U.S. economy its strong legs, and provided the prosperous ground Bill Clinton and his 60 percent approval rating are now standing on.

From this premise conservative intellectuals such as David Frum could become more insightful. Instead of temper tantrums and personal attacks, they might provide a more even-handed and accurate appraisal of our nation's improving condition. They might develop a more constructive, courteous and respectful relationship with Republican leadership efforts to enhance and enlarge Reagan's agenda and show the nation that the GOP can manage Congress and thus deserves re-election. Conservative thinkers might also consider innovative ways to promote even smaller government, even lower tax rates, even freer markets, even more personal responsibility, even greater family and community virtue, even more spiritual faith, and even stronger self-government. Most of all, conservatives must remember that in free democratic nations it is optimistic visionaries who succeed, pessimists who fail. Reagan taught us that. Clinton learned it.

2.13 STAY THE COURSE

August 12, 1997

C halk up the nasty financial market correction to a temporary relapse back to Phillips curve thinking. Prosperous economic reports on employment, purchasing managers, car sales, retail chain and department store sales have apparently triggered old fears that the economy will "overheat" its way toward a pick-up of inflation. Once again, experts are proclaiming that unemployment is too low and tight labor markets will generate cost-push wage inflation.

Somehow, bad old thinking never seems to die. Alan Greenspan did his best to dispel those fears by emphasizing the Information Age transformation of the economy in his mid-year Congressional testimony. Surging technological investment has expanded the supply-side of the economy's potential to grow, generating considerable productivity improvement along the way. This productivity has raised profits and controlled unit labor costs.

What's more, the post Cold War trend toward market-opening trade liberalization and the deregulatory removal of trade barriers at home have created recurring waves of intense competition, another price restraining factor. And let's not forget Joseph Schumpeter's dictum that large scale innovation creates more output at lower prices. Against this backdrop, solid economic growth has peacefully coexisted with low inflation. This was highlighted during the first half of 1997, when real GDP expanded at a 3.5% annual pace, while inflation averaged only about 1.4%. Orthodox economists on Wall Street and the Fed Board staff waved their Phillips curves and predicted higher inflation. However, measured inflation rates actually subsided. The pessimists were wrong.

Most important, classical economic theory dictates that inflation is always a monetary problem. In the absence of a formal price rule (such as the Bretton Woods gold link to the dollar) the most straightforward way of gauging future inflation risk is a careful perusal of inflation-sensitive market price indicators such as gold and precious metals, broad commodity indexes, the Treasury yield curve slope, and the dollar exchange rate. For example, strong commodities, a cheap dollar and widening yield curve spreads signal excess liquidity and rising inflation risk. But cheap gold, King dollar and a flat yield curve, such as we have today, signal monetary restraint and declining inflation fears. These market price trends accurately predicted this year's unwinding of inflation. Phillips curve models were dead wrong. Why should anyone believe them now?

Going one step further, two simple models can be used to forecast inflation for the next four quarters: (1) the year to year change in gold prices predicts a 1.6% rise in the GDP implicit price deflator for the next year (to mid-1998); and (2) the year to year change in the CRB precious metals index (gold, silver, platinum) projects a 1.9% year ahead rise in the deflator. In other words, inflation will stay low. Here is a brief performance review of key market price indicators. They strongly suggest price stability.

Market Price Indicator	*% Change From Year Ago*
Gold	–15.0%
CRB Futures	–0.1%
Precious Metals	–0.8%
Goldman Sachs	–1.9%
Journal of Commerce	0.4%
U.S. Dollar Index	16.5%
Treasury Yield Spread (30 year Fed Funds)	–37.0%

Inflation Forecast

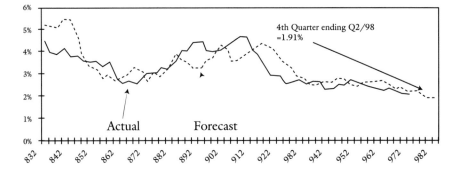

As for the economy, a simple econometric model using the slope of the Treasury curve and year to year changes in the Treasury bill rate suggests continued 3% real economic growth during the year ahead; no recessionary bust or inflationary boom. Actually, the entire 15 year bull market in stocks has coexisted with a 3% average yearly increase for real GDP. So investors should not fear 3% growth. During the prior 15 year period, characterized by sluggish 2.3% annual real growth, the stock market performed very poorly, losing 70% of its value (adjusted for

154

inflation). Actually, the slow growth period from 1967 to 1982 had an inflation rate that was roughly twice as rapid as the faster growth period from 1982 to 1997: 6.7% versus 3.2%. So the Phillips curvers have not only gotten it wrong recently, they've been off for a good 30 years. Message to Phillips curvers: change those coefficients.

Real GDP growth Forecast

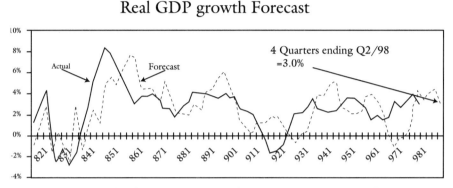

Fine tuning the forecast just a little more, it is noteworthy that M2 growth appears to be trending lower. Year to year M2 growth remains just under 5%. However, the higher frequency six month rate of change has slowed from 6.3% at an annual rate last spring to 4.3% currently. An even higher frequency three month growth measure shows a drop from 6.9% last winter to only 2.9% recently. In other words, the high frequency tail is dropping below the yearly trendline.

In a new world of price stability, where gold has become a fixed reference point and interest rate conditions have been increasingly less volatile, the link between M2 and nominal GDP is becoming more reliable. We have been using this link to cross reference the Treasury bill and precious metals forecasting approaches to real economic growth and inflation. Pulling all this together, the year ahead forecast looks like 3% real growth, 2% inflation and 5% nominal GDP.

M2

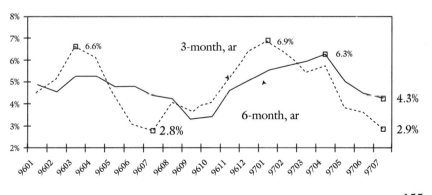

155

Over the past half dozen years, 30 year Treasury bond yields seem to trade about 150 basis points above the growth of nominal GDP. So that would suggest a fair valuation of 6½% for the long bond However, M2 and nominal GDP growth could be tailing down. What's more, 1½% to 2% inflation will eventually pull bond yields much lower than 6.50%. So let's set a range of 6% to 6½% for the long bond forecast. Over time, as price stability takes hold and inflation expectations continue to unwind, long bonds will drop into the 5% zone. First we need to bury the Phillips curve. Then we can lower the Fed funds rate. So investors should stay the course. Have patience. It's a long run game. Keep the faith. Faith is the spirit.

2.14 TAX CORRECTION

August 21, 1997

Financial markets in August are correcting and consolidating after the August run-up in stock and bond prices over the prior four months, especially July. Cross currents such as international currency risk, labor unrest, profit worries and the perennial Phillips curve threat (Will the Fed tighten to stop 3% growth? Absolutely not in my view.) have created a new wave of investor uncertainty. The late summer natives are restless.

Without denying the impact of these market worries, there is a simpler explanation for this correction episode: taxes. Especially the reduction in the capital gains tax rate. While complicated and diluted by unnecessary holding period qualifications, the bottom line story is a capgains rate reduction from 28% to 20% under the new tax law. This means investors take home 80 cents of the marginal dollar gained, rather than 72 cents. It's an 11% improvement in the incentive for risk taking and investment—a very good thing for economywide animal spirits and entrepreneurship, especially for our high tech information age new paradigm economy that thrives on innovation.

Under the new tax law investors are increasing their demand for companies that pay shareholders through capgains, while investors are reducing their demand for companies that pay through dividends. The latter of course is still taxed at the 39.6% income tax rate. Firms have a choice. They can return profits to shareholders in the form of dividends, or they can retain the earnings for capgains purposes. The wider differential between a 20% capgains rate and a 39.6% income tax rate is causing a significant portfolio restructuring by tax astute investors.

Big cap stocks typically pay out much more in dividends than small cap stocks, or micro-cap stocks, especially in the technology sector. Data for NASDAQ and Russell 2000 indices are hard to come by. However, the dividend share of corporate earnings for the S & P 500 (a big cap proxy) is a hefty 34.5%. By contrast, the dividend share of S & P Technology index companies is only 11.1%.

Assuming the S & P Tech is similar to the low dividend story for the NASDAQ and Russell 2000 small cap indexes, it's easier to understand the market correction. Since July 31, the NASDAQ (0.8% gain) and the Russell 2000 (0.6% gain) have outperformed the Dow (4% loss) and the S & P 500 (3.1% loss). No one is doing great in this choppy market, but the small caps are outperforming the big guys. This

157

is because capgains are worth more to shareholders on an after-tax basis than dividends. It's a question of tax rates and tax incentives affecting investor behavior. Quite rational.

Over time the large cap firms can be expected to restructure. They will find ways to increase shareholder value by converting away from investor returns taxed at ordinary income rates. Remember, $1.00 of corporate profit, taxed at the 35% corporate income tax rate, leaves $.65 to investors. If it's paid out in dividends, then it's only worth $.39 to investors. But if the earnings are retained and essentially paid out in the form of a higher share price as capital gains, then they are worth $.52, a 33% improvement. Until this 33% gap between dividend returns and capgains returns is significantly narrowed, the demand for capgains-heavy small caps will continue to exceed the demand for dividend-heavy big caps.

Because the economy's overall marginal tax rate is lowered by the reduction of the capgains tax, the whole economy will become more efficient on the margin, raising capital returns and increasing risk taking and innovation. So a rising tide will lift all boats. Our stock market outlook remains very optimistic. However, within that optimism, portfolio decisions under the new law are likely to continue to reallocate in the small cap direction. It has already begun. Taxes matter. Hold that thought.

2.15 SCHUMPETER'S COUSINS

August 22, 1997

With declining PPI reports, weak commodity trends, slumping gold and choppy markets, some observers have publicly expressed the view that deflationary pressures represent more of an economic threat than a rekindling of inflationary forces.

Actually, neither deflation nor inflation represents a significant risk. Instead, the U.S. economy is embarked on a long wave of prosperity coupled with price stability. Over the past fifteen years real GDP has expanded better than 3% per year, while the best barometer of monetary value, namely gold, suggests the current inflation rate is close to zero. With no inflation and 4.8% unemployment, Federal Reserve policymakers should toss their Phillips curves into the dustbin of history. Though you wouldn't know it from reading the business and financial pages each day, the only thing we have to fear is fear itself.

Deflation is a turbo-charged word, and more often than not it is misleading. In the 1930s, following Herbert Hoover's monumental policy mistakes of sharply increased protectionist trade tariffs and domestic income tax rates, the U.S. and the rest of the world did indeed sink into a deflationary depression. For ten years the U.S. unemployment rate averaged 20%. Because of this voters punished the Republican party for nearly 50 years.

However, during the late 19th century and early 20th century the U.S. economy experienced a tremendous burst of prosperity and wealth creation, which was accompanied by a slight decline of prices. Call it deflationary growth. From 1875 to 1896, real GNP (1958 $) expanded at a 4.8% annual rate, while the implicit price index *declined* by 1.8% each year. In fact, the whole period from the end of the Civil War to the beginning of WW I provided real growth of nearly 4½% per year while the implicit price index fell slightly.

This golden age, triggered by President U.S. Grant's policies to restore the gold standard and eliminate the wartime income tax, launched the U.S. as the world's greatest economic power. It was a period of extraordinary technological innovation: railroads, farming, heavy industry, autos, electricity, telephones and so on. From his studies of this period, classical economist Joseph Schumpeter coined the term "gales of creative destruction" to describe the entrepreneurial burst that transformed the American economy. Importantly, he saw that the technological boom generated substantially higher output, with greater product quality, accompanied by *falling* prices.

Today's 21st century economy is a near cousin to the high tech breakthroughs of a hundred years ago. Of course, now the productivity and profit enhancing innovations are Information Age breakthroughs in microchips, microprocessors, semi-conductors, fiber optics, and other knowledge-related products which are spilling over into every nook and cranny of our completely transformed economy. Along the way, output and quality are rising, while prices are falling. Witness declining price trends in personal computers and cellular telephones.

Rather than Hooveresque austerity, President Ronald Reagan helped launch this boom with his free market policies of lower taxes, smaller government, deregulation, free trade and price stability. The resulting 15-year stock market boom mirrors the economic upturn. But for an inconsequential eight-month recession in 1990–91, the U.S. economy continues in the longest cyclical upturn of the 20th century. The issue isn't deflation, it's prosperity. Trouble is, too many people have been too pessimistic for too long to see how completely the sunlight of the spirit has shined. And it's not over yet.

2.16 Schumpeter's Cousins (II): Bond Inversion

October 3, 1997

No two historical episodes are ever exactly alike, but the current bond market rally and Treasury yield curve flattening reminds me of yet another parallel to events of one hundred years ago. Remember the burst of technological innovation and investment that occurred roughly from the end of the Civil War to the beginning of World War I. It was a phenomenal long wave of prosperity driven by tremendous industrial advances in railroading, steam and then gas engines, autos, the electric light bulb and ultimately the telegraph and the telephone. Of course, today's Schumpeterian gales of creative destruction stem from unheard of breakthroughs in information age technologies such as computer memory chips, micro processors, bio tech, health care tech, financial services tech, etc. etc.

In macro terms, one key point linking both the industrial age and the information age is that bursts of innovation create more output, with better quality, *at lower prices.* This was one of Joseph Schumpeter's greatest insights. Think of the cellular telephone, which cost about $3000 in the middle 1980s, whereas today's model costs about $200, with many more battery minutes and other improvements. If you combine Alan Greenspan's hard money price rule, which has brought inflation down practically to zero, with Joseph Schumpeter's high tech dictum of more output at lower prices, essentially what you get is a price equilibrium process that combines *stable money chasing more goods.* This thought is the polar opposite of too much money chasing too few goods, which was the inflationist story from 1968 to 1982.

When President Ulysses S. Grant restored the U.S. greenback link to gold, he set the stage for a long wave of price equilibrium. And it didn't hurt that under Grant's presidency the Civil War income tax was repealed, thereby vastly improving economic incentives to take risks and innovate. So the long wave of price stability was linked to the long wave of prosperity. Today's story is very similar. The Reaganesque shift away from government economic engineering and toward free market tax cuts, deregulation, free trade and disinflation is very much like the Grant period, launching a long wave of technological innovation, economic growth and price stability. Not exactly the same, but worth the thought.

In bond market terms *both periods could produce sustained yield curve inversions.* For example, the period form 1890 to 1915 (this is the only 19th century interest rate data we could find) generated an inverted yield curve nearly half the time. During that period real GNP increased at a yearly pace of 3.5%, while the annual CPI rose only 0.5%.

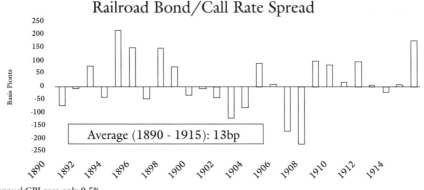

Railroad Bond/Call Rate Spread

Average (1890 - 1915): 13bp

annual CPI rose only 0.5%

In today's bond market, as a 10-year Treasury yields drop below 6%, the curve has flattened to less than 50 basis points. The economy's growth is trending around 3½%, while various inflation indexes are less than 2%. Economic forecasters usually anticipate recession as the Treasury curve flattens, and one rule of thumb is that actual curve inversion leads an official recession by roughly three or four quarters. However, in the current Greenspan-Schumpeterian spirit, where sound money chasers more (technologically driven) goods, yield curve flattening or inversion is actually a very positive development, much like it was one hundred years ago. This is because price stability is pulling long term rates lower, not because the Federal Reserve is tightening its credit policy.

Over the next year or so it would not be at all surprising to see an inverted Treasury curve. Ten year interest rates might blow right through the Federal funds rate as inflationary expectations continue to diminish. What's more, one of the powerful but invisible hand currents in the bond rally is the market's growing recognition that there is a *coming bond shortage in the new era of surplus politics.* During the next few years budget surpluses could average $50 billion to $100 billion. Treasury auctions might take place in Sotheby's, as would befit the sale of antique collector's items. In the current period of price stability, bond scarcity will raise prices and reduce yields. What fun. What a great story. Keep the faith. Faith is the spirit.

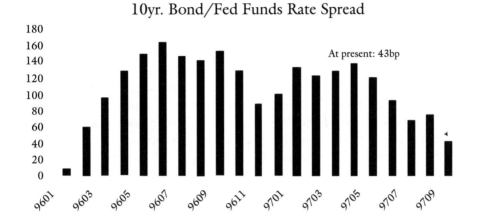

10yr. Bond/Fed Funds Rate Spread

2.17 A STOCK MARKET STORY

October 30, 1997

When questioned about the meaning of the stock market crash of 1987, President Reagan responded by calling it "a stock market thing; the economy is fundamentally sound." The same could be said about the 550-point loss on the Dow Jones index on October 27, 1997, perhaps more so. Brutish, short and painful market corrections are a necessary part of the free market's self-correcting and self-regulating process. Excesses in the stock market are periodically cleansed in order to make the financial architecture of capital raising and investment a more efficient mechanism to support a dynamic growth economy. It's the financial version of Joseph Schumpeter's *Gales of Creative Destruction*.

By themselves, these market shakeouts are largely unhinged from the Main Street economy. If anything, it is quite possible that the market's ability to rid itself of internal imbalances will actually prolong the long bull market and the long wave of prosperity we have experienced since 1982. In fact, sizable market adjustments took place in 1983–84, 1987 and 1990. 1994 witnessed a rolling correction. Briefer declines occurred in the summer of 1996, last winter and again last August: But none of these prevented the stock market from rack up total returns of 13% per year, adjusted for inflation, since 1982.

The capital-raising and wealth-creating functions of the second longest bull market in U.S. history (only the 1949–68 period was longer) have undergirded the longest period of economic prosperity in this century, beginning in 1983 and, with only a brief and shallow 1990 recession, continuing to the present. Led by an extraordinary burst of Information Age technological innovation and investment, which has transformed every nook and cranny of our new economy, and bracketed by free-market policies that have reduced taxes, virtually eliminated inflation, deregulated nearly all industrial, financial and labor market sectors, expanded market-opening free-trade, reduced the Federal budget share of the economy, and the deficit, and ended the Cold War, the completely transformed U.S. economy is the strongest in the world.

In 1997, the U.S. had produced $3\frac{1}{2}$% real economic growth, with only 1% to 2% inflation, S& P 500 profits were rising more than 10% (60% of corporations reported better than expected earnings in the September '97quarter), productivity gains matched $1\frac{1}{2}$% real wage increases, unemployment was below 5%, gold and silver prices were soft, King Dollar was strong and long-term Treasury bond rates hovered around 6%. Undoubtedly there will be another recession in my lifetime (we've experienced nine since World War II), but current economic trends suggest there is no downturn yet in sight.

Inevitably, stock market losses such as that of the 17th of October conjure up comparisons with 1987—though Black Monday's market dropped 23%, while Gray Monday's decline was only 7%. More to the point, then years ago the dollar was sinking while inflation and interest rates were shooting skyward. Today, of course, the strong dollar has nurtured declining inflation and interest rates. In 1987 large tax-rate increases on capital and real estate were taking effect, with a threatened tax increase on corporate mergers and acquisitions. By contrast, the 1997 tax bill (warts and all) reduced the capital gains tax, lowered the inheritance penalty and expanded IRA savings incentives. Indeed, as the possibility of budget surpluses grows larger, so does the opportunity for meaningful flat tax and Social Security privatization reforms. These approaches would substantially improve incentives for enhanced entre-preneurial risk-taking, saving and investment, sure to be capitalized into significantly higher future stock market valuations.

But even the soundest economic footing and efficiently valued stock market can be unnerved by shocks from outside the system or policy mistakes from within. This is why policymakers must pay attention to the message of market prices, especially when sharp price declines signal that policies have gone wrong. Without question, wide-spread currency chaos in the Asia Pacific Rim overloaded and tripped an internal stock market fuse. Rapid-fire currency devaluations last summer in Thailand, the Philippines, Malaysia and Indonesia, then spreading to Singapore and Tawain, raised the specter of likely recession and inflation among these formerly fast-growing Asian Tigers. Every one of their stock markets crashed, several by as much as 50%, signaling rough economic times ahead.

Despite the fact that developing country currencies never truly float, they sink, as most notably illustrated in the Mexico peso economic crisis a few years ago, these nations rejected monetary disci-pline by de-linking their currencies from the U.S. dollar. As is always the case when second and third tier countries break their promise of currency stability, international credit markets inflict swift punishment through the massive withdrawl of investment funds and liquidity. So interest rates blow sky-high, with rising inflation and unemployment sure to follow. Currency market prices *and* stock market prices both signaled that serious policy blunders had been made.

165

The entire Asia Pacific Rim accounts for only about 6% of all U.S. corporate profits and less that 10% of our exports stem from the Southeast Asian Tigers. but financial markets threatened to carry the Asian flu to Hong Kong, whose currency has been successfully pegged to the U.S. dollar since 1983, producing impressive results of 5% growth and minimal inflation. A devaluation of the Hong Kong dollar would have pulled the U.S., but the fragile economies of Japan and Europe. It was market rumors of possible Hong Kong devaluation that led directly to '97's Gray Monday seismic sell-off.

Fortunately, Hong Kong defended its currency peg to the dollar; it was a heroic decision, backed by roughly 80 billion in dollar reserves, with another 130 billion of China's dollar reserves standing ready to assist. PRC China itself has pegged its yuan to the U.S. dollar in recent years, accounting for a 9% economic growth rate with virtually zero inflation. Unquestionably, Greater China's currency defense was a crucial factor in the subsequent Tuesday stock market recovery in the U.S., and the Wednesday recovery worldwide. In Hong Kong the stock market has recouped over 20% of its prior loss. The HK defense of its dollar-linked currency board should serve as a shining example to all emerging nations.

But the Southeast Asian Tigers are still floating in a sea of valueless money, and thus far there are no plans to correct the problem. Neither Fed Chairman Alan Greenspan, nor Treasury Secretary Rubin, nor any other of the G-7 leaders has initiated any efforts to provide Asian currency cooperation. This despite the evidence that common currency cooperation is working in a Europe pegged to the German mark, and a Western Hemisphere pegged to the U.S. dollar. However, the ongoing currency crisis, which is again threatening Latin America and Central Europe, is a market cry for help from a world monetary conference to promote currency cooperation and stability. For it is clear that world financial markets want a currency price rule arrangement to govern monetary affairs and maintain currency value. As for Asia, international monetary expert Robert Mundell, formerly a senior IMF official and presently a professor of economics at Columbia University, told me in a recent interview that "Only a tough Asian link to the dollar, in the form of a currency board, will solve the problem. There is too much hostility to Japan. China won't accept the Japanese yen. But they're already tied to the dollar."

Beyond the stock market threat from Asian currency unrest, two homegrown U.S. policy issues have burdened the domestic market. First, on October 21st, 1997 the U.S. Justice Department sued Microsoft for "monopolistic practices." This action had an immediate chilling effect on high-technology share prices that preceded the overall market blow-off. While past anti-trust actions sought to protect consumers from predatory pricing strategies, the Microsoft action seeks to protect the software giant's *competitors* from aggressive marketing that combines the Windows system with an upgraded browser operation for use on the Internet Explorer. Even though consumers are getting an excellent product with declining prices, and Microsoft has only 35% of the browser market, the Justice Department is fining Microsoft $1 million per day. This is a naked attempt by government to take control, regulate and perhaps even tax Information Age technological innovation. It strikes at the very heart of the principal growth and profitability dynamic of the U.S. economy. Investor capital will migrate away from this crucial sector, with a combined hardware and software contribution of fully one-third of real economic growth, unless government contains its over-regulatory instinct.

And speaking of government interference with the market economy, only two weeks before the market's nosedive Alan Greenspan took it upon himself to scold the stock market for unrealistic price and earnings valuations. Also, he threatened to raise interest rates because unemployment growth was allegedly too rapid, wage increases would re-ignite inflation and the economy must be slowed. This outburst before Congress prompted a 150-point marked tailspin, with reverberations throughout global markets.

What gives with Greenspan? Arguably the best Fed Chairman since the Reserve System's founding in 1913, and presiding over the lowest inflation rate in over thirty years, surely he understands that more people working, producing and prospering cannot possibly cause higher inflation. Outside of the last remaining liberal-left economic fringe, mainstream economists today understand that inflation is a monetary problem caused by too much money chasing too few goods, leading to a decline in money's standard of value. One such yardstick of value is the price of gold, which stands at a twelve-year low. Actually, with surging investment and productivity, the current economy is experiencing a very positive interaction of sound money chasing more goods, a combination that is causing an *inflationary decline*, even while the economy is expanding rapidly.

University of Chicago Nobel Prize winner Gary Becker is quite unhappy with Greenspan's market scoldings, which include a December 1997 "irrational exuberance" charge. Becker argues "I don't think he knows any more than the rest of us about market valuations. It is presumptuous of him to think he has any more knowledge than other people. And it is dangerous to attempt to push the market down; it would be much better that Greenspan not get involved." Instead of attacking growth and a strong stock market, Greenspan should back off the discredited Phillips curve trade-off between unemployment and inflation, and instead maintain a steady dollar-gold exchange rate and a stable producer price index level, both of which would indicate that the new supply of money creation remains in good balance with the market economy's demand for money. This simple and direct approach will generate zero inflation, confidence in the dollar, even lower interest rates and help create a healthy economy.

Not Greenspan, nor the Justice Department, nor Asian currency chaos can obscure the fact that the dominant influence on today's economy is the pre-eminence of global free-markets and the rise of entrepreneurship. Governments are left to execute, but markets will dictate the direction of policy. Nations that impose currency barriers or trade barriers or regulatory barriers or tax barriers will experience capital flight and debilitating market shocks. World financial markets call the tune, and capital always seeks the highest after-tax return. The burst of information and communication technologies, operating across borders and through financial markets, is compelling nations to nurture the forces of free-market entrepreneurial capitalism. It is a relentless process, but one that gives voice to ordinary men and women around the world who desire economic growth and social progress. Governments may stubbornly resist market price warning signals, at large cost to their citizens, but the global financial market will relentlessly and sometimes punitively force recalcitrant leaders to mend their ways.

This is why I remain steadfastly optimistic and bullish about the future, including the stock market, which itself is a key barometer of wealth, growth and progress. Over the long-term, patient investors will prosper. Even dating back to the 1970s, an unsettling period of economic and moral decline in America, free-markets and free elections ultimately pushed the U.S. and the rest of the world in the right direction. For investors, a recent study shows that $5,000 placed in stock market mutual funds every year since 1970 would have grown to an $841, 099 retirement nest egg by today, yielding an annual return of 11.7%. Investing in mutual funds that performed in the top quartile would have grown to $1.06 million, with a yearly return of 13.26%. The populist wisdom of ordinary people understand this, that is why they stay invested over the long haul.

And that wisdom also accounts for the surge in stock market ownership. Today nearly the entire workforce, about 125 million people, own a piece of the rock. Because of this ownership stake they have no intention of permitting their elected leaders to stray from the free-market path. It was the ordinary man and woman from Main Street who stabilized the market on Tuesday and Gray Monday's harrowing setback. These are people who quite rightly have the necessary faith in America; and faith is always the right spirit.

Stock Market Story

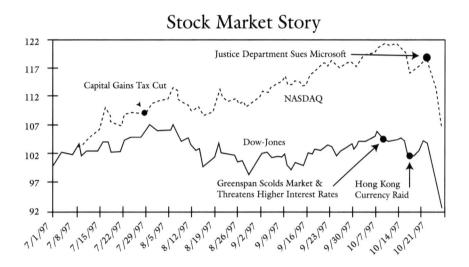

FROM ECONOMIC ABUNDANCE
TO MORAL PROSPERITY

The newspapers are so full of reports about falling crime rates in major American cities and nationwide that it cannot be a fluke. Rudy Guiliani was just re-elected mayor of New York City with a near 60% landslide vote, after a bare 1% victory four years ago. The major issue: crime. The National Development and Research Institute reports that the percentage of newly arrested criminals who tested positive for crack cocaine has been falling steadily since 1987 in Manhattan, Los Angeles, Chicago, Philadelphia, Detroit, Washington and Indianapolis. The biggest declines were registered by arrestees younger than 18.

Not surprisingly, with hard drugs on the decline, the FBI reports that U.S. property crime—burglary, larceny and auto theft—has been dropping steadily and significantly since the early 1980s. "One of the most remarkable things about the decline in burglary is that it is so substantial that it is unprecedented in magnitude compared to any other fluctuation in crime rate *over the last century*," (italics mine) said Scott Decker, a criminologist at the University of Missouri at St. Louis. Violent crimes per 100,000 people have dropped 20% since 1990, while since 1980, property crimes have fallen 17%, robberies have been reduced by 19%, and burglaries have descended by a remarkable 44%. Meanwhile, all the industrial democracies besides the United States have had huge increases in property crime from 1960 to 1990, ranging from 177% in Germany to 600% in Italy. Smaller countries like the Netherlands, Australia, New Zealand and Canada have experienced such large increases in overall crime rates that they now have just as many criminals per capita as the U.S.

Undoubtedly, better policing methods have contributed to the drop-off in crime. But that doesn't explain all of it. There's something else going on here, and I believe it is related to the long-wave of U.S. prosperity begun in 1982 and continuing to the present. American abundance is taking hold in the moral, or behavioral conduct, dimension as well as in the commercial sphere. *Webster's Ninth New Collegiate Dictionary* defines moral as "of or relating to principles of right and wrong in behavior; expressing or teaching a conception of right behavior; conforming to a standard of right behavior; sanctioned by or operative on one's conscience or ethical judgment." It's only part of the story, but it's a good place to start. Okay, okay. Now, how about what is not moral, starting with the Seven Deadly Sins: murder, lust, greed, gluttony, envy, sloth and pride. Then, switching to what *is* moral, at least in my view: faith, humility, temperance, respect, patience, honesty, kindness, charity, love, discipline, courage, gratitude, fidelity, cleanliness, unselfishness, to name a few.

How do we get from prosperity to morality? One bridge was put nicely by my former boss John O'Sullivan, editor of the *National Review.* In an essay entitled "After Reaganism," published April 21, 1997, John asserts that "Social harmony is easier to achieve in times of prosperity than during recessions." Another link was put bluntly by my friend Michael Cox of the Dallas Fed, who told *Investor's Business Daily* that "Free Enterprise is the greatest welfare program mankind has ever known." During her first campaign for governor of New Jersey, when she was brimming with ideas (unlike her second effort), a tax-cutting Christie Todd Whitman told voters that "having a good job is the best social policy."

Like Adam Smith's assertion in *The Wealth of Nations*, I agree completely that "work is its own virtue." This is good moral doctrine and good spiritual doctrine. That is, we must all put our God-given creativity to its best use. Which leads me to another vital (moral) code of conduct: personal responsibility. It is up to each of us to behave in socially responsible ways. And that includes *accepting the consequences* of our actions. Blaming others when events go against us, often called victimization, is one of the worst of the liberal-left dogmas of the past thirty years, a dogma that led to huge government spending programs to "take care" of those "victimized by society."

Nonsense. We all have choices to make. If we act irresponsibly, we must pay the price. That's what character building is all about. Hopefully, through pain and suffering comes personal growth. However, the huge Welfare State that grew up over the past three decades undercut individual responsibility and character building, and did more to erode the moral conduct of behavior necessary for a prosperous society than anything I can think of. In so many cases the Welfare State, or the Entitlement State, enabled, excused and subsidized irresponsible behavior, including chronic jobless welfare dependency, children born out-of-wedlock, family break-up, drug and alcohol addiction, teen pregnancy and crimes of all sorts. At least in financial terms, the Welfare State said to people who refused personal responsibility, and refused to be held accountable to anyone or anything, "It's all right. It's not really your fault. Society did this to you. Let me help. Let me ease the problem."

William Bennett was completely right when he noted in his book, *The Index of Leading Cultural Indicators* (1994): "The last quarter century has taught politicians a hard and humbling lesson: there are real limits to what the state can do, particularly when it comes to imparting virtue and forming character." This is why I believe that one of the greatest economic decisions of this century was the Congress's 1996 decision to disentitle welfare, and to create strict time limits and tough work rules. President Clinton tried to water this down in the 1997 budget by re-imposing a bunch of Federal mandates such as unemployment compensation, minimum wage, job training, Davis-Bacon and minority set-asides, but most states will simply ignore the costly regulations or get the courts to throw them out. For the voters and taxpayers have spoken: get a job, because we refuse to subsidize personal irresponsibility.

All that noted, here's an interesting development: the U.S. experienced a substantial drop in welfare recipients and welfare costs *several years before* the path-breaking legislation was passed.

- The percentage of the U.S. population on welfare *peaked in 1994* at about 5.4%, according to the U.S. Department of Health and Human Resources.

- Nationwide, the number of AFDC recipients has fallen from 14.1 million to 11.4 million *since January 1993*, also according to HHS.

- 46 states out of 50 have seen their caseloads of welfare recipients decline in the *last four years*. (HHS, 4/97)

- 1.2 million people have been dropped from the welfare roles since August 22, 1996 (the date the welfare law was signed). (HHS, 4/97)

Now, I'm certainly not going to argue that economic growth and job creation alone were responsible for the drop-off in welfare. Without question, for many years there has been an increasingly loud public muttering about welfare expansion, and the revolt of taxpayers and culturally conservative voters, which helped propel President Reagan to two landslide victories, were a backlash against welfare. And it is also true that the 1996 welfare reform bill was preceded by Newt Gingrich's highly publicized 1994 Contract with America, which designated "ending welfare as we know it" as one of its key policy goals. However, a case can be made that a long wave of prosperity, and the thirty-four million new jobs it has created, has played an important role in welfare decline.

First, a lot of new entry-level jobs have been created, not only in fast-food outlets, but in services, light industry, retailing and numerous other small businesses that have cropped up during the most prosperous period in this century. Second, with so many new people employed, and making a decent living, with newfound self-respect, I'm willing to bet that this example of work effort either incentivized or shamed welfare recipients to try it themselves. Peer pressure to work, take home good wages and become a provider has undoubtedly created an environment of change, where every government dependent thought new thoughts and shifted their behavior as they saw friends and family members going to work with a new sense of mission and achievement. There's good pride, and then there's hubris. Good pride is a good thing. It rubs off. And it's a good thing that the prosperous economy has been throwing off a huge number of new job opportunities.

Data show that the welfare population is pretty evenly divided among white and non-white recipients (though probably not true for inner cities, which have produced an extraordinary volume of drug and welfare-related pathologies). But, it is worth noting a recent study published in the *Wall Street Journal* that shows the three major minority groups—African-Americans, Hispanics, and Asian-Americans—have made tremendous economic strides during the long wave of prosperity. The study shows a "significant pattern" of minority progress that argues against "an outdated mindset" that their influence is marginal, according to Alfred L. Schriber of Graham Gregory Bozell, one of the companies conducting the analysis. Of course, mainline economists were skeptical, according to *Journal* staff reporter Joseph N. Boyce, but the study coincides with a Harvard University Joint Center for Housing Studies report that minorities account for nearly 30% of the nation's *new* homeowners, while they make up only 15% of homeowners.

And the Census Bureau recently reported that the homeownership rate for native-born citizens in 1996 was about the same as that for foreign-born citizens, and that *foreign-born Hispanic citizens were more likely to own a home than those born in the U.S.* As well, a study by Target News, Inc., a Chicago-based market research firm, found that middle-class black households are purchasing computers and on-line services at a faster clip than whites. The Bozell study created a Multi-Cultural American Dream Index, which showed that while the three minority groups in the period from 1986 to 1996 increased by 3%, compared to only 1.67% white population growth, minority-owned businesses grew by nearly 10% between 1987 and 1996, and college degrees by more than 7%. Mortgage originations advanced by more than 13% between 1993 and 1996.

AMERICAN DREAM INDEX (1989–1996)

	Black	Asian	Hispanic	White
Mortgage originations*	15.1%	4.9%	15.9%	4.5%
Owned businesses	7.6	8.1	11.9	1.5
College degrees	5.7	8.3	8.8	2.4

*1993–1996

Sources: Graham Gregory Bozell, MSR Consulting, DemoGraph Corporation, *Wall Street Journal.*

In terms of income, the Census Bureau reports that Asian-Americans have already passed whites, with median household income in 1996 of $43,267, compared to $24,906 for Hispanics, $23,482 for African-Americans and $37,161 for whites. "In terms of absolute numbers, ethnic Americans have not yet reached overall parity, but the speed at which growth rates have advanced, almost doubling over the last ten years, is phenomenal," says Laura Teller, chief executive of DemoGraph Corp.

If having a job is good social policy, then the tremendous economic improvement for minorities shows just how much American social conditions have improved during the long-wave of prosperity. Jack Kemp had it exactly right when he repeatedly argued over the years that "a rising tide lifts all boats." Uninterrupted prosperity since 1982 has in fact produced an "opportunity society." In an economy that has grown by 57% in real, inflation-adjusted, terms, where non-corporate establishment, brand new small businesses have been the engine of growth, God-given talents of creativity have been put to work by minority and non-minority groups alike. Actually, I've never felt entirely comfortable with all these socio-economic aggregate labels. It is *people* who are working hard to take advantage of prosperity, no matter what their color or income status. Free markets are color-blind, the ultimate equal opportunity organizer of the economy. Color-blind free markets foster all manner of wealth producing gales of creative destruction. Risk-taking and innovation are also color-blind. So is hard work and personal responsibility.

While minority economic gains are soaring, social pathologies are starting to decline. Here I do not mean to cast aspersions on minority groups with respect to declining social conditions; whites (Caucasians) contributed their share. This is simply a factual discussion, not a comprehensive sociological analysis. The good news is that four categories of social decline are starting to show improvement.

- The teen birth rate dropped an estimated 3% from 1994 to 1995, and 8% from 1991 to 1995. This is the fourth straight year that teen birth rates have declined; teen pregnancy rates are also declining.

- Out-of-wedlock births, the birth rate for unmarried women, dropped 4% from 1994 to 1995. This is the first decline in nearly two decades. The number of non-marital births also declined 3% in 1995, and the proportions of births to unmarried mothers fell two percent to an estimated 32% in 1995.

- For violent crime, preliminary homicide rates fell sharply in 1995, by an estimated 15% accounting for the largest decline among leading causes of death between 1994 and 1995. Mortality from firearms also declined between 1994 and 1995.

- There were fewer violent crimes committed in 1995—total, not per capita—than there were in 1973. Violent crime fell 12.4% in 1995, the biggest drop in the 22 year history of the National Crime Victimization Survey.

- The overall use of illicit drugs among Americans of all ages remained flat from 1995 to 1996, but illicit drug use among teens 12 to 17 years old declined for the first time since 1992.

- Overall drug use in America has fallen by half in 15 years. (Marijuana is by far the most prevalent drug used by illicit drug users.)

- The number of occasional cocaine users (people who used in the past year but on fewer than 12 days) was 2.6 million in 1996, similar to what it was in 1995. The number of users was down significantly from 1985, when it was 7.1 million.

- However, there were an estimated 141,000 new heroin users in 1995, and there has been an increasing trend in new heroin use since 1995. The rate of heroin initiation for the age group 12–17 reached historic levels. Heroin is still a big, big problem.

- Per capital alcohol consumption is lower today than at almost any other time during the past quarter of a century. The rate of alcohol-caused deaths per 100,000 people has trended down since the early 1980s.

- Household surveys by the U.S. Department of Health and Human Services show that alcohol consumption among 12–17 year-olds is near its lowest point since the surveys began in 1974.

- The number of fatal highway accidents involving teenage drunk drivers has declined by 68% since 1982.

176

Another link from economic prosperity to social progress comes from Brandeis University historian David Hacket Fischer. In his recent book, *The Great Wave: Price Revolutions and the Rhythm of History* (1996), he shows a clear connection between *inflation and social consequences*, arguing that sharp inflation increases, or long waves of price increases, cause profound economic, human and social suffering. Studying the renaissance of the twelfth century, the renaissance of the fifteenth century, the age of the enlightenment, the Victorian era and the twentieth century, he argues: "The darkest tendencies of our troubled times—the growth of violence and drug use and family disruption which many people identify as the most urgent social problems of our age—are closely connected to price movements."

He also argues that waves of price inflation cause economic decline, drops in real wages and increases of income inequality. In other words, nothing good comes from waves of rising inflation. Nothing. Fischer warns in his conclusion:

> The historical record of the past eight hundred years shows that ordinary people are right to fear inflation, for they have been its victims—more so than the elites. And ordinary people who live in free societies have a special reason for concern. . . . A society that seeks to make its political decisions by open elections, and also hopes to regulate its economic decisions by the operation of the free market, is specially vulnerable to the effect of unstable prices.

However, the good news from Fischer's study is that "price equilibrium" in the Victorian period (1800–1896) in England and the U.S. (except for the Civil War period) produced many good things. Their economies grew rapidly, real wages rose buoyantly, interest rates fell steadily, the distribution of wealth became more equal, and crime, bastardy, and alcohol consumption fell substantially. What's more, Fischer tracks the beginning of progress in the U.S. over the past fifteen years. He charts the decline of inflation from 1980 to 1996 (inflation has dropped significantly more in 1997), and shows how theft, homicide, use of marijuana, and alcohol consumption have fallen, in sync with the disinflationary wave.

What I conclude from all this is very simple: as long as the U.S. pursues a monetary policy of price stability, as it has under Reagan and Clinton, with Volcker and Greenspan at the Federal Reserve's helm, both economic and social trends will continue to improve. Disinflation, which is an economy-wide tax cut, has not only been the backbone of our long wave of economic prosperity, it has been a driving force for the improvement of social conditions and moral conduct. In part, this is because price stability promotes growth and jobs and better incomes, so it pays to work. And work makes very good behavioral discipline: showing up on time, being well-groomed, following suggestions and directions, working in cooperative teamwork with others, being responsible for one's own actions, and being accountable to others on the job. Again, Adam Smith had it right: "Work is its own virtue." So price stability and economic prosperity create *cultural as well as material change.*

Another example of conservative cultural change is cited by Nobel Prize winner Robert W. Fogel, who teaches at the University of Chicago Graduate School of Business. In a *Wall Street Journal* article published in January 1996, Fogel calls it "The Fourth Great Awakening" (soon to be published as a book), where the U.S. is experiencing an upsurge in religiosity, an intensification of religious beliefs, and the mobilization of believers to shape political and social institutions. He writes that: "The new religious revival is fueled by a revulsion in the corruption of contemporary society. It is a rebellion against preoccupation with material acquisition and sexual debauchery; against indulgence in alcohol, tobacco, gambling and drugs; against gluttony; against financial greed and against all other forms of self-indulgence that titillate the senses and destroy the soul."

Though Fogel traces this movement from the early 1960s, it is gathering steam and gaining more and more influence during the long way of prosperity that began in the early 1980s. Fogel notes that while membership in the principal Protestant mainline churches has declined by 25%, membership of "enthusiastic churches" has nearly doubled. By the end of the 1980s enthusiastic religions had about 10 million people including fundamentalist, Pentecostal, and Protestant charismatic denominations, with about 31 million "born again" Protestants, Catholics and Mormons. Fortunately, as Washington University in St. Louis economist Richard McKenzie has shown, charitable contributions of time and money are surging. In 1995, 93 million Americans donated 20 *billion* hours of their time to charity. In the so-called "Decade of Greed" of the 1980s, individual financial contributions surged by 58% in real terms. From 1984 to 1988, corporate giving rose nearly 10% to $7.5 billion, while personal giving jumped 16%. According to data collected by the Social Welfare Research Institute, Americans give on average about 1.3% of their total household income to charity. But Fogel's upturn of religiosity and McKenzie's rise of charitable giving are two sides of the same coin: the long wave of prosperity has spawned sizable gains of spiritual thinking and unselfish action.

178

I find myself agreeing with the father of free-market capitalism, Adam Smith. In his "Theory of Moral Sentiments," written a half dozen years before *The Wealth of Nations*, Smith argued that the commercial spirit must be fused with the moral spirit. Freedom does not mean rebellion, defiance, disobedience and disrespect. It must be rooted in moral virtues. We are not just producers and consumers, but we are fathers and mothers, church and temple-goers, members of fellowships, part of our community, civic minded and public spirited. During the Welfare State period now ending, the Federal government and HHS crowded out our religion and morality. The secular temples of entitlement and victimization blocked spiritual progress.

However, during the long wave of prosperity, cultural attitudes are changing. We are all learning that while self-sufficiency and self-reliance may sound like good capitalist virtues, if they are carried too far they become inimical to our own moral and spiritual health, and may ultimately undermine the free-market economy. From my own personal experience, I have come to believe that life is not only about what we can accomplish, but how we behave as we accomplish. It's not only about what we do, but how we do it. Most of all, we must play by the rules. That means respecting other people, respecting institutions and respecting the community around us. In the end, it means learning, respecting and following God's will. For whatever our spiritual higher power might be, we must be responsible to it. Think of it as a spiritual tax cut. It makes the economy, and all of us within the economy, more prosperous. That is why I believe we must keep the faith. For faith is always the spirit.